THE
ILLUMINATI
CONSPIRACY

THE ILLUMINATI CONSPIRACY

THE SAPIENS SYSTEM

BY
DONALD HOLMES, M.D.

INTRODUCED BY
ROBERT ANTON WILSON, Ph.D.

1993
NEW FALCON PUBLICATIONS
PHOENIX, ARIZONA, USA

International Standard Book Number: 1-56184-051-3

Library of Congress Catalog Card Number: 87-80596

First Edition 1987
Second Printing 1993

Cover Art S. J. Black

Mass Market German Edition Droemer Knaur 1990

NEW FALCON PUBLICATIONS
655 East Thunderbird
Phoenix, Arizona 85022 U.S.A.
(602) 246-3546

Dedicated
To
Lincoln Steffens

OTHER CONTROVERSIAL BOOKS
FROM NEW FALCON

Equinox Of The Gods
Eight Lectures On Yoga
Gems From The Equinox
Magick Without Tears
The Worlds Tragedy
The Law Is For All
The Heart Of The Master
Little Essays Toward Truth
   By Aleister Crowley
Undoing Yourself With Energized Meditation
Secrets of Western Tantra
The Tree Of Lies
   By Christopher S. Hyatt, Ph.D.
Enochian World Of Aleister Crowley: Enochian Sex Magick
   By Aleister Crowley • Lon M. DuQuette • C. S. Hyatt
The Way Of The Secret Lover: Tantra, Tarot & The HGA
   By Christopher S. Hyatt, Ph.D. • Lon Milo DuQuette
Taboo: The Ecstasy Of Evil
   By C. S. Hyatt, Ph.D. • Lon DuQuette • Gary Ford
The Illustrated Goetia: Sexual Evocation
   By Lon Milo DuQuette • C.S. Hyatt, Ph.D. • David P. Wilson
Pacts With The Devil
   By S. Jason Black • Christopher S. Hyatt, Ph.D.
Freedom Is A Two Edged Sword
   By Jack Parsons
Cosmic Trigger I
Cosmic Trigger II
Sex And Drugs
The New Inquisition
Quantum Psychology
   By Robert Anton Wilson
Info-Psychology
Game of Life
   By Timothy Leary, Ph.D.
The Complete Golden Dawn System Of Magic
   By Israel Regardie

And to get your free catalog of all of our titles, write to:

NEW FALCON PUBLICATIONS
Catalog Dept.
655 East Thunderbird
Phoenix, AZ. 85022 U.S.A.

TABLE OF CONTENTS

INTRODUCTION
The Spaghetti Theory of Conspiracy
by
ROBERT ANTON WILSON

WHO'S IN CHARGE HERE?

Pay no attention to that man behind the curtain!
— Oz the Omnipotent

It is characteristic of the primitive conditions on this backward planet that virtually nobody knows any of the basic facts about how the human race is actually governed. For instance —

1. Governments are not nearly as important as most people think. Since we live in a post-barter economy—a money economy—those who **control the money supply** effectively **control the planet**. Governments gave up all attempt to coin or control money in the 19th Century, mostly because they did not trust one another, i.e. no nation had faith that the coinage or currency of another nation was really worth what it claimed to be worth. The great International Banks stepped into this vacuum and, by demonstrating more fiscal rectitude than governments had in the past, became the creators of money in the modern world.

After the banks had control, they no longer needed to be quite so prim in their fiscal rectitude. Nobody could challenge them.

3

This means that governments cannot do *anything*—good or ill, wise or foolish—unless the banks first lend them the money for the project. The power is in the banks. The governments survive on the permission of the banks. If the banks cut off their credit, governments die. Any government that resists has its credit cut off and dies.

As Buckminster Fuller stressed in all his writings (especially *Critical Path* and *Grunch of Giants*) this means that, in the modern world, banks **act** and governments only **re-act** to the situations the bankers have ordained. Even earlier, historian Brooks Adams wrote of the British financier Samuel Loyd, in *The Law of Civilization and Decay,*

> He comprehended that, with expanding trade, an inelastic currency must rise in value; he saw that, with sufficient resources at command, his class might be able to establish such a rise, almost at pleasure; certainly that they could manipulate it when it came, by taking advantage of foreign exchange.

In other words, as soon as the great multi-national banks had control of the money supply, they saw that they could manipulate cash and credit to maximize profits. They would have been rather dense if they had not seen this. Nonetheless, while these financiers quite sanely and legally maximize profits, the rest of us are at their mercy; but we never elected them to this position of power, and, by and large, we do not even know who they are.

2. In the present decade, it costs $50,000,000 to run a campaign for the presidency of the United States, $10,000,000 to run a campaign for the Senate and $5,000,000 for the House of Representatives. (These figures are documented in Buckminster Fuller's *Grunch of Giants*.) This means that the U.S.—the strongest country in the West—is not only "owned" (in trillion-dollar debt to) the banks, but also governed by persons who are either (a) millionaires or (b) heavily in debt to millionaires. In the words of ex-Senator Pettigrew, we now have "government of the corporations, by the corporations, for the corporations."

3. As Edward Luttwak documents in his cheerfully Machiavellian little text, *The Coup d'Etat*, more governments have been changed, since World War II by the *coup d'Etat* than by any other method. More governments have been changed by *coup* than by all the democratic elections and revolutions combined.

Since every *coup* is by definition a conspiracy, this means that conspiracies have had more effect on the past 40 years of world history than all the electoral politics and all the popular revolutions added together. That is rather ominous, in a period when "educated" opinion holds that it is infamous, nutty, eccentric or downright paranoid to think about conspiracies at all. We are, in effect, forbidden to think about how the planet is actually governed.

4. If governments cannot act without permission of the banks—without loans or "lines of credit" granted by the banks—and if the U.S. government is "owned" by the multi-millionaire (or billionaire) banking and corporate elite, and if other governments are, more often than not, changed by conspiratorial *coup*, the major portion of humanity is economically-politically controlled by persons who are largely unknown to the general public and/or have never been elected to any office. Democratic theory is beautiful and inspirational, but has nothing to do with the actual situation of the domesticated primates of this boondocks planet.

5. If the masses of the planet are politically-economically controlled by shadowy financiers and conspiratorial adventurers, the same masses are *intellectually* controlled by persons who are more visible but equally unpalatable to the Rationalist view of history. In blunt language, nearly 300 years after the Age of Reason was prematurely announced, most people in most nations most of the time are mentally in total bondage to religious leaders who operate on sheer bluff, i.e. on the basis of claims that cannot be proven and appear clearly insane to everybody who hasn't been raised within their frameworks.

The Methodist can see how absurd are the beliefs of Roman Catholics. The Catholics can see the obvious insanity of the Sikh militants who blow up airplanes because there are a few Hindus aboard. The Sikhs, no doubt, can see how nonsensical Scientology is. But none of the people processed by any of these cults can see how crazy their own cult is. It is often quite hard for a rational observer to determine if the leaders of these cults are just cynically raking in the cash or are genuinely as deluded as their brainwashed followers.

One can acquire a reputation as a satirist, a wit, a cynic, etc. simply by stating blunt facts. For instance, it is quite clear from the above that the human race is largely governed politico-economically by unknown financial cliques and criminal scoundrels and governed intellectually by borderline psychotics and charlatans. But we have all been so conditioned and indoctrinated that to state the facts simply makes it sound as if one is being sarcastic or perhaps even trying to be "shocking."

Let us look at the situation of this planet in a little more detail.

SOCIOBIOLOGY OF DECEIT

All men are born liars.
— Liam O'Flaherty, *Autobiography* (first sentence)

Conspiracy is the first manifestation of intelligent life.

The original organic molecules formed affinity groups and conspired to exploit the resources of this planet. Working in small cells originally, these DNA conquistadores quickly developed organizations of higher complexity and spread a network of hungry, predatory Life over the previously dead Earth. In less than 3,500,000,000 years this network has expanded from the ocean beds to the very peaks on the Himalayas. No square centimeter of Earth is uninfested.

The trapdoor spiders formed their own secret society and went underground. They lurked silently, hidden beneath a plausible surface of twigs and soil, waiting to pounce out and devour any beetle or other tasty-looking morsel that happened to pass by.

The day of the undercover agent had come.

This technique of cover-up and disguise has proven an evolutionary success and is widely copied everywhere. Thousands of species of conspiratorial insects even today still hide behind ingenious make-up that deceives us into thinking they are only branches or rocks.

Other species got even smarter even faster. Polar bears donned white fur coats to fade into snowy landscapes. The leopard's spots make it hard to distinguish from speckled sunlight on foliage. The Norway rat (*mus rattus Norwegious*) learned to hide by day and come forth under cover of darkness.

The first human beings looked about them and very sensibly concluded, "It's a jungle out there."

Human psychology has remained jungle psychology. As historian Carl Oglesby writes in *The Yankee and Cowboy War*

> . . . a multitude of conspiracies contend in the night. . . . Conspiracy is
> the normal continuation of normal politics by normal means . . . and
> where there is no limit to power, there is no limit to conspiracy

As soon as we find evidence of human beings on this planet, we find evidence of secret societies. Paleolithic paintings show that they met, typically, in the deepest, darkest caves, and they plotted sorcery and mischief against all competing species.

In every tribe known to anthropology, we still find secret societies. Most tribes have all-male secret societies, but many also have all-female secret societies. Most readers will probably remember that they had their own secret societies as children, with passwords and quasi-Freemasonic grips determinedly hidden from the adults.

From this evolutionary perspective, every paranoid is partly right. The major error of the paranoid appears to be his characteristic belief in one jumbo Mega-Conspiracy that explains everything. This is impossible, because it violates basic laws of primate psychology. Domesticated primates like wild primates are mischievous, sly and have a keen sense of humor: **the double-cross is their most characteristic invention**.

George Washington, who rose to power by conspiring against his king, said with blunt honesty, "Nations have no permanent allies, only permanent interests." This is why governments, corporations and other large-scale conspiracies all have a *natural life-span*, like other living systems. There is no government on this planet that has existed in its present form for more than 200 years; aside from the Dutch East India Company, most corporations rise and fall within 100 years (average). Outside of paranoid fantasy and Romantic fiction, most conspiracies collapse of their own "internal contradictions" within months or years. (Thus, if there actually is one big jumbo-conspiracy governing this planet, it must be, as Donald Holmes wittily suggests in the following pages, of non-human origin.)

The study of conspiracy *as a branch of primate psychology*, has great interest in itself, as Machiavelli knew; but real conspiracies are not as clever or long-lived as the ones that paranoids and ideologists imagine; they are simply much dirtier.

It is one of the ironies of our time that conspiracies and secret societies have proliferated more than ever **at precisely the same time it has become impolite and uncouth to discuss them**. In this sense, the Nazis defeated the Liberal Democracies in World War II, because they have achieved a form of Thought Control over the Liberal Mind. Liberals are afraid to think of conspiracies because that might lead to the One Big Mega-Conspiracy, i.e. to "thinking like Hitler." But a mind chained by Tabu is a mind unfree. I believe it is time we broke Hitler's power over our minds and began to think in terms of the facts instead of being restrained by Tabu.

Disguise, deception and group-action have a long evolutionary history, and primates have all these traditional evolutionary habits, which in political jargon are called conspiratorial habits. Even if it is Tabu to think about it, that seems to be the way things are on this planet.

TRUE CONFESSIONS

When four sit down to conspire, three are
fools and the fourth is a government agent.
— Duncan Lunan, *Interstellar Communication*

Frankly I myself never dared to violate the Liberal Tabu—"Thou shalt not think about conspiracies"—until I was virtually *forced* to think about them.

In the 1960s in Chicago, I was involved in the anti-war movement. Congressional investigators later revealed that there were over 5000 government agents assigned to infiltrate peace groups in Chicago alone—some working for the Federal Bureau of Investigation (FBI), some for the Central Intelligence Agency (CIA) and some for Army Intelligence. From 1968 on, the FBI was following a program code-named COINTELPRO. The purpose of COINTELPRO was to make sure the anti-war movement *knew* it was infiltrated, in order to spread suspicion, distrust and paranoia among individuals and groups who might otherwise have cooperated harmoniously. Working in the peace movement in those days was, accordingly, like living in an Eric Ambler novel. In any given week I would be warned perhaps three times that somebody I trusted was really a government agent, and, of course, somebody who was accused one day might very well be around to accuse somebody else the next day. Over 20 years later, I still don't know who was a government agent and who was not. I enjoyed it all rather than being terrified only because I basically agree with Helen Keller that "Life is either a great adventure or it is nothing."

I encountered the same Spy Story atmosphere in the early 1970s when involved in the campaign to secure the release from prison of the controversial scientist, Dr. Timothy Leary. At one time or another, everybody in the Leary Defense Committee suspected everybody else of being a government agent (I think the poet, Allen Ginsberg, suspected me for over a year) and eventually government "leaks" in the press attempted to persuade us that Dr. Leary himself had become a government agent. I still relish that classic John Le Carre touch, especially since some people believed it.

Eventually it was confirmed that Leary's son-in-law, Dennis Martino, had been entrapped into becoming a government agent. Dennis later died in Spain and three press reports in two days claimed the cause of death had been murder, suicide and accident. That mystery is still unsolved, at least in America. Presumably, the Spanish authorities finally came up with a coroner's verdict, which may or may not be the truth, but by then the U.S. media had lost interest. As far as you can learn from American sources, Dennis Martino accidentally overdosed, committed suicide *and* was murdered, all on the same day. Evidently, nobody in the U.S. media wanted to find out what the hell really happened.

But there are wheels within wheels in this modern Machiavellian world.

During the last year of my employment as Associate Editor of *PLAYBOY*, a certain executive came into my office one day and closed the door behind him. He told me that my home phone was tapped and that I was under heavy surveillance by the Red Squad of the Chicago Police Force.

I was stunned, and asked how the hell he knew this.

He replied that certain people in the *PLAYBOY* empire had made an arrangement with a Chicago police official. The official received regular money through some circuitous route that was not explained to me; in return, he notified his *PLAYBOY* contacts whenever an executive of the firm was under police investigation.

That was when I first realized how often there are spies spying on spies.

Incidentally, my informant told me *why* I was under heavy surveillance. A police informer in the Black Panthers, he said, had reported that I was involved with a group of white radicals who were buying guns for the Panthers.

Despite my cynicism about cops, I was shocked. I explained heatedly that there was no truth in this at all. "We know, we know," said the executive, who was very close to Hefner. "We trust you."

And they did trust me. They never made any attempt to ease me out the back door, or dissociate the Bunny Empire from me. They even offered to pay my legal expenses if the police ever busted me on this absurd charge.

It was years before I wondered why the Bunny Empire decided to trust me in such an explosive matter. My guess, now, is that they had me under surveillance, too, along with their other editors—but that's only a guess. Maybe it was just that I have an honest face. I'd like to think that.

Of course, I was *not* buying guns for the Black Panthers. I had met a few Panthers at Peace rallies, and the informer had seen me. He or she had probably "improved" the story to impress the Red Squad. A *PLAYBOY* editor talking to Black Panthers is not all that sensational, but a *PLAYBOY* editor buying guns for the Panthers was a story that made the informer seem on the edge of discovering a major conspiracy.

I could tell several similar stories, but I would again have to conceal the names of my sources and you would probably not believe me. Truth is much, much stranger than melodrama.

Instead I will examine the neuro-economics of conspiracy and then relate some notable conspiracies that have become matters of public record. We will see that the theories outlined by Dr. Holmes in this book are, however shocking, no more bizarre than the world in which we live.

WEALTH AND "MONEY"

A banker is a man who will loan you money if you can prove you don't need it.
— attributed to Mark Twain

Just as most people have no idea how this planet is governed at this barbaric stage of evolution, most people have no concept of where "wealth" comes from. This is because most of us have never learned to distinguish between wealth and *money*.

Money was originally created by the State, as I mentioned at the beginning; this is why King Lear says his persecutors can't accuse him of counterfeiting. The State was, in those days, the only legal creator of coin: a legal coin was, by definition, a State coin.

As States learned the advantages to be gained by issuing debased coinage—a matter discussed with great clarity and wit in Jonathan Swift's little-known but brilliant *Drapier Letters*—every State and every individual became the potential victim of coins that did not contain the amount of gold stamped on them. Eventually, no State would trust any other State in this area and, more and more, the *paper* of the great banking firms began to seem the only "safe" medium of exchange.

The U.S. Constitution, amusingly, says that Congress shall have the power to coin money and regulate the value thereof, but Congress has not exercised that power in over a century. Official U.S. money is issued by a private bank, just like the money of all other nations (except Albania, a lonely heretic), but, because U.S. money says "Federal Reserve Note" on it, most Americans assume it is issued by the Federal government. It is issued, actually, by the Federal Reserve Corporation, a private bank, owned largely by the Rockefellers and Morgans. We do not "owe the National Debt to ourselves" as the late Franklin Roosevelt once said; we owe it to the Rockefellers and Morgans.

Irish money says "Bank of Ireland" on it and English money says "Bank of England," and so on; all across Europe, most people know that the banks are in control of the creation of money. Only in America, because the word "Federal" in **Federal Reserve** is thought to mean *"federal"* and because the Constitution says Congress shall coin money, is there a lingering belief that the government is still a sovereign entity not owned by the bankers to whom it is in debt.

None of this has anything to do with Real Wealth in the sense of classical economics.

Real Wealth, in the economic sense, consists of tangible assets. It includes, not only plants in operation "owned" by individual or corporate capitalists, but known resources, inventions, bridges, roads, scientific data—all the creations of human intelligence that can be concretely applied to make the human environment more pleasant for somebody or for everybody.

Thus, if all the Real Wealth disappeared over night, *the world would be entirely different.* We would literally be back in the Old Stone Age, and no amount of Federal Reserve Notes or other paper would change our situation. We would have to re-invent and re-create all the science and technology of the past 30,000 years step by step.

On the other hand, all the money in the world—all the Federal Reserve Notes, Bank of England notes, etc. and all the stocks and bonds—

could disappear over night and *the world would be exactly the same physically.* There might be a hell of a fight over *who* owned *what,* but the human world of Real Wealth would still be here.

In kindergarten language, Real Wealth consists of "things" that can't be stored in banks or computers, while money consists of "tickets" or symbols that can be stored in banks or computers.

Of course, Real Wealth is more than solid "things." I have been arguing for 30 years, in various publications, that Real Wealth is essentially pure information. It has finally dawned on me that nobody understands that but a few mathematicians and computer buffs, so I now say, more simply, that Real Wealth is **ideas that work.** In the terminology of General Semantics, Wealth is ideas that are similar in structure (isomorphic) to the energy systems of space-time.

Wealth is created by analysis: by extracting higher-order structure from the raw signals perceived by the senses. You can starve to death in a wheat field if your mind has not analyzed the energy system of space-time sufficiently to recognize that wheat is edible and nourishing.

Money, then, is not Real Wealth, but consists of tickets for the exchange of Real Wealth. Such tickets are necessary in an advanced technology-economy-society, because barter becomes cumbersome and unwieldy.

Most money, however, does not exist in tangible form at all, not even as *paper.* Most money, in today's advanced techno-society, exists only as computer records or, in less advanced outposts, notations in ledgers. Banks may legally lend up to *eight times* the amount they have on deposit, and as Penny Lernoux documents in her invaluable *In Banks We Trust,* they often go far beyond this and hope to cover their tracks before the bank examiner comes around.

Michele Sindona, a kingpin of the Vatican/Mafia/P2 clique and founder of the infamous Franklin National Bank, was convicted of murdering a bank examiner in Italy, after being convicted of 65 counts of bank fraud in the U.S. His principle flaw appears to have been that he was more reckless than older and wiser financiers who have been running the world longer and more judiciously. (We shall return to the Sindona/P2 case history.)

When banks lend eight times what they have on deposit, or more than that, they are gambling that everybody will not come in and withdraw their funds on the same day. It is a safe gamble, most of the time. But it means that paper wealth has become even more metaphysical and ghostly than the most debased coinage of the most corrupt Tudor or Stuart monarchs. It means that, by a species of magic, the Real Wealth of the planet can be manipulated as the ghostly paper is maneuvered from one computer to another. And it means that the really bold adventurers and pirates can alchemically transform totally unreal paper into ownership of resources, factories, roads, bridges and whole nations on occasion, as they, following Samuel Loyd, "establish a rise . . . at their pleasure," or just as easily establish a fall.

The reader should consult some of the books I will be summarizing here—especially illuminating is Richard Hammer's *The Vatican Connection*, which tells how Johnny Roselli and his friends in the American Mafia printed one billion dollars worth of counterfeit stocks which disappeared into the Vatican Bank/Banco Ambrosiano feedback loop in such a manner that the New York District Attorney's office, which had wiretaps on most of the felons, never did find out where the $900,000,000 of the $1,000,000,000 finally landed.

Buckminster Fuller, in *Grunch of Giants*, describes the modern world as governed by MMA&O—Machiavelli, Mafia, Atoms and Oil. You know the Mafia. Atoms and Oil are the multi-national corporations. Machiavelli is the symbol of the paper-magic wizards, or international banks, who make the whole system possible. GRUNCH stands for GRoss UNiversal CAsh Heist. It's another book you really ought to read.

NEURO-GEOGRAPHY OF CONSPIRACY

Go West, young man.

— Horace Greeley

As I pointed out in *Prometheus Rising* (Falcon Press, 1983), the Real Wealth of the world has been doubling every generation since statistical economists started collecting data in the 18th Century. This is a side-effect of the accelerated doubling of knowledge that has been occurring in the past two milleniums. (Information, or ideas-that-work, is the source of Real Wealth. Remember?) As George Anderla, a French statistician, determined, if we take all the knowledge of 1 A.D. as our base, then knowledge has doubled at the following rate since then:

1 AD	1 unit
1500 AD	2
1750 AD	4
1900 AD	8
1950 AD	16
1960 AD	32
1967 AD	64
1973 AD	128

A glance at world-historical trajectories indicates that this doubling of knowledge-and-wealth has followed a western (and mildly northern) vector, as has been documented e.g. in Brooks Adams' *Law of Civilization and Decay*, Timothy Leary's *The Intelligence Agents* and Buckminster Fuller's *Critical Path*.

Bronze Age tools first appeared in Southeast Asia, followed by large-scale agriculture, slavery and war. By 1 A.D. all the technology thusfar produced was being processed through the schools and banking establishments of Rome. By the time this knowledge/wealth doubled in 1500, the universities of North Italy and the great Florentine banking families like the Medici held the hot center of power. By 1750, the next doubling was occurring mostly in England, the first Empire "on which the sun never set."

By 1900, the U.S. was becoming a rival to England; by 1950, the American Empire had replaced the English Empire. The years since 1950 have witnessed what Prof. Oglesby calls "the Yankee and Cowboy war" as Eastern bankers like the Rockefellers try to hold on to control and are challenged by Western mavericks like Howard Hughes.

The more adventurous and innovative persons—those with nervous systems programmed by maverick genes and/or bizarre imprints and conditioning: the "misfits"—have been moving steadily westward for about 5000 years. They have been moving away from centralized Authority, out into the perimeters and frontiers, because that is where misfits and geniuses can function.

Clausewitz described war as a continuation of politics by other means; Oglesby calls conspiracy "the normal continuation of normal politics by normal means." Conspiracy, the murky territory between politics and war, is part of our glorious primate heritage, which is why Ambrose Bierce defined peace as "a period of cheating between two periods of fighting."

The role of conspiracy in human history, I suggest, is a period of cheating during which two power centers are struggling, one of them Eastward and representing established ideas and old wealth, the other Westward and generally representing maverick ideas and new wealth. Enclaves of "outlaws" move in the shadowy territory between these two power poles, running their own games and exploiting the paranoia of each side where and when they can.

Anthropologist William Irwin Thompson has suggested, in a recent address in Oslo, Norway, that the Reagan administration's Strategic Defense Initiative—the so-called "Star Wars" program—is more radical, and less reactionary, than it looks on the surface. Thompson alleges that, under the pretext of military bluster, SDI actually represents the total re-alignment of American society into a scientific-technological paradigm. Only the most "patriotic" rhetoric, Thompson says, could sell to the American people a program which amounts to the most expensive and most daring scientific research-and-development project humanity has ever attempted. In this context, Reagan represents the "Cowboy elite" that Oglesby sees as being on the edge of toppling the Rockefeller and other Yankee empires. The Cowboys are looking for a High Frontier, and they are computerized Cowboys now.

Werner von Braun used Disneyworld—both the amusement park and the TV show—to "sell" NASA's more adventurous ideas to the politicians by first selling them to the people. General Graham, who gave the "Star Wars" idea to Reagan, is following the same scenario. Amid the 24 separate-and-interlocking conspiracies struggling over the turf on this planet, the Cowboys are struggling for higher and more imaginative lands in the stars. Why not? They are, in the 20th Century, the same sort of mavericks the Yankees were in the 18th Century—namely, "the products of the Protestantism of the Protestants and the dissidence of dissent," as Edmund Burke said of the wealthy radicals who wrote the Declaration of Independence. The coming dominant looks to be, like California, a mad mixture of Hollywood, computers, special effects, apocalyptical visions and dope. Reagan does not fully understand the neuro-geography of the historical forces he represents.

The next dominant will probably be further west and more technological.

If we revise our chart of the doubling of knowledge (Real Wealth) to include these factors we find:

DATE	KNOWLEDGE FACTOR	CENTER OF POWER	PRINCIPLE ENEMIES
1 AD	1	Rome	Greece, Egypt

DATE	KNOWLEDGE FACTOR	CENTER OF POWER	PRINCIPLE ENEMIES
1500 AD	2	Florence	Turks
1750 AD	4	England	France, Spain
1900 AD	8	England	Germany
1950 AD	16	New York	Russia
1960 AD	32	California	Russia
1967 AD	64	California	Russia
1973 AD	128	California	New York
?	Japan	California	

The rising power always seems to the West or Northwest of the declining power that struggles against it; it is always richer and more powerful than any previous Empire; it always seems to the older power center (and its kept intellectuals) exactly what California seems today— a kind of sociological Granola made up of equal parts of fruits, nuts and flakes.

THE C.I.A. & THE MAFIA

Patriotism, sir, is the last recourse
of the scoundrel.
— Dr. Samuel Johnson

In the 1960s, the CIA conspired with two Mafia leaders, Sam Giancana and Johnny Roselli. Mr. Giancana and Mr. Roselli provided professional Mafia assassins and the CIA trained them and sent them to Cuba to kill Fidel Castro. Like most real conspiracies, this was unsuccessful; Senor Castro is still alive. This conspiracy was also well documented in Congressional hearings and broadcast in the news media internationally, so you are not considered a crank if you write about it.

You will begin to understand what I call the Spaghetti Theory of Conspiracy when I remind you that Johnny Roselli was also involved in printing one billion dollars ($1,000,000,000) worth of counterfeit stock for the Vatican Bank. That is documented fully in *The Vatican Connection* by N.Y. *Times* reporter Richard Hammer, which I again recommend to your attention.

According to Anthony Summers' book, *Conspiracy*, there is a good *prima facie* case that Johnny Roselli was also an instigator of the assassinations of both John and Bobby Kennedy, in collaboration with Sam Giancana—the same Giancana who had previously collaborated with Roselli in providing assassins for the CIA. While Summers' evidence is not conclusive, it is chillingly plausible.

The House Select Committee on Assassinations concluded, on the basis of the hard scientific evidence of acoustics, that there were **two** gunmen shooting at John Kennedy in Dealy Plaza, one from the front and one from the back. On the basis of softer but persuasive supporting evidence, the Committee concluded further that a conspiracy of more than two persons was probable and that the possibility of Mafia involvement was worthy of deeper investigation.

The Chief Counsel for the Committee, Prof. Howard Blakey, was willing to be more definitive in a press conference. "I am now firmly of the opinion that the mob did it," he said. "It is a historical truth." (Quoted by Summers in *Conspiracy*.)

Sam Giancana was shot dead in June 1975, after testifying once before the committee and while negotiating with their investigators about further questions they wished to ask him under oath. Giancana was shot through the mouth—the *sasso in bocca*, traditional Mafia punishment for suspected informers.

Johnny Roselli was shot dead in July 1976, after he, too, had been called once before the Assassinations Committee. According to journalist Jack Anderson, Roselli had told him that he was not involved in the Kennedy assassinations but another Mafia "family" was.

The Mafia has acquired its international empire only because the most popular drugs of our time are illegal. In the past 40 years, the rulers of the Mafia have graduated from multi-millionaires to billionaires *only* because these absurd anti-drug laws remain on the books.

It is permissible in "liberal" "educated" circles to say that these laws remain in force because of stupidity or conservatism or superstition. If you say the laws remain because somebody is making a profit out of them, you are supposed to be eccentric or downright nutty.

Nonetheless, the ancient Romans knew that the basic question about any social policy was—**cui bono?** (Who profits from it?)

INTERLUDE & *KOAN*

In CIA jargon, a "useful idiot" means somebody who is working for them but doesn't know it.

My involvements with controversial politics have left me with one lasting legacy. Whenever I suspect that I am taking myself or my theories too seriously, I stop and ask myself, "Have I become a *useful idiot* yet?"

THE STATE AS CONSPIRACY

The more laws that are written,
the more criminals are produced.
           — Lao-Tse, *Tao Te Ching*

It is likely that the State as we kow it is an innately conspiratorial organism. As the sociologist Franz Oppenheimer pointed out in his remarkable book, *The State*, there is no anthropological or historical evidence that anything like Rousseau's "Social Contract" ever happened in pre-history; on the contrary, the State appears in human affairs only after conquest by armed force. It is to maintain themselves in power over the conquered that a conquering elite create those institutions— police, army, taxation—that make up the skeleton of the State as we know it historically. There is no record of a tribal people peacefully "contracting" to set such a machinery of oppression above themselves. Conquerors impose it upon them.

Bakunin argued in *God and the State* that nobody has ever *seen* "God" or the "State." This, although startling, is true. Human beings, called priests, claim to represent "God," and other human beings, called civil servants, claim to represent the "State," and this metaphysical sleight-of-hand is alleged to justify acts which would be regarded as not only criminal but barbarous if it were remembered that mere human beings were doing these things. Similar verbal magic—meaningless words like "heresy" and "treason"—are used to convince the victims that resistance is evil, escape or flight is just as evil, and even thinking that you are being victimized is somehow sinful.

In simple language, anybody who robs you is a thief, unless he claims to be an agent of the "State"—in which case, he is not a thief but only a tax-collector. By the same metaphysical trick, anybody who murders millions is a lunatic, unless he claims to be an agent of "God"—in which case he is a Crusader. You can resist an ordinary bandit with a perfect sense of righteousness, but you feel guilty about resisting the Churchman or Statesman, since that is called "heresy" or "treason."

Since the State was founded in conquest and is maintained by metaphysics (or, in the Logical Positivist jargon, "abuse of language"), it follows Oglesby's rule—"where there is no limit to power, there is no limit to conspiracy."

We have already cited Anthony Summers' book *Conspiracy*, to indicate that there is real evidence, not mere paranoia, behind the claim that the Mafia was involved, perhaps centrally, in the Kennedy assassinations. According to Summers' more recent book, *Goddess*, there is also good evidence that Sam Giancana and Johnny Roselli had arranged for the electronic bugging of the bedroom of a house belonging to Peter Lawford, where Marilyn Monroe and Bobby Kennedy met for romantic dalliance in what they thought was privacy. Jimmy Hoffa of the Teamsters' Union, who had been imprisoned by Bobby's "get-tough" Justice Department, was allegedly also involved in this plot, which was intended to obtain material with which Bobby could be blackmailed. A BBC documentary on Summers' book—"Say Goodnight to the President," BBC-TV 1985—supported all of Summers' charges.

Giancana and Roselli were both shot in the mid-1970s, as we have seen. Jimmy Hoffa simply "disappeared" and has never been found dead or alive. Rumor claims he is buried beneath an interstate highway in Illinois.

Norman Mailer, many of you might remember, became convinced, while researching his biography of Marilyn Monroe, that there was some kind of "cover-up" connected with her death. Mailer even implied that there was a definite possibility of murder.

According to Summers' *Goddess* and the BBC documentary previously cited, there was indeed a conspiracy in which Marilyn's death was concealed for three hours while persons unknown removed from her house all documentia of her love affairs with John and Bobby Kennedy. The weight of circumstantial evidence suggests that this conspiracy was instigated by Peter Lawford, who had, as we noted, loaned his house as a trysting place for Marilyn's affairs, and who was also brother-in-law to the Kennedys. It is not demonstrable that Lawford ever thought, or allowed himself to think, that he might also be concealing clues in a murder case. He probably thought, or wanted to think, that he was merely concealing politically embarrassing sexual dalliances. The possibility of murder remains only a possibility, although it is still insisted upon by Hank Messick, a former consultant to the New York Joint Legislative Committee on Crime. Massick claims that unnamed informants in the Mafia told him Marilyn was killed to lure Bobby Kennedy into a trap and then blackmail him into ending his crusade against the Mob.

All one can say about that theory is "Maybe."

Nonetheless, another of John Kennedy's mistresses—although he did not pass her on to Bobby—was one Judith Exner. Ms. Exner, the House Select Committee on Assassinations later noted, was, curiously enough, the mistress of Mafioso Sam Giancana before, during and after her affair with the President. The Committee was of the opinion that it was probable that Mr. Giancana more or less shoved Ms. Exner into the President's bed, for blackmail purposes. Mr. Giancana, you may remember, was also suspected by the Committee of having a hand in JFK's assassination, and died of gunshot wounds—through the mouth—while under investigation.

Another of JFK's *amours* was with a Mary Pinchot Meyer, a most interesting lady. She was married to Cord Meyer, a top CIA official who happens to be the only man to have received the Agency's Distinguished Intelligence Medal three times. Mary Pinchot Meyer was also a dear and good friend of Dr. Timothy Leary; and, according to his book, *Flashbacks*, Mary told Dr. Leary in 1962 that the CIA wanted to stop him and other scientists from publishing LSD experiments, because they wanted to keep the mind-altering properties of LSD one of their own little secrets.

In 1964, about a year after John Kennedy was assassinated (or about two years after the somewhat mysterious death of Marilyn Monroe), Mary Pinchot Meyer was shot dead on a street in Washington.

Thereafter Dr. Leary was repeatedly arrested, and although every case against him except one was dismissed by the courts, he was finally convicted in that one case, which involved alleged possession of one half of one marijuana cigarette. He was sentenced to 37 years—although the penalty for that crime in that state (California) was normally six months—and was released after serving over five years. Dr. Leary claims he was framed by the arresting officer; he also claims there was a cover-up in the shooting of Mary Pinchot Meyer. Nobody much cares what Dr. Leary claims, because for over a year before his release government officials had leaked to the press claims that he had become an informer. There is no record of any person or persons convicted on the basis of Dr. Leary's testimony, oddly, but the rumor has stuck to his name and "everybody knows" he is a government agent these days.

As the French say, it gives one ferociously to think.

PROPAGANDA DUE (P2)

Make him an offer he can't refuse.
— Don Carleone

As most people know by now, the first degree initiation into Freemasonry contains the warning that if the candidate ever betrays his fellow Freemasons he will be hunted down and hanged where the rising tide will cover his dead body. We are not supposed to think about that at all. That is only "ritual" and isn't meant to be taken literally. Besides, Hitler had delusions about Freemasons and therefore to think about Freemasons hanging people means that we are becoming weird and might turn into Nazis overnight if we don't watch ourselfes.

On the morning of 18 June 1982, the body of Roberto Calvi, a Freemason, was found hanging from Blackfriars Bridge in London, where the rising tide had covered his dead body.

Liberal opinion—or as it also calls itself Education Opinion—absolutely forbids us to think a rather obvious thought at this point.

Still, it does seem **possible** that Signor Calvi was killed by Freemasons **or by persons who devoutly wish us to believe he was killed by Freemasons.**

At the time of his death, Calvi was in flight from Italy where he had been indicted for massive stock and currency frauds. As president of Banco Ambrosiano, Calvi had been one of the principle managers of Vatican financial affairs, due to the close symbiosis between Banco Ambrosiano and the IOR or Vatican Bank; his financial piracy had left the Vatican in debt hundreds of millions of dollars. His widow, Clara Calvi, has repeatedly asserted that persons "high in the Vatican" ordered the murder of her husband.

Mrs. Calvi's claim is not supported by English journalist Stephen Knight who argues in *The Brotherhood* that Calvi was killed by his fellow

Freemasons in the notorious **P2 (Propaganda Due)** lodge. Two other investigative journalists, Foote and della Torre, however, offer a third verdict; in their *Unsolved: The Mysterious Death of God's Banker* they endeavor to prove that Calvi, who had admittedly been "laundering" Mafia drug money through Banco Ambrosiano and the Vatican Bank, had been killed by the Mafia for double-crossing them in a heroin deal.

The first coroner's hearing on Calvi's declared, admittedly on the basis of incomplete evidence, that the banker hanged himself. After widespread press criticism, a second coroner's hearing returned an "open" verdict, meaning that the cause of Calvi's death is unknown. The major argument against suicide, discussed in all the books on the case, is that Calvi was hanging from an under-girder of the bridge which appears to be difficult of access even for a trained acrobat—and Calvi was 62 years old, overweight and never seems to have been concerned with exercise or physical fitness at all.

Is it paranoid or extravagant to suspect conspiracy in the Calvi death?

Calvi was found with bricks stuffed down the front of his trousers, a hard fact to explain rationally; but the symbolism reeks of Freemasonry.

The day Calvi was found hanging from the bridge in London, his secretary Graziella Carrocher, died mysteriously in Milan: she fell or jumped or was pushed out of a window of Calvi's Banco Ambrosiano.

The quasi-Freemasonic secret society to which Calvi belonged, **P2**, has been accused by Italian investigating magistrates of multitudinous financial frauds, laundering Mafia drug money, infiltrating over 950 agents into the Italian government, carrying out terrorist bombings, and conspiring to install a fascist government in Italy by *coup d'Etat*. Financial reporter Penny Lernous, in her book, *In Banks We Trust*, adds to this that there is considerable evidence that **P2** was the main financial backer of fascist regimes in Latin America and helped many Nazi war criminals, including the notorious Klaus Barbie, find new identities and employment in the **CIA**-backed death squads which maintain the power of these fascist governments. P2, Lernoux documents, was largely responsible for the return to power of the fascist Peron regime in Argentina, and Peron personally thanked Licio Gelli, Grandmaster of P2.

In 1978—four years before Calvi died in London—the editor of a Rome magazine, *L'Osservatore Politico*, Mino Pecorelli, sent Pope John Paul I an issue of his journal in which he named over a hundred **P2** members and/or members of other Freemasonic lodges who had jobs in the Vatican (especially in the IOR or Vatican Bank, which worked so closely with Calvi's Banco Ambrosiano). The Pope died shortly thereafter in ambiguous circumstances—no autopsy was performed and the Vatican has refused to show the death certificate to enquiring journalists.

David Yallop's controversial *In God's Name* is an attempt to prove that the Pope was poisoned by a conspiracy of Vatican officials who were members of, or allied with, **P2**. Mr. Yallop does not, in any legal sense, prove his case, but he does make it highly plausible.

Whatever the facts about the death of Pope John Paul I may be, there is no mystery at all about the death of Signor Pecorelli, the editor who sent the **P2** list to the Pope. Pecorelli was shot dead in his car. Both fatal bullets entered through the mouth, in the classic Mafia form of execution—the same *sasso in bocca* that was used by the killers of Sam Giancana. It seems undeniable, then, the Pecorelli was killed by the Mafia **or by persons who devoutly wish us to think he was killed by the Mafia.**

COCAINE, THE C.I.A. AND THE POPE

Cocaine is just nature's way of telling you that you have too much money.
— Richard Pryor

The most provocative moment in the famous "Watergate tapes" occurs when President Nixon agrees to pay E. Howard Hunt $1,000,000 not to spill "that whole Bay of Pigs thing." It is hard to imagine what Bay of Pigs "thing" had not been revealed by 1973, when that conversation took place, or why Nixon would pay such a huge sum to keep it covered up.

Part of the answer probably relates to the odd symbiosis between the CIA and the Mafia which we have already noted. Mr. Hunt was an employee of the CIA at the time the Agency was involved in assassination plots with Mr. Roselli and Mr. Giancana, and while the Bay of Pigs invasion was being plotted.

Another part of the answer, perhaps, lies in the story of the World Finance Corporation, a bank in Miami, Florida, which went bankrupt after its top officials were indicted, in 1981, for knowingly laundering the cocaine money of various Latin American dictators. The President of the World Finance Corporation was one Hernandez Cataya, who had also served in the CIA with Mr. Hunt while the Bay of Pigs was being plotted.

Two other executives of the World Finance Corporation also turned out to be former CIA employees.

To be a "former" CIA agent can mean one of two things. It can mean that the person has left the Agency and has no more connection with them, or it can mean that the person is still working for them and receiving compensation through a numbered Swiss bank account although no longer on the records as their employee. Only God and the CIA know what it means in the case of the World Finance Corporation and its lucrative cocaine business that also supported some of the Agency's favorite dictators.

Financial reporter Penny Lernoux, who discusses this curious bank at length in her *In Banks We Trust*, quotes members of both the District Attorney's staff of Dade County and a Congressional Committee who say bluntly that attempts to discover the exact role of the CIA in the World Finance Corporation were blocked by a CIA smokescreen.

However, it was learned that the cocaine money was laundered by the WFC sending it on a strange carousel that began with an even shadier bank in the Bahamas, called Cisalpine. The major owners of the Cisalpine Bank were Roberto Calvi (remember him?) and Archbishop Paul Marcinkus of the Vatican Bank. Ms. Lernoux believes the drug money passed through Calvi's Banco Ambrosiano and the Vatican Bank on its way to some financial Black Hole where law enforcement officials will never find it.

Lernoux claims—as does David Yallop in his *In God's Name*— that this profitable conspiracy was masterminded by Licio Gelli, the Grandmaster of the **P2** secret society. Gelli, who has been indicted in Italy for conspiracy, murder, fraud and plotting to overthrow the government (among other things) is presently hiding out in Uruguay, after being arrested in Switzerland and escaping, in less than a week, from an allegedly escape-proof prison.

It *seems* that **P2** was Signor Gelli's invention from the beginning, but this has been challenged by various investigators. Stephen Knight in *The Brotherhood* claims that Gelli was working for the KGB and tries to prove that **P2** was a Soviet experiment in destabilizing a Western government; Knight bases this chiefly on the claims of a British Intelligence agent, from which we may deduce either that Gelli was working for the KGB or that the lads in MI5-London have their own reasons to wish us to believe he was working for the KGB.

Both Yallop in *In God's Name* and Lernoux in *In Banks We Trust* indicate that, while there is evidence that Gelli was recruited by the KGB at one point, there is even stronger evidence that he had been recruited by the CIA even earlier—in the 1950s, he arranged the assassinations of several Italian labour union officials whose politics were distasteful to Washington—and the weight of the data strongly suggests that Gelli was deceiving both sides in the "Intelligence war" for his own profit.

Many Italian journalists have tried to prove that Gelli and **P2** were both "fronts" for another, older Freemasonic group. Larry Gurwin of the *Institutional Investor* (London), in his book, *The Calvi Affair*, quotes one former **P2** member as saying this mysterious lodge was headquartered in Monte Carlo.

But Gurwin also notes that Gelli was a member of the Grand Orient Lodge of Egyptian Freemasonry before **P2** came into existence. The Grand Orient is well known to students of conspiracy literature. It was founded in 1771 by the duc de Orleans and the enigmatic "Count Cagliostro" and is believed by many to have manipulated events during the French Revolution so as to advance Orleans to the kingship. If so, it was as unsuccessful as most such plots—Orleans, of course, ended on the guillotine, not the throne. Nonetheless, the Grand Orient has played a role in so many political adventures and high crimes that British Freemasons refuse to recognize it as a "real" Freemasonic lodge.

Grandmaster Licio Gelli's escape from a supposedly "escape-proof" Swiss jail has led many to speculate that P2 is as strong as it ever was, despite the prosecutions of hundreds of its members in Italy. Both Yallop and Lernoux indicate that P2 lodges are still very active throughout Latin America; Yallop insists that there is still a powerful P2 lodge in the United States.

Here it is worth noting some opinions of Roberto Calvi, as a man in a position to know what goes on below the surface of things. According to Yallop and Gurwin, Calvi recommended Mario Puzo's novel about the Mafia, *The Godfather*, on numerous occasions, saying it was the one book that tells "how the world is really run." Calvi believed in what Italians call *potere occulto*—hidden power that operates behind the scenes. His son, Carlo, says Roberto was "fascinated by secret societies" and

Calvi's lawyer said to Gurwin that Roberto Calvi believed "the world is run by conspiracies."

The plural is significant. Amateurs in this field always seem to fall into the trap of thinking in terms of One Big Conspiracy, singular. This is because conspiracies, like a bowl of spaghetti, contain endless entanglements and overlaps; but to mistake the spaghetti for a coherent or intelligent organism is like mistaking the debris and flotsam on a beach for the outline of an invading army.

It is noteworthy that Gurwin, although employed by the conservative *Institutional Investor*, concludes *The Calvi Affair*—after tracing the criss-crossing paths of the Vatican, the Mafia, the CIA and Freemasonry through jungles of fraud and double-dealing—"Roberto Calvi's world view may have been far more accurate than anyone realized."

LOONY TUNES AND MERRY MELODIES

The chessboard is the world . . . the player
on the other side is hidden from us.
— Thomas Henry Huxley, *Collected Essays*

All secret societies have their own myths, like the Freemasonic allegory of the Widow's Son; but for that matter, all human groups seem to feel the need for symbol or transcendental "truth"—i.e. for myth and allegory.

Some secret societies, of course, may have real secrets, because conventional "history" and conventional "truth," in any tribe or nation, always turns out to be, as Marx said, the myth of the ruling class. The truth is always "hidden with seven seals," because **nobody is more paranoid than professional conspirators**, and the ruling elites are always afraid to let any real knowledge get into general circulation.

Those who horde money, land titles, etc. also horde information; it is a mammalian reflex. It is always a key rule of strategy in all competitive games, as von Neumann and Morgenstern documented mathematically in their *Theory of Games and Economic Behavior*. Hiding information and spreading false information are successful strategies in poker, economic competition and hot and cold wars. All the existing government stamps saying **TOP SECRET** or **FOR YOUR EYES ONLY** are exemplifications of this primate habit of hoarding information.

In this connection, consider first Father Juan Kronh, who attempted to assassinate Pope John Paul II at Fatima in 1982. Father Krohn told the court at his trial that the Vatican has been taken over in recent decades by a conspiracy of "Freemasons and Satanists." This was the doctrine of the renegade Archbishop Lefebvre in France, who ordained Father Krohn and played a large role in Krohn's intellectual development. Many have wondered why Lefebvre, whose denunciations of the Vatican are now legendary, has never been excommunicated. According to Lincoln, Leigh and Baigent in their controversial and speculative *Holy Blood, Holy Grail*, a disciple of Lefebvre's, in England, claims the dissident prelate holds an "earth-shaking weapon" over the Vatican.

Whatever Lefebvre's "weapon" may be, it is probably not any inner knowledge of the Freemasonic/**P2** infiltration of the IOR (Vatican Bank); that has already been widely publicized, and the Vatican handled it as priests have always handled unwelcome news, as witness the *Irish Press* for 23 June 1983 in which the Pope replied to an enquiry about the frauds and drug-dealing of the Vatican Bank with the following well-chosen words:

> Many incredible things can be read in the newspapers, things which have no basis in truth. You must never let your faith be shaken by what you read in the newspapers.

W.C. Fields could not have replied with more aplomb.

We are still in the dark as to what "earth-shaking weapon" the heretic Lefebvre holds over the Vatican. According to Father Malachi Martin, S.J. (in his *The Decline and Fall of the Roman Church*), Lefebvre sent the late Pope John Paul I a portfolio of documents concerning Freemasonic affiliations of Vatican staff members—together with photos of Cardinals with their boy friends and other such unsavory matters—but the Pope was taken suddenly dead before he could respond in any way. Lefebvre's right-hand man, the Abbe Ducaud-Bourget said to the French press on the Pope's demise, "It is hard to believe this death is natural."—which was some kind of new high, or new low, in the propaganda war between the Lefebvreites and the Vatican—but something still remains unexplained, one feels.

According to Jean Delaude's *Le Cercle d'Ulysse*, both Archbishop Lefebvre and the Abbe Ducaud-Bourget are members of the Priory of Sion. Delaude identifies the Priory of Sion as an ancient Catholic order, strongly conservative, which is currently pledged to make Lefebvre the next Pope. Delaude also says the Abbe Ducaud-Bourget is the current Grandmaster of the Priory of Sion, having succeeded Jean Cocteau in 1963.

A rather different view of the Priory of Sion is given in Gerard de Sede's *La race fabuleuse*. As de Sede tells it, the Priory is made up of persons descended from Merovingian kings and certain allies who are devoted to the Merovingian cause. Another group, not named by de Sede but sounding suspiciously like the Vatican, has been persecuting and assassinating the Merovingians for over a thousand years; they killed the last Merovingian king, Dagobert II on 23 December 689 and (perhaps out of a sense of symmetry) they killed de Sede's principle informant, an elusive "Marquis de B." on 23 December 1971. At the very end of this odd and undocumented saga, de Sede reveals the secret of the Merovingians and the Priory of Sion—they are superhuman beings, descended from the intermarriages in ancient Israel between the Tribe of Benjamin and extraterrestrials from Sirius.

De Sede does not mention Archbishop Lefebvre at all; but then, he doesn't need to. The extraterrestrials are exciting enough.

The Swiss journalist, Mattieu Paoli, gives a different account in his *Les Dessous d'une ambition politique*. Paoli does not mention Archbishop Lefebvre either. He says the propaganda of the Priory of Sion is circulated in Switzerland through the Grand Loge Alpina, the largest Freemasonic lodge in the country and the one that allegedly controls Swiss banking. (Curiously, Yallop's *In God's Name* indicates that the Freemasons in the Vatican Bank included members of the Grand Loge Alpina along with members of P2.) Paoli found that *Circuit*, the newsletter of the Priory of Sion, was distributed through the Grand Loge Alpina, was devoted mostly to obscure articles on astrology and occultism, and, according to its title page, was published by the Committee to Secure the Rights and Privileges of Low Cost Housing, indicating some hermetic humor on the part of some of the Priory. *Circuit* was actually published, Paoli discovered, out of the offices in Paris of the government department called the Committee for Public Safety.

The directors of the Committee for Public Safety at that time were Andre Malraux, the well-known critic and novelist, and Pierre Plantard de Saint Clair, about whom we will soon learn more and understand less. Both Malraux and Plantard served under de Gaulle in the Free French forces during World War II, and both had remained close associates of his after the war. Paoli was admittedly stumped in trying to fathom what the Priory of Sion was, but the conclusion of his book is that the Priory reaches very high in the French government and has considerable influence on Swiss banking.

De Sede's book on the extraterrestrial-Hebraic roots of the Priory had not appeared when Paoli published *Les Dessous*, so it is amusing that he reproduces without comment the cover of one edition of the Priory's magazine, *Circuit*. The cover shows a map of France with a Star of David superimposed on it and something that looks like a spaceship hovering above . . . I suspect hermetic humor again. That cover seems well calculated to push the paranoia buttons of both anti-semites and the more demoniac UFO theorists.

It is only a coincidence (I hope) but Paoli was shot as a spy in Israel shortly after his book was published.

Literature on the Priory of Sion continues to proliferate.

According to Lincoln, Baigent and Leigh in *Holy Blood, Holy Grail*, the secret of the Priory of Sion is that, as de Sede claimed, its leaders are descended from the Merovingian kings—but the Merovingians themselves were descended, not from extraterrestrials, but from Jesus Christ and Mary Magdalene. The authors also claim (as de Sede only hinted) that the Vatican murdered Dagobert II, but they do not imply that the Vatican is still trying to murder off all the descendants of Dagobert (i.e. also of Jesus). They identify Pierre Plantard de Saint Claire, not the Abbe Ducaud-Bourget, as the Grandmaster of the Priory of Sion, and attempt to prove that Plantard is a direct descendant of Jesus and Magdalene.

M. Plantard actually gave an interview to the authors and was brilliantly occult and evasive. He did not comment on his own bloodline but volunteered that the Priory of Sion is in possession of a treasure that belongs to Israel, that the treasure is not material but spiritual, and that it will be returned to Israel "at the proper time." That may contain some broad hints, or it may be magnificent misdirection.

According to Michael Lamy's *Jules Verne: Initiate et Initiateur*, Verne was a member of the Priory of Sion, which was originally a front for the Illuminati conspiracy in 18th Century Freemasonry—of course, the Illuminati and the Grand Orient, from which **P2** is descended, were virtually identical—and the great inner secret of the Priory is that they

know a temple in Rennes-le-Chateau which has, in the basement, a
hole leading down to the center of the Earth, where there is a race of
immortal superhumans. Verne hinted at this in several of his novels, of
course.

Like de Sede's yarn about the extraterrestrials mating with Hebrews,
this thesis that some of Verne's science-fiction was science fact is not
well documented. There *is* a temple in Rennes-le-Chateau mentioned
in most other books on the Priory of Sion. It was built in the 1890s by
an eccentric priest named Father Sauniere, is dedicated to Mary
Magdalene, and, for some odd reason, Sauniere wrote over its door the
gnomic inscription, **THIS PLACE IS TERRIBLE.** (Of course, to an
orthodox Catholic the thesis that Jesus had a child by Magdalene and
their descendants are all around us would be rather terrible.)

According to Eon Begg's *The Cult of the Black Virgin*, the mysterious
Black Virgins in European churches—there are over 400 of them,
regarded as inexplicable by most historians and a profound embarrass-
ment to the Vatican—were placed in the churches by the Priory of Sion
in the 13th Century. Begg, who is more given to esoteric hinting than
to clear exposition, says the Priory also introduced the Tarot cards to
Europe at that time and that all this has something to do with Mary
Magdalene and the Sufi Order of Islam.

Going back a bit, *Holy Blood, Holy Grail* insists that Father Sauniere's
temple to Mary Magdalene in Rennes-le-Chateau has some distinctly
odd Stations of the Cross, including one which seems to show Jesus
being carried out of the grave during the night as if by conspirators
planning to fake the Resurrection. Another one, not so blasphemous
but rather spooky if you think of it, shows a Scotsman in kilts watching
the crucifixion.

Father Sauniere was, all sources agree, an associate of, and perhaps a
member of, the Hermetic Brotherhood of Light, in Paris. This was
another secret society, which at various times included composer
Claude Debussy, Gerard Encause and Aleister Crowley. Debussy was,
according to several of our sources, a Grandmaster of the Priory of
Sion. Encause, better known under his pen-name, "Papus," wrote one
of the most influential books on the Tarot and was later closely
associated with Rasputin in Russia, and thus with shadowy doings
before the Russian Revolution. Crowley also wrote an influential book
on the Tarot, and became Outer Head of the Ordo Templi Orientis
(yet another secret society, which alleges descent from the Sufi Order
and the Knights Templar). Crowley also worked for German intelligence

in World War I, although he oddly remained a good friend of the acting chief of British Naval Intelligence, leading some to think he was at least a double-agent.

According to Francis King's *Satanism and Swastika*, the Outer Head of the Ordo Templi Orientis before Crowley, Dr. Theodore Reuss, was also an employee of German intelligence and assigned to spy on no less a personage than Karl Marx.

It is useless to try to make sense of all this in terms of a rational paradigm. Remember the bowl of spaghetti metaphor, and remember that conspiracies, like nations, have no permanent allies, only permanent interests. It is worthy of note, however, that Father Sauniere, who built a temple to the Magdalene and called it terrible and who associated with the Hermetic Brotherhood of Light and the Priory of Sion, became a very rich man by unknown means. According to *Holy Blood, Holy Grail*, Father Sauniere was given his riches in one huge gift from the Archduke Johann von Hapsburg.

According to Maynard Solomon's *Beethoven*, the *Emperor Joseph Cantata*, Beethoven's first Major work, was commissioned by the Illuminati. The *Cantata* glorifies Emperor Joseph von Hapsburg as a bringer of light and a foe of "darkness and superstition." The Emperor's enlightenment seems to have been demonstrated chiefly by the facts that he made Freemasonry legal in Austria (including, of course, the Illuminati lodges) and that he closed the Catholic schools, replacing them with public (secular) education.

We might jump to conclusions when noting that one von Hapsburg in the 18th Century was a friend to Freemasonry and a hero of the Illuminati and another von Hapsburg in the 19th Century gave huge wealth to a strange priest associated with the Priory of Sion.

We might even think strange and Romantic thoughts if we were to put these facts together with the Merovingian geneologies in the Bibliotheque Nationale, attributed to Leo Shidlof. According to these geneologies the von Hapsburgs are of Merovingian descent. They are thus related to Jesus and Magdalene, if one believes *Holy Blood, Holy Grail*, or to extraterrestrials from Sirius, if one believes *La race fabuleuse*.

The current scion of the family, Dr. Otto von Hapsburg, has attracted the attention of conspiracy buffs, however, because he is one of the leading members of the Bilderbergers—the secretive group of financiers who meet once a year (always at a different place) and never answer press enquiries about what they discuss or what their purposes are. Along with Dr. von Hapsburg, the two best known members of the Bilderbergers are David Rockefeller, who virtually controls American banking, and Prince Bernhard of the Netherlands.

Prince Bernhard also has Merovingian genes, according to the Shidlof geneologies. This means either that he is descended from Jesus, or from extraterrestrials, or that some members of some secret societies enjoy planting false leads to baffle profane investigators.

TRILATERAL SPAGHETTI

Every bank of discount is downright corruption, robbing the public for private individuals' gain; and if I said this in my will the American people would pronounce that I died crazy.

> — John Adams, letter to Benjamin Rush
> *Works*, Vol IX, p 638

David Rockefeller is, of course, the principle financial backer of the mysterious Trilateral Commission in addition to owning Chase Manhattan Bank and belonging to the esoteric Bilderberger club. Lyndon Larouche, the eccentric right-wing former Trotskyist, believes that the Trilateral Commission is nothing else but Rockefeller's attempt to take over the world; but then Larouche also believes Queen Elizabeth II is the mastermind behind the international drug trade. Others far less bizarre than Larouche have worried about the Trilateralists. For instance, Sean MacBride—winner of the American Medal of Justice, the Lenin Peace Prize, the Dag Hammerskold Medal of Honor of the UN and the Nobel Peace Prize—has also claimed that the Trilateral Commission is a front for Rockefeller's banking interests.' MacBride also finds it sinister that even so small a nation as neutral Ireland has a Prime Minister and two cabinet members who are also members of the Trilateral Commission. Throughout the Western world, Trilateralists are found in higher numbers in all the NATO governments.

Penny Lernoux, in *In Banks We Trust,* treats the Trilateral Commission as David Rockefeller's major folly, arguing that if it is intended to further Rockefeller's financial interests, it is a total failure, since its members seem to spend most of their time quarreling.

Again we must return to the spaghetti metaphor and remind ourselves that most conspiracies are not nearly as clever as they think they are. The Trilateralists are not "running the world" yet, but they are intertwined like spaghetti with every other affinity group that wields considerable power. Through Prince Bernhard, they have a communication channel at least to the Bilderbergers and, probably, the financial wing of the Priory of Sion, which, for all its mysticism, once operated out of an office of the de Gaulle government and which is cozy with the Grand Loge Alpina and the "Gnomes of Zurich" (Harold Wilson's name for the Swiss banking cartel). Through Chase Manhattan, Rockefeller was involved financially with the World Finance Corporation and its strange links to the CIA and the Mafia; through Chase Manhattan, Rockefeller is still financially involved with the Vatican Bank.

Licio Gelli, incidentally, was not only Grandmaster of **P2** and a sometime employee of both the CIA and KGB, but also a Knight of Malta. The Knights of Malta, one of the most secretive of Vatican orders, dates from the 12th Century; membership in it gave Gelli a fraternal bond to William Casey, head of the CIA, and who is also a Knight of Malta, and to General Alexander Haig, another Knight of Malta, who was advisor to President Nixon and Secretary of State under President Reagan. This may explain why Gelli's colleague in the cocaine trade and bank frauds, Michele Sindona, was a guest at Nixon's inaugural ball and why Gelli himself was a guest at Reagan's inaugural ball.

David Rockefeller is also a major financial backer of the Republican Party, and two of his brothers became governors of New York and Arkansas respectively. The spaghetti metaphor must be invoked again to explain why Nixon, who, like all Republican Presidents, owes a great deal to Rockefeller, was also a good and dear friend of Rockefeller's arch-enemy, Howard Hughes.

The war between Rockefeller and Hughes is the major theme of David Tinnin's *Just About Everybody VS Howard Hughes*, a book just as important for one who wishes to understand modern Capitalism as Machiavelli's *The Prince* for one who wants to understand politics. Briefly, David Rockefeller set out to capture control of Trans World Airlines from Hughes, who vowed he would "burn down the plant" before allowing Rockefeller to take it over. The conflict was protracted, lasted over decades and left Hughes a clinical paranoid, convinced that

Rockefeller owned the U.S. government lock, stock and barrel. The question is: did Hughes think such things because he always had a tendency to paranoia, or did he become paranoid because of what happened to him in fighting Rockefeller in the American courts?

One of the loose ends left over from Watergate is the question of why President Nixon loaned "the plumbers"—his own private espionage and dirty tricks gang—to Howard Hughes, for whom they burglarized a newspaper office looking for God-knows-what. As Carl Oglesby indicates in *The Yankee and Cowboy War*, Hughes had previously given Nixon's brother, Donald, $1,000,000; Hughes had been equally lavish in buying the affections of literally hundreds of Western politicians, in his endeavor to fight off what he saw as the death grip of Rockefeller upon Eastern seaboard legislators and judges. By the end of it all, Hughes was not only paranoid, locked in a room, fearful of human contact, but had his financial empire heavily infiltrated, as Oglesby proves, by the Mafia, whom he had been fighting for control of the Las Vegas gambling casinos.

The Knights of Malta, to which Licio Gelli, William Casey of the CIA and General Haig all belong, is discussed in Gordon Thomas's *The Year of Armaggedon*. Thomas claims that Pope John Paul II has weekly meetings with CIA officers in Rome and uses the Knights of Malta as couriers of secret communications with CIA headquarters in Alexandria, Virginia. It all tends to remind me of a remark I once heard from the philosopher Alan Watts: "The principle error of academic historians is their belief that the Roman Empire 'fell.' It never 'fell.' It still controls the Western world through the Vatican and the Mafia." Our evidence, however indicates that the Vatican/Mafia group does not control the West, but only tries to, and that in the huge bowl of spaghetti which is primate territorial politics, every other affinity group is aiming at similar control. They all cooperate at times, and they all double-cross each other whenever that is to their advantage.

The Franklin National Bank, which went through the most shocking bankruptcy of the 1970s, was also a client of Chase Manhattan and Mr. Rockefeller. Franklin National was founded by Michele Sindona, manager of Vatican finances in the United States and a member of P2. Sindona, who started his career as a lawyer for several Sicilian Mafia families, bought huge shares in Paramount films, Procter and Gamble and the World Trade Center for the Vatican; he also seems to have looted $55,000,000 from Franklin National, right under Rockefeller's nose—Chase was the major guarantor of Franklin's loans—and was convicted later, in New York, of 65 counts of stock and currency fraud, and in Rome, of the murder of a bank examiner. Sindona died in prison while awaiting trial on the further charge that he conspired with Roberto Calvi, Licio Gelli (Grandmaster of **P2**) and General Musemicci, chief of the Italian Secret Police, in the 1980 Bologna railway bombing. Reports differ as to whether Sindona killed himself or was poisoned by his former associates. The motives of the Bologna bombing are not clear, either—one's interpretation depends on whether one regards **P2** as chiefly a tool of the CIA or of the KGB or as a band of adventurers exploiting both sides in the Cold War for their own financial gain. The only sure thing about any of this is that Lord Acton was right when he said all power tends to corrupt and absolute power corrupts absolutely.

Author's Advisory

"It's a jungle out there."
"It's a dog eat dog world."
Or is it?

All of our received, recorded human history appears to be a dreary and depressing tale of endless warfare, poverty and pestilence. It seems a random and rambling series of largely tragic happenstances, only occasionally relieved by moments of grandeur; of monarchs, musicians and philosophers, yet all of it against a dark tapestry of human baseness and suffering—of unbridled money-lust and savage territorial conquest.

This is the *accidentalist* school of human history, the one officially subscribed to by virtually every institution of learning in the world. It is the history interpreted and promoted by honest and conscientious scholars who faithfully pass it on from one generation to the next throughout the centuries. It is the history you believe in, and the one I also believed in until . . .

A brief autobiographical blurb is needed here in the interest of fairplay. You are entitled to know something about the sources of this information and how this book came into being. This is advance notice, then, necessary to your appreciation of what lies ahead, and what lies ahead may well be the greatest astonishment of your life.

As an allopathic physician specializing in psychiatry—an M.D. with two specialty certifications—I am still practising after some thirty-five years in the field. Following a pleasant and altogether unremarkable childhood and adolescence, the beneficiary of good parenting and with probably fewer than usual emotional insults against my earliest imprints, I completed my WW II hitch in the United States Marine Corps (at the time a dreadful waste but later to prove a profoundly meaningful experience), then on to medical training and a few scrappy but happy years on the faculty at the University of Michigan, "The Berkeley of the Midwest."

In that time of tempestuous social ferment, during most of the '50s and all of the '60s, I eagerly played out my natural role as armchair radical, lecturing and writing on behalf of civil rights, minority rights, world peace, militant feminism and most of the other liberal causes at the forefront of public consciousness in that era.

In 1970, ready for a change, my family and I moved to Arizona where I entered the "real world" of community psychiatry and began to learn—among other things—about the psychology of money. I brought my white horse with me and continued to gallop abroad for all the right causes until, on an overcast afternoon late in January, 1976, I was stunned to my foundations by an utterly unexpected, very personal and to me plainly miraculous experience.

At that moment I was spraddled on the floor of my study writing a book on the psychology of the American Manchild (as I described him then) at the invitation of a major American publishing house. Surrounded by mounds of reference books and articles, and with two or three hundred pages of my own rough manuscript at my side, still mildly interested in the subject but less than inspired, I lapsed into a garden-variety brown-study. My mind was a blank and comfortable void, unconflicted, empty and undirected. And then it happened.

Over an interval of no more than two or three minutes my mind was abruptly and inexplicably flooded with what was to me, the fashionable radical, utterly alien information. It was not an auditory hallucination of the kind that gave Richard Bach his now famous *Jonathan Livingston Seagull*; nor was it the sort of dictation received by famed country musician Mel Tillis ("We don't really compose that music—it comes from somewhere else and we just write it down.")

At the time, and probably in response to some ego need on my part, I explained this stunning experience as the unplanned culmination of years of extensive reading in every field relevant to the human experience. The problem with this theory is that I had never really read all *that* much, and though reasonably quick-witted I was also not that bright.

Looking back I found myself inclined to a considerably more modest and, to me, more credible explanation. The subjective sensation was one of having had an ethereal floppy disc slipped slyly into my frontal lobe circuitry and the "printout" button then pushed by some invisible finger.

If I had merely *reasoned* my way to the astonishing conclusions described in this volume I would never have had the brass to write it, as I do not have that much faith in the power of human reason nor in my own mental capacities. But as the information *did* come to me I could only assume that it had been niftily slipped into my mental network for a purpose—this present one.

There were few stauncher skeptics than I—until it happened to me. The clarity of this staggering realization was so unmarred, so perfectly detailed, I could only believe that a few hundred other professional writers were racing to their typewriters to "scoop" me—not realizing at the time that I had been given an exclusive.

The resulting novel was *Skinnerball!!!*, after psychologist B.F. Skinner of operant conditioning fame, and our own planet earth. In the present writing a discreetly revised version of it has been retained, chiefly because it is difficult to improve on the prose born of fresh inspiration. Though fictional in form, the original dust-jacket pitch makes it clear that the theme is not, and it also neatly synopsizes the fictional vehicle that carries the factual message:

President Kennedy spoke warningly of them as "the little gnomes of Zurich." The John Birchers revile them repeatedly as the ill-famed *Illuminati*, the ruthlessly wealthy and powerful supranational *Insiders*—the money manipulators who are hell-bent on gaining total control of the world's money systems and through this its national governments—thus to enslave us all.

To the man-on-the-street the dark and age-old rumors of this international conspiracy are part paranoid legend, part ominous reality.

Convinced of T.H.E.I.R. existence and of their malignant purposes, noted psychiatrist Adam Trasy Solon recruits a highly specialized cadre of dedicated allies to pursue them to their innermost circle and expose them to the world.

Through field investigation, exhaustive and scholarly research, and an agonizing siege of deductive reasoning that brings him to the edge of madness, the secrets of the mysterious *Illuminati* are at last revealed to him: their strategies, their objectives, and who they are.

The discovery is as stunning as it is incredible. But how incredible is it, really? Fact or fiction?—let the reader decide for himself.

For this is a story, or an account, about the breeding, cultivation, training, and harvesting of the most recent crop of the species *Homo sapiens*, now becoming *Sapiens excelsior interstellus*.

1

The Roots of Illumination

How are we to keep the human herd from breaking out again?
— Plato's *Dialogues*

Adam poised on the edge of the granite cliff and looked down at the clear, cold water in the lake below, then up at the brilliant blue dawn sky over the desert, feeling every inch like Howard Roark at his towering and indomitable best.

Then Candy called across the ravine from the deck of the house, "You look like Howard Roark!"

"He was a piker," then taking a fast glance at her glistening facade he added cheerfully, "I'm a breast stroker myself!"

"You're a cop-out. He dove completely naked!"

With both hands Adam smoothed his minimal, flesh-colored briefs from the front around to his butt, all bunched for the plunge. He looked back across the ravine at Candy, who was standing insolently nude on the deck like a bronzed statue, with her maddeningly blonde hair cascading halfway down her body, stilted on one leg, shading her eyes from the brilliant morning sun and waiting for him to finish his morning rite. He called back to her:

"Then he was nuts to risk his jewelry against all that surface tension down there at" (. . . he paused and did a quick mental calculation starting with thirty-two feet per second then converting to . . .) "about twenty-two miles per hour!"

"Stop bragging! Do your thing and come have breakfast with me!"

He glanced briefly over his shoulder at the rising sun, brilliantly illuminating hundreds of square miles of desert chaparral around him, then he scowled. "Illuminating," he repeated to himself—a sudden alien blight on an otherwise perfect morning. "Those arrogant bastards—I'll get 'em yet."

Consoled by the thought, he spread his arms to the side, tensed and drove forward from the cliff's edge, holding nearly horizontal at first, then piking suddenly at the last moment to enter the little lake cleanly, almost vertically. As he decelerated in the chilly morning water, exultant with the force of its tearing at his face and body, he arched and glided upward to the surface, which he broke with a lunging stroke toward the opposite shore some two hundred yards away.

Candy dropped back into the deck chaise to watch him, silently granting him 9.5 points for the dive and a biased observer's gold medal for his long, effortless freestyle. *How much simpler it would be*, she thought, *if he had just turned out like any other bejowled, gray-haired, pot-bellied and spindly-legged middle-aged daddy.* The sun was warming her breasts and belly and thighs, and she was returning the heat from an inexhaustible source within.

Moments later he was beside her on the deck, toweling himself dry.

"What do you want for breakfast—the usual?"

"Please. Fine."

She bounced up from the lounge and he watched her retreating figure admiringly as she strode toward the door, with her apple cheeks rolling smoothly against each other, and all but escaping concealment by her incredible veil of hair. When she disappeared he shook his head sharply to erase the disturbing image from his mind, then picked up the pen and daily log book from the table at his side. He stared off across the desert for a minute to fire up his train of thought and began to jot:

"The feeling is still there, getting stronger every day.... Something is going to happen—something huge and imminent . . . powerful intuitive feeling, undoubtedly a fragmentary surfacing of accumulated unconscious data that's still assembling before print-out is ready . . . related somehow to my expose book on the Insiders, the Illuminati, which is coming together.... But something major is missing—a link as big as an elephant.... Feel that I'm looking right at it but it's in my blind spot and I can't see it . . . something pitifully obvious but infuriatingly elusive . . . will keep trying to associate to it . . . maybe I'm afraid of it because it's too mind-blowing . . . must keep feeding in data, reading, thinking, computing, and most of all—writing—tease it up to where I can see the whole thing—whatever it is. . . . "

Candy reappeared with a serving tray and set the table between them. Small glass of chilled orange juice, hot black coffee, and a modest bowl of mixed natural grain cereals with chopped dried fruit and sunflower kernels, floating in cold non-fat milk. He tossed down the juice, took a sip of the coffee and then had a spoonful of the cereal mix.

"Not bad at all for what it is, but," he reminisced fondly, "I still miss those murderous old breakfasts of my youth; ham and eggs, bacon gravy on hot homemade biscuits, fresh hot bagels slathered with whipped cheddar cheese and chopped onions and bacon bits—warm Danish pastries—peanut butter and jelly on toast—hash browns with a couple of soft-boiled eggs on them—goddamn those meddling, spoilsport, metabolic, cardiovascular internists and their crummy research. . . ."

"Hang in there, pappy," Candy said philosophically. "Sunday will soon be here and you can sin again."

"I know, but to a man who needs to indulge his vices daily—as desperately as I do—Sunday seems forever. What's on your agenda today, routine school?"

"Nope. It's a national holiday—no school."

Adam was perplexed. "It is? What national holiday?"

"It's National Be-Kind-To-Candide-Day, so I'm not going to school. And before you say anything be advised that I'm still number one in the whole school, am carrying a four-point, am a month ahead in all my subjects, and am bored absolutely shitless!"

"Okay, okay—cease and desist. If they hand you any hassle give Dan Winthrop a ring and have him threaten to haul them into court again. . ."

Candy nodded. "No sweat. I haven't had any trouble since I bloomed into gorgeous womanhood, like a year or two ago. Old man Hitchcock—the vice-principal in charge of discipline?—every time I walk into his office he has to sit down with his legs crossed . . . That time I missed a whole week to do my own private desert flora trip, he tried to chew my ass but his voice was trembling so much he couldn't even finish the job."

"Splendid. Glad to know you're using all that power to good advantage."

She suddenly glanced over his shoulder and frowned. "Hey Dad—we're being watched. Just saw a reflection from a spotting scope."

"I know—I sensed it. Likely just a normal, red-blooded voyeur.

Forget it."

"Anyway," she continued, "I'm going to be working for you most of the day . . . which reminds me—you owe me thirty-six small green ones for my eighteen hours last week."

"Fair enough. Dun me again when I have my checkbook with me. Have you come to the Alumbrados and Afghanis yet?"

"A little. I'm still on the Bavarian branch—coming up with more material than I expected. Getting into some original sources, too, which is going to cost you extra."

"Anything big?"

Candy cocked her head and thought: "No, nothing huge. Just lots of interesting little tidbits to feed into W.H.I.Z. K.I.D."

"Like?"

"Well, the Afghani Roshaniya—the Illuminated Ones—flourished in the fifteen hundreds, but they probably derived from the House of Wisdom in Cairo, which had been going strong for at least three or four centuries prior to then. Both orders had eight degrees of initiation and a strong link between them recurs repeatedly in both the oral and written traditions. . . ."

"And their tie to the Bavarian sect?"

"A little tenuous, maybe, but believable. About forty years after the last religious and military leader of the Roshaniya vanished from the scene, the mysterious Adam Weishaupt came up with the Ingolstadt operation—also called the Illuminati. That was in 1776, when he was a young professor of Canon Law at the University of Ingolstadt. . . ."

"And Washington was elected to the presidency in 1789. . . ."

"Right—thirteen years later—when Weishaupt would have been like in his mid-forties. That does make for a considerable age difference between the two, but with a little makeup and a set of wooden teeth, it's possible that he could have been thrown in as a ringer for old George during the White House years, but still not too likely."

"Okay. Do keep digging on that one. But, meanwhile, back in Bavaria, why all that governmental antagonism toward Weishaupt when he was only trying to replace a Christianity of superstition with one of reason—was it just old-fashioned religious bigotry?"

"That, too—but some of their methods were a bit flaky. One of their honchos, a lawyer named Zwack, was busted ten years after the order was founded for possessing impressions of the personal seals of a few hundred VIP's along with instructions on how to forge and substitute them on influential documents. He claimed it was just a hobby, but the government found that hard to swallow."

"Is that where the women came in?"

"Yep. It was then that the Illuminati's plan for recruiting women—especially young ones—was uncovered. The theory was reasonable enough—that women could influence powerful men as effectively as money or the promise of more power."

Adam nodded grimly. "It'd sure work with me."

"With most men, except maybe the gay ones. Anyway, I have a strong intuitive hunch that today, exactly two hundred years later, women are very, very strong in the organization—which is as it should be, natch." She smiled smugly.

"Good. Good." Adam sat back and rubbed his chin thoughtfully. "How about the concept of Illumination itself? Getting anywhere with that one? I mean, in the literal sense it's such a benevolent idea—what's wrong with being Illuminated?"

"Exactly. That's a mystifying paradox. Illumination is really a very old religious concept—a stage of spiritual development following purification of the soul and preceding an ultimate union with God. After that, one is able to detach himself from things of the material world—wealth and food and sex and such—and progress thereafter at a strictly spiritual level."

Troubled by the thought, Adam frowned and sighed. "Guess I'm not ready for that yet. Still a pleasure-loving spiritual barbarian."

"But you're still growing, daddy. Anyway, the concept of Illumination is almost universal. It appears in Buddhism, Islam and Christianity—especially in Augustine's neoplatonic epistemology. So don't give up on yourself yet, pater—remember: *Ewige Blumenkraft!*"

"*Ewige Blumenkraft*," Adam pondered, "supposedly a favorite slogan of the Enlightened Ones. Means something like 'Let Power Bloom Forever,' doesn't it? That would certainly fit those birds. It surely applies well to Mayor Daley, who was reportedly seen mouthing the phrase at the Democratic National Convention in Chicago when he got pissed off at some remark made by Abe Ribicoff."

Candy insisted on a more disciplined approach to the analysis. "Look," she said firmly, "this is very fuzzy history we're dealing with here—and fuzzily dealt with. I mean, Shea and Wilson and Saul Goodman and his sidekick Muldoon—they actually had very little to go on. Flimsy stuff at best and all of it a part of the public record. In fact, there was a minimum of scholarly digging involved in bringing this stuff to public attention."

"No high-powered espionage?" Adam asked.

"Nope. It's all from publicly published works. In his book *Violence*, Jacques Ellul dates the movement back to an eleventh-century religious leader named Joachim of Floris, who has most interestingly been condemned by William Buckley as the fount of contemporary, bleeding-heart liberalism.

"And, next," she continued, "is Daraul's *A History of Secret Societies*, published in 1961, which also traces them back to the eleventh century, but brings them to the modern era as the Aga Kahn's Ishmaelians, and to the Spanish *Alumbrados*, the French *Guerinets* and, of course, to good old Adam Weishaupt's eighteenth-century *Illuminati* in Bavaria. And then there's the Wilgus book on *The Illuminoids*, a scholarly windup but no pitch."

"Not exactly esoteric sources, are they," Adam observed.

"Hardly! And it gets even flakier. Next they cite the *Encyclopedia Britannica* on the Weishaupt caper. Then they move on—now get this—to the April, 1969 issue of *Playboy*, repeating some hearsay about the *Illuminati* being the moving force behind the recent wave of assassinations here in America. They're depicted as international financiers who were exposed by Ian Fleming, in the guise of fiction, of course, as *Spectre*, for which indiscretion they did him in. This same note then cross references to an item in *New Yorker* magazine holding that one of Jim Garrison's investigators of the JFK assassination truly believes in the active existence of these self-same *Illuminati*.

"And next," Candy smiled impishly at her raptly attentive father, "comes an admirably unimpeachable source from my own peer level, an article on "The Conspiracy" by one Sandra Glass in the March, 1969 issue of *Teenset*. It also dates the movement from the eleventh century, grassdoping assassins, the *Hashishim* and their latter day student, Adam Weishaupt, who allegedly attracted luminaries like Goethe and Beethoven to membership in his branch of the Society. It's also the article that speculates about Mayor Daley's impassioned utterance of the *Illuminati* slogan at the 1968 convention.

"After that," Candy hesitated as she leafed through her notes, "come our not-so-crazy-as-they-sound cohorts from the lunatic fringe of the John Birch Society."

"A nice coincidence," Adam smiled picking up a copy of *American Opinion* magazine from the rack under the table. "I subscribed to their journal for a few months, trying to get a line on their thinking . . . "

"That much, I suspect, you're already pretty familiar with. A major Birch thesis is that diamond mogul Cecil Rhodes founded a secret

Illuminati branch in the late nineteenth century, which supposedly operates through Oxford University, the Rhodes Scholarship fund, and our own council on Foreign Relations."

Adam nodded. "Good. We have Peter Newton up there now doing a photographic survey of CFR activities—should be revealing. I'm not yet ready to knock the Birchers, but I don't understand the Cecil Rhodes thing—I thought the Birch theory implicated Weishaupt all the way . . . ?"

"They do. They simply link Rhodes to him, but time and again they refer to Weishaupt as the 'monster' who's really responsible for founding the modern Order."

"Fuzzy is the word for it, all right," Adam murmured.

"And it gets fuzzier. The remaining references are a sort of hodge-podge of poorly documented hypotheses and assertions. For example, they purport to confirm that following his banishment from Bavaria, Weishaupt did in fact come to this country, killed the real George Washington and then took his place for at least those two terms he served in the White House. Our flag has the Illuminati colors, red, white and blue, and the thirteen stripes in it correspond to the thirteen levels of the Order's symbolic pyramid.

"They also point to George Washington's backyard crop of marijuana as a distinctively Weishauptian feature—he used to do the same thing back in Ingolstadt—and not unreasonably they make a point of his strong Federalist stance, which would have the effect of concentrating political and economic power in as few hands as possible, thus making said reins all the more accessible, I presume, to the grasping if invisible clutches of the Enlightened Ones—whoever and wherever they might be.

"Which is not to mention that almost taunting smile on the face of the Gilbert Stuart portrait, or the baleful eye in the pyramid on our one-dollar bill, or the Reverend Morse's charge that Thomas Jefferson, like Washington-Weishaupt, was also an agent of the Illuminati. . . ."

"Boggles the mind," Adam said, blinking his eyes and shaking his head in perplexity.

"Inevitably," Candy answered drily, "because these theorists leave no base untouched. Also implicated, one way or another, are the Houses of Morgan and Rothschild—who've supposedly financed the whole operation—the Masons, Yippies, Black Panthers, Mafia, Bank of America, the Mental Health Movement, Mao Tse Tung, Black Muslims, Nelson Rockefeller (supposedly a Primus Illuminatus, if you can believe that), Richard Nixon, *Playboy*, Mark Lane, and the Democratic Party—to mention only a few."[1]

Adam sighed and observed philosophically, "So, historical chaos appears to reign. We have Robert Anton Wilson's quasi-fictional demivillains, the Birchers' infamous *Insiders*, *The Illuminati*, along with Neal Wilgus' thoughtful and painstaking recital of one secret society after another, from Biblical to present times. With it all, I'd say we must remember: it is entirely likely that those of us who write on this subject are not talking about the same people at all."

Then he stretched lazily. "I can believe almost anything these days, while believing none of it. But from all that, the one thing I reject out of hand is the suggestion that Nelson Rockefeller was a Primus. That violates Solon's first law: 'If they're visible, they're not of the Inner Circle.' "

Smiling, he looked at his brilliant and beautiful "little" girl with undisguised admiration. "Well, you really have been digging into it. What's a girl like you doing in a dumpy school like the one you're going to?"

"That's what I keep trying to tell you!"

"Want out? Do your own program?"

Candy laughed. "Not really. That's where my friends and most of the action are—and the work's a cinch. Just a minor annoyance, as long as people don't get too snotty about the attendance bit."

Adam stood up, drew Candy to her feet and embraced her warmly. "Okay, Patoot—great. Write it up and I'll send it along to Gilth to feed to our hungry K.I.D. And don't let me forget what I owe you."

"No way," she murmured, nuzzling and pressing against him. "Know if you'll be home tonight?"

"I think so. If not, I'll call you. Now, into my duds and off to work."

Candy called after him: "Hey! Don't forget—you were to call Gilth this morning!"

"Thanks," he fired back over his shoulder, "I nearly forgot. Later!"

After dressing, Adam let himself into his top-security inner sanctum and flipped on his transceiver. Seventeen randomly layered combinations of audio and frequency modulation had, the electronics experts at G.R.I.P.E. believed, assured them of freedom from monitoring by the Insiders. He flashed the alerting signal to the Alpha Orion mobile unit and waited. Only seconds later Gilth Ypres' voice, calm and dispassionate as ever, came through the speaker: "Dr. Solon I presume."

All these years and Gilth still persisted in the formal address. "Right on Gilth. Listen, if you and I got married would you call me by my first name?"

"Definitely not, Dr. Solon," the disembodied voice continued, with the merest trace of amusement. "Rank-ordering is a necessity in any viable organization, and you are the chief—and would remain so even after the wedding."

Adam couldn't resist one more dart: "If I'm the chief, Gilth, then why are you running everything from that luxurious pleasure craft in the tropics while I slave my poor peasant's ass off back here in never-never land?"

"The staff and I are merely keeping house and tending the ledgers, awaiting your next orders and looking forward to your return and personal leadership."

Adam dropped the banter and went serious. "Speaking of that, how are preparations coming for the quarterly meeting next month?"

"All in order," Gilth replied evenly. "Full attendance is expected and the business agenda is ready. Any new recruits for the staff, doctor?"

"Yes. Not a legion, but what I have are premium quality. Should give us some good additional coverage in oriental language translation, cryptography, and I also want to bring my daughter in for security clearance, to help with historical research, and a few of her carefully selected juvenile recruits for general espionage tasks. I'm still looking for a first-rate computer expert to help you with that end of things, and another expert on international law. That much should see us handsomely through the next meeting, anyway."

"Excellent, doctor—we here look forward to meeting them all. Speaking of computers, I do have some new information for you."

Adam paused and thought. "Hold a minute, Gilth. Do you still think we're safe on this frequency?"

"Our countermonitoring gives no indication that they have tapped into us."

"Good, but let's be doubly careful. Feed your information through the K.I.D. to my component here, in code AA-34, okay?"

"Immediately," Gilth answered obediently.

Adam activated the code-reception circuit on his component console and patched it into the decipher and printout unit. After a few seconds of muffled chattering he tore off the decoded printout and read it: "Believe we have succeeded in sequestering a small but significant segment of the world computer system for communication piracy purposes. Should permit more extensive and rewarding incursion into

Illuminati intelligence banks without detection by their countermonitors. Hope to learn much more about what those triple-distilled diabolists of the solar system are currently up to with Operation Caesar. Our new technique holds much promise for future expansion, though the way to The Top is not yet clear."

Adam's face glowed with pleasure as he dropped the message into the incinerator slot. "Hot fudge sundae," he whistled under his breath, then went back to voice communication.

"Beautiful, Gilth. Marvelous. Keep up the good work and we may yet topple old Zeus himself. Glory to Mankind, Gilth! See you next month at Rendezvous Stat-I."

"Glory to Mankind, doctor. Roger and out."

Jasmyn entered the bright domed chamber with a series of graceful pirouettes, the flowered hem of her frock swirling about her bare thighs.

Sandol was lounging on the dais sipping a glass of cool pilta while scanning the array of monitors on the opposite wall.

"Any happy happenings?" Jasmyn asked lightly.

"Soporific," he answered. "I am perpetually amazed by their snail's pace."

"That stir in South Africa, though . . . "

"Taken care of. I relayed it to media HQ for maxplay. Slow but sure, they're headed the right way."

Jasmyn eased down at his side and stroked back the hair across his ear. "How's my favorite dark horse doing?"

"Well and not well. Still stolidly in the paranoid stance. Pathetic but amusing."

"He'll make it."

"Really? He's not that bright."

"But determined, relentless, perhaps inspired."

Sandol smiled thinly. "You're irrationally partial to him. Most likely, I think, because of his chronic adolescent ways."

"Charming, and quite bright by local standards. He'll make it."

"Never," Sandol murmured confidently. "None of them have made it in the fast fifty years, earth time."

"A small wager then?"

"Certainly. Shall we say five billion?"

"Fine. Five billion what?"

"Whatever," he smiled. "Your friend Adam is too easily distracted. Instant pleasure is his first concern."

Jasmyn tapped a sequence of touch pads on the remote control console and glanced at the affected monitor. "We shall see."

"In any case," Sandol muttered, taking the console from her hand, "I'm going to pique his paranoia with the old cake-jumper bit."

"You're a meanie, Sandol," she pouted prettily. "If you do that, then I reserve the right to drop him a little hint later on—right?"

"It won't help anyway—be my guest." Then he pressed the required pads.

1. R. Shea and R. A. Wilson, *Illuminatus!* Part I, "The Eye in the Pyramid" (New York: Dell Publishing Company, 1975).

2

Cake Jumping Girls

Adam bounded up the four floors to the Psychiatric Admitting Ward three steps at a time. Deb Suners, the charge-nurse, glanced at her watch, then at him, and strove with small success to conceal the expression of pleasurable anticipation that rose to her face.

"Good morning, Dr. Solon," she said politely for the sole benefit of others present: Dr. Telman Durst, a surly and overbearing young staff psychiatrist who was unloved by all but his own mother, and two very cute student nurses who had recently begun their rotation on the service.

Adam took them all in with a cheery good morning and a wave, bravely managing to include Telman with the others. Patting Deb fondly on her delightfully taut rump, he winked intimately at Satin Frisbe, the student nurse he'd met several days earlier (on the tumbling mat in the patients' gym, after hours) and asked "Who's your colleague, Ms. Frisbe?"

With her face carefully composed Satin replied formally: "Oh, excuse me. Marcey Sapinet, this is Dr. Adam Solon, Chief of Service." Adam drank her in appreciatively, deciding at once that she, too, was an emphatic "yes," then with some exercise of will returned his thoughts to prosier tasks at hand.

"Any new admissions?"

Deb answered casually. "Just two. A slightly dotty old-timer and one flasher."

Telman shot her a superior look and butted in officiously. "That's not exactly DSM III terminology, Ms. Suners." He turned to Adam. "The first is a ninety-one year old white male . . . "

"What species, Dr. Durst?" Adam interrupted drily.

"Huh?"

"A white male of what species—for the hundredth time—equine, bovine, or *sapiens*?"

Telman squirmed unhappily. "Oh, sorry—forgot. A ninety-one year old white *man* with an obvious organic brain syndrome secondary to cerebral arteriosclerosis, with moderate psychosis . . . "

"Okay. Save the details for staff—we'll do him first. The other one—in twenty-five words or less?"

"A twenty-three year old white fem . . . uh . . . lady . . . uh . . . woman, post-doctoral fellow in theoretical mathematics, arrested yesterday morning for lewd and lascivious behavior in public, held in jail overnight, transferred here early this morning when her keepers decided she was crazy because she persisted in her L and L performance behind bars . . . My diagnosis is schizophrenia, paranoid type, with sexual sociopathic features . . . "

"Naturally," Adam said acidly. "If they aren't schizophrenic, then what are they doing in here—right?"

Telman again bit back his anger and went on.

"She has some unmistakable manifestations of either latent or overt homosexuality . . . "

"Dr. Durst, please," Adam interrupted again. "Surely you've heard that homosexuality, latent or otherwise, is no longer an official disease—by act of the American Psychiatric Association?"

Telman decontrolled, red-faced and bubbling saliva. "Goddammit, Dr. Solon, I just thought it might be relevant, that's all! So lesbies are supposed to be normal now, huh! Well, they're still queers in my book! So you can just stop picking on me, see! I got my boards in psychiatry, too, just like you—and I deserve to be treated like a colleague and not get picked on all the time. Everyone picks on me! How come, huh? Just tell me that, Dr. Solon—how come all you guys keep picking on me?"

"Because you're there, Telman," Adam answered coolly. "Because you're there."

Telman slammed the chart down on the desk and huffed out the door, heading for the conference room. Satin giggled and said, "Wow, he sounds kinda paranoid." After giving her a quick, dark look of admonition, Deb returned to Adam:

"We still have fifteen or twenty minutes before staff meeting and I need to talk with you about a little problem we're having on the ward. Can you come to my office?"

"Sure. Lead the way."

When they were out of earshot, Satin nudged the other girl and giggled again: "The only problem Ms. Suners is having on this ward is with her own flaming libido. They're going to her office now so Dr. Solon can put out the fire for her."

Marcey was shocked but intrigued. "Really? Right there in her office? How d'ya know?"

"Never mind—I know. Give 'em a couple of minutes to get rolling and you can go down and listen outside the door if you don't believe me," and after a moment of staring dreamily out the window she added generously, "Not that I blame her—he really is something special."

"You mean . . . you mean you've . . . you've . . . ?"

Satin turned to her, open-eyed: "You mean you haven't tried him yet?"

Marcey recoiled. "My god, Satin, I've only been here three days . . . "

"So? Have you tried him yet?"

Deb turned to Adam and smiled as they slipped from her office and walked down the corridor: "How much do I owe you for that one, Adam?"

"Ah, Deb. That one's on the house—it was that good."

"She shook her head emphatically. "No dice, or I won't feel free to call on you next time. I'll send you a check next week for the whole month, usual rate. You just don't realize what a great thing it is for a woman like me to be spared the time and energy and emotional wear-and-tear it takes to deal with your average calf-eyed, jealous, controlling, possessive, sloppy, sentimental, sophomoric bunghole of a man."

"Okay," Adam laughed, "I do appreciate your patronage though."

As he and Deb walked to their seats, Marcey nudged Satin and whispered: "Check Ms. Suners hosiery—on the insides."

Peering around the head in front of her, Satin caught a quick glimpse before Deb sat down and modestly pressed her knees together: "Oh, wow. Did ya hear anything?"

"Plenty—right now I feel like I should be confined to a padded cell—or get some immediate psychiatric therapy."

Satin giggled. "So—are you gonna hit on him?"

"You bet your sweet bustle I am—right after conference—all in the line of duty, of course!"

Deb quieted their hushed giggling with another black look as Dr. Durst began the conference with a chart presentation of the elderly man, then asked Ms. Sapinet to bring him from the ward for an interview. As she left to do so, Adam addressed himself to the staff:

"This may be redundant, but please remember your manners. Our patients are our employers. They are not to be treated as specimens. Show respect. No whispering or giggling during the interview. Only one person at a time will converse with the patient, and everyone be prepared to answer his questions about you as readily as you ask them about him. Okay?"

Heads nodded silently around the room. Everyone present knew of Adam's reputation as a real bear about what he called "common clinical courtesy." Even so, there was a suppressed and generalized gasp when Ms. Sapinet returned with the patient. Adam, like the others, had expected the usual doddering old man on a cane or in a wheelchair, and was as surprised—even startled—as the others to find him quite otherwise. He had to stoop slightly to get through the six-and-a-half-foot doorway and his massive shoulders barely cleared the sides. His thorax was also enormous, and proportionately so, rather than with the pathologically increased front-to-back dimension associated with emphysema and other pulmonary diseases.

He was dressed in a faded blue shirt, denim trousers and leather sandals. His eyes were also pale blue and as tranquil as the rest of his face, and his head was covered with a great snowy white mane that reached to his shoulders. His shirt, unbuttoned almost to the waist, revealed a thick pile of chest hair as white as that on his head. He was immaculately clean and, to all appearances, in superb physical health. The visual impact he made was awesome. As Ms. Sapinet brought him to the front of the room, Adam rose and extended his hand in greeting:

"Mr. Gonman, I'm Dr. Solon, staff psychiatrist here at the institute. We appreciate your joining us—hopefully for our edification. Would you mind answering a few questions for Dr. Durst?"

The old man's voice matched the rest of him—a soft but quite distinct, rolling baritone: "Not at all. Glad to be of service any way I can." He and Adam sat down and Telman Durst began his usual sweet smiling, agonizingly condescending interrogation.

"Now, then, Mr. Gonman, the officers who brought you in said they found you wandering around the park talking to the sun and apparently lost—is that the way you remember it, sir?"

The old man nodded and replied pleasantly. "That's right. I came into town to have a look at what people were up to these days, and when I came to the park, well, it was such a beautiful day I just thought I'd stroll around and enjoy it."

"Were you talking to the sun—can you tell us what that was about?"

The patient smiled and nodded: "Oh, yes, I do that almost every day—just expressing my appreciation."

"Oh? Appreciation? For what, sir?"

Adam winced and constrained himself as the old man, understandably showing mild surprise at the inane question, replied: "Why, for everything it gives us. Light. Warmth. Sustenance for all growing things—life itself."

"I se-e-e-e," Telman intoned wisely, obviously not seeing at all. "Now, then, sir, would you mind telling these good people what the date is today?"

Smiling tolerantly, he answered, "Well, doctor, I guess that depends on what calendar we're going by."

A ripple of laughter went around and Telman failed to conceal his annoyance: "I was thinking of the Christian calendar—the *true* one."

"Ah, yes—the Christians—I know them well. So, by that calendar I'd guess we're somewhere near the middle of the twentieth century."

Telman tossed a smug smile to the staff and thought, *good!—disoriented as to time.* "Very well, sir. Now can you tell us where you live?"

"Glad to. In a cave, up close to the top of my mountain, about two days' walk out of town. . . ."

"Alone, sir?"

"Oh, no, not at all. Got a big old eagle living in an aerie right next to mine, and a pack of coyotes a couple a boulders down from me, and the sun, and . . ."

"Uh, sir, excuse me for interrupting, but I was referring to human company."

The old man touched his fingers thoughtfully to his chin and answered slowly: "Well, no, not exactly human, I guess."

"Not exactly human—I see." Telman straightened up self-importantly, signalling to the staff his cleverness at eliciting what was obviously a major thinking disorder with pronounced organic features. "Now, then, what *direction* from town is your—ah—residence?"

Perplexed, Mr. Gonman raised a log-like arm and pointed due west: "Perhaps I don't understand directions as you do, but it's that way—two days' walk."

Splendid, thought Telman—*disoriented in space*. Sounding more and more like a prosecuting attorney with every question, he went on: "And now, Mr. Gonman, would you please tell us who is presently the president of these United States."

The old man shrugged: "Last time I noticed—you see I don't pay much attention to details like that—it was a wheeler-dealer type from New York—'Little Van' they called him. That's it, Martin Van Buren..."

"Uh, sir—that would have been over a hundred years ago—I think," Telman finished lamely. "Didn't you tell me you're ninety-one years old. . . .?"

"Seemed the polite thing to do at the time, you were so eager for an age. Don't rightly know how old I am." He turned to the staff, his tone almost apologetic: "You see, I don't reckon time the way most of you folks do. It's something people invented a long time ago because they can only think one thought at a time and say one word at a time. The concept of linear time gives them a sort of sense of continuity and connectedness they need. To me, you see . . ." he hesitated, reaching for words that would be understandable to his audience, "my being alive now equates to being alive before and hence, here in the Spacious Present—though I suspect that doesn't make much sense to most of you."

It made sense to Telman, who was inwardly delighted at having caught the old-timer with grandiose delusions of immortality and omniscience.

"One last question, then, if I may, Mr. Gonman. You seem in good spirits now, but do you ever feel otherwise, like anxious, say—or depressed?"

A suggestion of tears rose on the old man's lower lids as he answered sadly, "Only when I dwell too long on the condition of the human species."

Labile affect! For Telman that wrapped the case up completely. Turning to the staff he launched into a pontifical lecture on mental status findings in organic brain syndrome, strutting, gesturing, playing the professor as he had always imagined a professor should be.

But Adam could stand it no longer. Scooting his chair up close to the old man's, behind Telman's back, he leaned forward and asked in an intense whisper: "Look, Mr. Gonman, it's glaringly obvious to me that there's not a damn thing wrong with your mind. Why did you let him railroad you like that?

With a peaceful smile the old man answered softly, "Why should I detract from his illusion of happiness?"

"Two reasons. One, he's an overbearing, ignorant, self-righteous snot who sees himself as a Levitican prophet, a self-ordained guru marvelously informed on esoteric theoretical trivia and—as you can hear in the background—much given to declaiming publicly on the ideal human being, with himself as the obvious model and finest living example of 'a warm, helping person' . . . He's an intellectually pretentious phony, a tight-ass Portnovian hypocrite who delights in helping innocent, suggestible and gullible people into a state of chronic helplessness . . . a pious prick, a self-bedazzled bastard who needs the kind of help you can give him. Second, I don't want these impressionable young people on our staff thinking that he's what a psychiatrist is supposed to be. He's easy enough to unhorse, but if I do it directly I'm, well, frankly afraid I might overdo it and martyr him. It's much better done by indirect demonstration."

"I see," the old man nodded, "but aren't these little moral defects things that he will have to recognize, in time, and correct in himself— by and for himself?"

Adam hesitated. He himself, over the years, had become all but disenchanted with teaching. And yet, with the misguided faith and idealism of a Johnny Appleseed he still went about dropping his little seedling notions wherever he went though knowing all the while that human thought changes very slowly—perhaps not at all?

He shook his head: "All right. I know what you're talking about, but I still delude myself that *some* people can learn a *few* things if they're approached properly . . . dramatically, spontaneously, and in a way that lets them think they've learned the lesson themselves without having to credit anyone for having taught it to them. . . ."

The old man's eyes opened in admiration. "Well said, but with that view of things these people on your staff must think you're insane."

"A few do, of course, but most of them regard me as a brilliant but harmless eccentric, which is probably true. Anyway, I'd appreciate it if you'd answer a few questions I have for you."

The old man chuckled good-naturedly. "All right, I'll go along with that—if only for the fun of it."

By this time half of the staff were yawning and the other half were futilely straining their ears trying to hear beyond Dr. Durst's stentorian performance to tune in on the strange Dr. Solon's hushed but animated conversation with the even stranger Mr. Gonman. When Telman finally finished his discourse and laid the expected damning diagnosis on his patient, he started to announce a short coffee break. Adam held up his hand: "Two or three minutes more, Dr. Durst, before we break. There are several questions I'd like to ask Mr. Gonman."

Telman nodded uneasily and sat down, anxiously sensing that his nemesis, the flamingly mad Professor Solon, was somehow arranging to throw him in a bad light again—as usual. "So, go ahead, you old fart," he muttered to himself, "I double dare you to try and break down my diagnosis."

Adam, very relaxed, turned to the identified patient and asked amiably: "Mr. Gonman . . . by the way, is that how you like to be addressed?"

"It doesn't matter to me. My first name is Rockford, and people I'm at all acquainted with usually call me Roc."

"Good. Now, would you mind telling our staff why you don't know *our* direction to your dwelling?"

Once again the old man's tone bordered on the apologetic. "Well, it's just that I'm no longer accustomed to thinking in terms of your four cardinal directions of Thorn, Shout, Teas and Stew.. . . . "

Adam laughed abruptly: "Excuse me for interrupting, but did you anagram those on purpose or was it a Freudian slip?"

"Oh! forgot myself for a moment. Anagramming words is one of my little amusements but I didn't intend to do it here."

As a confirmed anagramophiliac himself, Adam was able to appreciate the little lapse: "Do go on, then, Roc, if you would. . . . "

"I use my own variation on conventional celestial navigation, with the help of this little device. . . . " He drew a short, tubular instrument from his shirt pocket and unfolded it. . . . "which operates on the same principle as an ordinary nautical sextant. So, you see, it's just that I find your cardinal direction system somewhat imprecise by comparison."

Telman stared wretchedly at the floor and thought, *Shit, piss, and goddam,* as Adam continued:

"What about the navigational data and conversion charts?" he smiled. "Do you have them on microfilm in your hip pockets?"

"Oh, no," Roc said, trying to think of a way to explain it without appearing immodest. "It's just that I'm quite old and have a good deal of time on my hands, so, well, I just thought I might as well go ahead and memorize them. . . . "

A murmur of wonderment and disbelief went round the room, as

Telman continued with his litany of self-castigation—*Bastard, stupid asshole, sonofabitch . . .*

"What about the calculations, then?" Adam continued mildly. "Do you use a pocket calculator?"

Again the old gentleman effaced himself carefully: "Well, with a little practice and a few short cuts one can train himself to handle reasonably small arithmetical operations mentally."

"I see. Would you mind, then, if I tested you a little?" Glancing quickly at Telman he added with just a trace of cyanide, "because it *is* an important part of the standard mental status examination."

Telman, now quite wretched: *Oh, sweet Jesus, I forgot to do digit span and serial sevens. Oh, Solon, you double-dyed bastard for humiliating me in front of . . .*

Adam turned to the audience and secured a volunteer with an electronic pocket calculator: "Okay, let's have the product of, say, 27, 33 and 268."

Roc answered quietly with less than a second's hesitation, "That would be 238,788," and a moment or two later an awed voice called out, "That's right—right on."

Adam nodded, "and could you give us its reciprocal?"

"That's .0000041."

"Correct again!"

"Last one. Could we have that multiplied by, oh, 11,569.72?"

"That's .0474358."

"My god," the voice called out again, "right on the button!"

Some of the staff were now darting amused glances at Telman, who, staring catatonically at the floor, was urgently and devoutly wishing himself dead and buried.

Adam glanced at his watch. "Thank you very much, Roc, for an amazing performance. We'll break in a moment here, but I'm sure that many of our staff share my curiosity about why you don't happen to know the name of our incumbent president."

Roc nodded his head understandingly. "Yes, it's not easy to explain." Looking directly at the rapt faces before him he continued calmly. "That kind of information is, I know, very important to you, but in my own personal experience it classes as insignificant trivia. Kings, emperors, presidents, you see, just come and go. They serve a certain figurehead function in the human drama. It is an important function, true, but apart from that they have little to do but play their part in the unfolding of quite inevitable events which they only appear to cause. Like the rest of us they are very important units in the comprehensive program, but they actually do little, if anything, to affect it measurably."

Mouths were gaping as Adam stood up, thanked Roc for his "time and contribution" and announced the coffee break. Dr. Telman Durst fled silently through a rear door, and the room buzzed electrically as people rose to leave, all hotly embroiled in a dozen small, impromptu debating circles. Adam sat down again and whispered to Roc:

"Let's eavesdrop for a minute or two and see if we did any good. . . . "

A few phrases were intelligible through the din.

". . . but everyone knows Solon is plain skitzo. . . . "

". . . bullshit—like a fox. . . . "

". . . coulda been a parlor trick—collusion. . . . "

". . . y'know, it really doesn't matter who's president. . . . "

". . . it does to us Democrats, goddammit. . . . "

Adam smiled happily at his new-found friend: "You see—it worked. That's about all we can do, isn't it, those of us who think of ourselves as teachers? Entertain and startle them. Jar their convictions even a micron or two. Give them their choice and let them think their own way to a solution, because that's the only one they'll ever accept anyway. . . . "

Roc nodded and returned the smile. "Again, well said, Dr. Solon." He held out his hand. "It's been a pleasure meeting you. Am I free to go now?"

Adam shook his hand, wincing a little from its power: "Actually, you have been all along. Ever since Dr. Szasz and the A.C.L.U. rocked the boat a few years back, these places have become easier and easier to get out of. But I was wondering, before you go, uh . . . "

"If you could come calling on me sometime?"

"Yes, but if you'd prefer that I not . . . "

Again amused, Roc answered, "I'm not the world's most sociable creature, but you would be welcome," and Adam quite understood the ellipsed "as long as you don't make it too often."

"That mountain there," he continued, pointing out the west window, "just beyond the horizon . . . go up the steeper slope, about a two-hour climb, and as you approach the top you'll come to what appears to be an impassable boulder across the trail. There you'll be raucously greeted by the clan of coyotes I mentioned earlier. Don't be frightened. Just hold up your hand and say distinctly and slowly to the leader, 'Take me to Roc,' and they'll show you the trail up. The same words will mollify my eagle friend should he decide to strafe you with his terrifying screams and flappings . . . "

"Good. Thank you. And I can see that any casual climber would be profoundly discouraged from ascending beyond a certain point."

Roc smiled, nodded, and departed with a long, strong stride.

Adam sat down again and picked up Roc's hospital chart. Perusing it absently, he recalled William Faulkner's observation that one can tell a lot about a person by his name—if it's read the right way. "Mmmm. Roc—big mythical bird—could be. Or, Cor, for heart. . . . "

His thoughts were interrupted by an excited little yelp behind him. Half-turning he recognized the legs immediately as belonging to Marcey Sapinet, the cute little student.

"Dr. Solon, I just wanted to say what a fantastic performance I thought that was . . . just marvelous . . . how did you know?, etc., etc. . . ." Adam instantly identified her bubbling panegyric as the human version of any good mammal's instinctual courting-approach behavior. Beginning to look for a way out, he spotted a small diamond ring on the tell-tale finger, and lifted her hand for a closer inspection.

"Oh, that," she interrupted herself, "that's nothing. I mean, I *am* engaged but I'm not about to get married . . . and I was wondering if I could talk with you sometime . . . " Sensing his coolness, she swiftly shifted her tack again, ". . . I mean, my twin sister and I, we're really fascinated . . . "

Adam's eyes were suddenly bright with interest: "Twins? Monovular?"

"Oh, yes. Identical—like two peas in a pod. . . . We'd both love to talk with you sometime. . . . "

"I think that can be arranged. Is she a student nurse, too, and what's her name?"

"Mesta. Yes. She's on medicine rotation now. We both get off duty around four-thirty."

Adam sat back and scanned her again, openly. Very pretty. Lovely legs and breasts—albeit standard. She was somewhat smaller than his usual preference, but, what the hell, matched bookends—a new experience: "You know that university parking structure by the arboretum?"

Excitedly, "Oh, yes."

"On the top level, in solitary splendor, sits my luxurious motor pad. See you both there around five to five-thirty?"

Eyes dancing and grinning happily, she bobbed her head and turned to go, thrilled with her success.

"Hey, Marcey," Adam halted her. She stopped and turned expectantly. "I'll bet that identical twin feature works every time—right?"

She nodded and grinned impishly: "Every time," then left.

Deb Suners appeared at the door: "Adam, would you pick up that extension—some chick from Universal Charge Cards wants to talk with you."

Adam grumped: "Wonder what they want now. Okay." He picked up the phone and covered the mouthpiece with his hand: "Better get people together for the rest of rounds, Deb. It's getting late and we have to haul-ass."

"Will do."

From the phone: "Dr. Solon? This is Clare Upton—Universal Charge's main office."

"I sent my check in ten days ago."

"It's not about that, sir. You'll be receiving a letter of explanation but I've been directed to call and tell you personally that your account is being cancelled."

"Cancelled? What the hell for?" Adam snapped impatiently.

"For excessive use, sir."

"Excessive use!" he barked. Ms. Upton went on in an unruffled and business-like way, inured as she was to telephonic temper tantrums and serial insults. "Exactly what is 'excessive use'?"

"You account, sir, is $2,300 overdrawn."

"Impossible!" he exploded. "I've never charged that kind of money in my whole life! What are the charges for?"

"All those scantily clad dancing girls, sir, jumping out of cakes. In Dayton, Cleveland, Albuquerque, Flagstaff—a total of twenty-three at $100 per jump. Cake-jumpers don't come cheap, you know."

Adam's face sagged with disbelief. "You and your whole company are crazy. I never hired a cake-jumper in this or any other life! I'd know if I had—right?"

"So it would seem, sir, but policy is policy, and by the terms of your agreement with the company you are now obliged to cut your card in two and mail it to this office at once."

"All right," Adam said grimly, "I'll not only do that but I'll also pre-lubricate it so the chairman of the board can more easily put it where the sun never shines."

"If you wish, sir. Good-bye."

Adam slammed down the phone and rubbed his forehead: *Scantily clad cake-jumpers! That doesn't make any sense at all—absolutely none whatever! Those goddamn Insiders again, harassing me for getting on their case. Maybe I'm closer than I realized. Won't do them any good, though—I'm not about to ease up on the pressure. If they mean to stop me they're gonna have to kill me. All that money they have—the incredible power—what a stupidly silly sadistic way to use it, frigging around with nonsense like that. Why not put one of their hit men on me and get it over with?*

With Telman Durst conveniently called away to answer a consultation request on the orthopedics floor, the one remaining patient was staffed much more expeditiously. Word of the earlier bloodletting had spread all over the institute during the break, so that now there was standing room only, with staff from every corner of the complex, eagerly hoping for another spectacle.

When Deb came through the door with the young woman who had been busted for L. and L., Adam realized that they could not possibly be entirely disappointed. Dressed in a filmy tennis outfit, he saw at once that she was pretty lewd and lascivious just standing there: tall, leggy, melon-breasted, and with short and softly curled sandy blonde hair around a lightly freckled Doris-Day face. *Jesus,* Adam thought—*life would be so much simpler if there weren't so many of these gorgeous women in it.*

Deb introduced them. "Ms. Cameron, this is Dr. Solon. Adam, this is Bairny." (The familiar first-naming of the chief was Deb's sly way of letting the rest of the staff know that she was right in there with him.)

Adam gestured for her to sit down, and the entire staff watched her do so with a sort of collective, ill-concealed gulp and gape.

"Thank you for joining us," Adam said in what he hoped was his coolest and most euphonious voice. "And how do you like to be addressed?"

She smiled at him and cocked her head quizzically, apparently enjoying the encounter already: "Oh, Bairny's fine. Or maybe Diogenesa."

"Good. Now, looking over the nursing notes from yesterday afternoon and last night I gather that you're intelligent, sociable, and are suffering from no form of mental illness—major, minor or otherwise. Is that correct?"

In the back of the room one of the psychiatric residents whispered to another, "Good lord, he's an examiner for the American Board and he calls that a mental status examination," and the other whispered back, "Right on, man—it would take that idiot Durst half-an-hour to get the same information." Adam ended the illicit whispering with a withering, split-second glance.

Bairny nodded. "Correct. Mentally and emotionally I'm in great shape."

Adam would have lopped a resident's head for doing it, but he couldn't resist the opening. "Just for starters, it would seem to me."

There was a round of amused laughter, and again she nodded, this time with an appreciative smile, deciding on-the-spot that in this benign-looking super-shrink she really had a live one.

"Would you tell us, then, as much as you comfortably can, about just what happened that prompted the police to arrest you, jail you, and then later transfer you to us?"

She shrugged. "Sure. It was all a silly tempest in a teapot—I still don't know what all the commotion's about . . . "

Adam encouraged her with an interested nod and a somewhat less than professional smile as she continued airily:

"I'd just finished a couple of sets of tennis and I wanted to do another because I was really on, but my partner had to go to work. So I just sat down in a chair on the sidelines, maybe ten or fifteen yards back from the courts, and watched the other people play. And they were all so, well, beautiful—the men with their tanned, hard-muscled legs and arms and graceful strokes; and the ladies, too, soft-skinned and pretty and curvy . . . " She sighed contentedly as she reviewed the scene in her mind.

"And it was such a perfectly lovely sunny day that, you see, the combination of the beautiful day and the beautiful people and the sun warming my whole body and a gentle breeze stirring over me—I just developed an acute case of the hots like I haven't had for a long time . . . "

Adam nodded again and the expression on his face clearly conveyed "of course, what could be more natural," while most of the staff were registering startlement at the young woman's candor.

"So I was thinking about calling up a friend to get together for an emergency de-horning session but I had a busy day ahead of me that was going to call for some heavy thinking, which my extreme horniness would surely have interfered with, or vice versa, yet time was short, so I was really in kind of a bind. . . . "

Anticipating her, Adam grinned, "So, that's when you decided to go, as they say, 'Lewd and Lascivious in a public place'?"

"Ri-i-ight! Well, actually, there wasn't that much of a decision to be made. I was thinking about taking my happy burden home and discharging it there but I didn't want to run a chance of losing the mood, so what really settled it was when just at that time, across the park lawn at the far end of the courts, came this beautiful old giant of a man with a really outrageous pile of shiny white hair and . . . "

Adam interrupted: "You mean the one who was just in here?"

"Right. Roc, he calls himself. We were busted about the same time and rode down to the pokey in the same cop car . . . "

"And exactly what did you do that brought the wrath of the law down on your head?"

She shrugged again: "Nothing particular—just what comes naturally. I put my right ankle on my left knee, to sort of conceal things a little, then slipped my hand down into my panties and started getting myself off—y'know?"

Adam sensed a distinct reaction of generalized dismay among his staff, which irritated him tremendously. Seeking to counteract it he said: "Naturally—what else? And the word 'public place' is a relative thing, isn't it? Was any one in the area bothered by what you were doing—as far as you could tell?"

"Not exactly! The guy playing in the court nearest to me lost quite a few points glancing over my way, and Roc stopped to watch me—wow!—that old gent must have eyes like an eagle to have picked up my action from that distance. So, no, no one was bothered but this young cop who snuck up behind me and, you know, real uptight-like, put the old pinch on me—the whole thing was really silly."

"Agreed," Adam said. "I guess most people in the world simply don't know how to react when they see something sexually arousing, so they either assault it, kill it, throw a bucket of water on it, arrest it, or faint dead away—instead of just relaxing and enjoying it."

Bairny bobbed her head: "Yep, I guess that's just what happened."

Adam went on: "Then according to the record here, you were later transferred from jail to here because you, quote, persisted in your lewd and lascivious behavior, unquote—right?"

She giggled. "Really. By then I was way into the whole thing. The cop who arrested me had an obvious hard . . . uh, I mean . . . erection, and was all bashful and red-faced and confused trying to be tough while he was so turned on. And by that time his partner had good old Roc in tow, bringing him across the courts to the cop car, and all the people had stopped playing tennis to watch the great drama—it was just like one of those cop shows on the tube—really exciting!"

"So you figured you might as well be hanged for a sheep as a goat—or however that goes?"

"Sort of, but by then I guess I was partly into just burlesquing the whole thing. I couldn't believe it, you know? I mean people are so incredibly hypocritical about all that—it's like they're delusional. They pretend to themselves that they can really keep their naughty little secrets to themselves and that's just not possible. They, you know, those weird invisible overlords at the top of it all—*they* know everything about every one of us anyway—so why do we even try to hide anything?"

A current of alarm ran through the room. It suddenly appeared that the flawlessly smooth Professor Solon had goofed gigantically in failing to elicit this glaringly delusional ideation during his truncated mental status exam. Doubly irritated, Adam started to set them straight, but Bairny, who had also picked up the reaction, took care of it herself:

"Oh—excuse me," she said to the audience in a patiently explanatory tone. "That must sound very paranoid to you, but it wouldn't at all to the people in my field. . . ."

Adam interjected, "Bairny is a post-doctoral fellow in theoretical mathematics, specializing in large scale computer arrays and networks. . . ."

"Right. You see, those of us who are closest to the world-wide computer system know that you can trace it only so far—then it simply vanishes. But we know it has to end somewhere, so we reasonably assume that in ways not known to us it terminates invisibly with a very secret and very powerful group of people that we . . . well . . . really know nothing about. . . ."

Alan Bregan, a notoriously aggressive-gay clinical psychologist, intruded sarcastically. "This wouldn't be the old International Banking Conspiracy you're talking about, would it?"

A troubled murmur arose noisily and Adam raised a restraining hand. "Conspiracy is a heavily loaded word, Dr. Bregan. None of us who are involved in this work know very much about T.H.E.M., but a few of us are trying to learn more. Consider for a moment: this young woman is an expert in the world computer system and she doesn't know where the Ultimate Computer Monitor is—do you?"

Dr. Bregan minimized the question with a harumph. "I suppose it's a theoretical possibility, but what's all this business about *Them*—god, that sounds paranoid—knowing all our secrets? Are you suggesting we all have taps on our phones and bugs in our bathrooms and bedrooms . . . ?"

Again Adam arrested the ensuing disturbance with an upraised hand. "Entirely unnecessary—that's all done by a remote and very high level computer analysis of an endless stream of information that we ourselves innocently feed into the system, like how we use our credit cards. . . ."

Bairny added enthusiastically, "Our bank accounts and investments."

"School, military and other public records. . . . "

"The Federal census. . . . "

Adam paused and looked at her uncertainly. "The census? I'd class that as a red herring, a diversionary camouflage to conceal the extent and intricacy of the real information-gathering process."

Bairny returned his look thoughtfully and replied, hesitating, "I hadn't thought of it that way . . . could be . . . the census questionnaire *is* limited to awfully crude information. . . . "

Another surge of commotion in the audience prompted Adam to quiet them and abrupt the interview. "I'm afraid this conversation goes well beyond the interests of most of you here today so we'll wind it up now. . . . "

Still on the muscle, Alan Bregan tried to put the professor in a corner. "What's your diagnosis in this case, Dr. Solon?"

The room was hushed. Adam locked gazes with him and answered evenly, "The formal diagnosis here is: No Psychiatric Diagnosis— which, I might add, is one that is not used nearly often enough around here!" Bregan, who was almost as bad a hanging-judge as Telman Durst, dropped his eyes uneasily from Adam's accusing stare.

He turned to Bairny again: "Do you have a good lawyer?"

She nodded. "Dan Winthrop—do you know him?"

"Oh, yes—very well. You'll have no trouble at all beating this bum rap."

"But what about a shrink, Dr. Solon—do you have a private practice?"

"Yes, I do—but do you *need* one?"

"Oh, no, not a psychiatrist, but . . . " she leaned forward, put a soft hand on his and smiled sweetly into his face . . . "you and I do have things to talk about, don't we?"

Covering her hand with his free one, Adam leaned forward, teasingly mimicked her seductive smile and replied in a like tone, "Indeed we do—but not in a clinical setting . . . let's take another short break, everyone . . . !"

Stirring, chairs scraping and excited buzzing. Marcey giggled to Satin, "Oh damn, but at least Mesta and I will get to him before she does—I think . . . "

A few more fragments of parting dialogue drifted up to Adam and Bairny as the room cleared:

" . . . but he doesn't think anyone's crazy—what kind of a shrink is that . . . ?"

". . . conspirators my royal ass . . . pure paranoid delusional. . . . "

". . . normal, okay, but right out in public . . . ?"

". . . grossly inappropriate dress for a conference . . . "

". . . one gorgeous set of lungs, though . . . "

And from one of the psychiatric residents, laughing, "It may not be grass roots medicine but it's a hell of a lot more fun than sticking thermometers up febrile ani. . . . "

Adam said to Bairny, "Now, I ask you, aren't they something else?"

"They're funny—kind of crazy though, aren't they?"

"Definitely crazier than our patients, but that's how it is world 'round—it's a perfect system, actually. . . . "

Retrieving his hands, Adam picked up the chart and checked the face sheet for Bairny's address. "Ah, that's very close to where I'm parked." Remembering the Sapinet twins, he asked, "Okay if I pick you up around 6:30 or 7:00?"

"Fine. What should I wear?"

"Something casual and outdoorsy—and don't have dinner. We'll go out to my little Shangri-la and work up an evening. . . . "

Meanwhile, in the nursing station, Deb was playing her second favorite indoor sport, which was an even blend of teasing Telman's cock while systematically wiping out his ego.

"Now see? You say Dr. Solon is crazy but he wasn't nearly that unkind about you."

"Huh? What'd he say about me?"

"He said you are an uneducable pain-in-the-ass."

Telman flushed angrily but bit his tongue. Lusting as he was for her excruciating body, and feeling himself dangerously close to being both outwitted and outvirtued by her, he decided to compensate his earlier pettiness with a gesture of magnanimity. "Well, he may be crazy but I've got to hand it to him for his energy. I hope I have his kind of drive when I get to be that age."

"You won't," she snapped.

Taken aback, he stepped right into the trap: "Huh? Whaddaya mean—how do you know I won't?"

She smiled at him sweetly: "Because you don't have that kind of energy now, and where you going to get it between now and then?"

Struck down, all hope gone of ever gaining access to her tender flesh, his day a shambles, Dr. Telman Durst ambled wretchedly onto the ward and commenced looking for some woman patient he could talk with and feel vastly superior to. That, according to Dr. Solon, was one of a mental patient's more important social roles—to help the staff improve their comparative self-esteem. "The crazy bastard," he muttered to himself, "I don't have to do that—I *am* superior."

3

Up From Marriage

Marcey and Mesta, wearing loafing clothes, were sitting in the shadow of Adam's Landau waiting for him cross-legged, finishing off a joint between them and grinning happily fron its effects. Adam extended both hands and helped them to their feet. "My god, I'd have to brand your foreheads to tell you apart—okay if I just call you both sweetie or darling, or something inanely general like that?"

They both leaned against him, smiling and eager, and one of them said, "Sure—just don't call us late for bed!"

Adam unlocked the door and they went in. His was the only vehicle on the top deck and he had parked it so the side picture window looked out over the rolling acres of rich, green arboretum. One of the twins gasped, "Wow! Some pad," and the other added irreverently, "A regular bachelor's meat wagon!"

Closing the door and locking it, Adam apologized: "Listen, I didn't mean it to be this way, but I'm a little more pressed for time than I expected to be . . . do you mind if we pare the preliminaries to a minimum and sort of get on with the program?"

Smiling, the girls chorused "far out," and began shedding what little they had on at a brisk rate. Then Marcey teased, "I know why you're in

73

a hurry, Dr. Solon. I saw you making big time with the beautiful Bairny broad right in front of the whole staff—you looked like you were about to screw each other on the spot . . . which I, for one, was all set to scope in on."

"Not that I didn't want to," Adam admitted, expertly peeling to the buff with a few quick moves, "but we have enough flashers around these days without my getting in on the act."

The twins were ready. Adam drank them in lovingly as they stood there expectantly, side by side, two lovely little French dolls, then asked, "Which one is Marcey?"

"Me," piped the one on the right, holding up her hand.

"Okay, then," he laughed, "now I can at least tell you apart when you're naked. That little birthmark just above the anterior superior iliac spine—Marcey's is on the right side and Mesta's is on the left. And by the way, for my interest, which one of you has the dextrocardia?"

"Me," Mesta said, aping her sister.

Adam approached them slowly, circled his arms around their waists and herded them gently back toward the amply cushioned romper room at the rear, saying, "You know, this is a first for me but I feel oddly at ease—maybe I've been secretly conditioned for it over the years by that chewing gum commercial on the tube." He began to sing, " . . . double your pleasure, double your fun, with double good . . . " then tumbled them both back on the pillow and dropped down between them.

Mesta chimed in, "You're a first for us, too, Dr. Solon."

"Please call me Adam—considering the circumstances. In what way am I a first for you—oldest? First professor? First married man? Homeliest?"

"No," Mesta giggled, "you're our first status fuck."

"A—what's a status fuck?"

"You know—you're famous. Some evening you'll be on the Johnny Carson Show or some other big talk show and we'll be watching it with some friends and one of them will say how brilliant and witty you are, then Marcey and I, we'll just smile casually and say 'Yep, and he's great in bed, too.' See?"

Bairny, wearing a plain cotton shirt and the traditional denim cut-offs with pockets showing fashionably an inch or so below the ragged hems, was waiting for him when he rolled up to the curb. She jumped in and slammed the door with a happy hi. Adam said, "Sorry I'm a little late but something came up."

"You're not late—it isn't seven yet . . . " then turned toward him suddenly, wrinkling her nose in mild distaste, "Jesus, Adam, I guess something did come up. This otherwise fantastic palace smells like a five-dollar Memphis whorehouse on a hot Saturday night."

Adam leaned forward and flipped on the toggle switch for the exhaust fan. "Well," he said laconically, "guess I'll have to take your word for that, as I, for *one*, have never been in a five-dollar Memphis whorehouse on a hot Saturday night."

She laughed and punched his arm. "You dog! Neither have I—but I can dream can't I?"

As they rolled past the hospital, Adam spotted the twins approaching the phone booth at the corner. One of them went into the booth— Adam couldn't tell which with their birthmarks covered—and the other turned toward the street to wait. When Mesta saw him waving she broke into a delighted smile and waved back, blowing him a hasty kiss as the huge motor home drove by.

Bairny glanced at Adam. "Was that the student nurse from the ward?"

"Or her twin sister. They're identicals—can't tell 'em apart with their clothes on."

Bairny looked at him with a brow arched in suspicion. "They both looked pretty rumpled and sweaty to me, and so do you, come to think of it. Couldn't be, could it, that you dropped them off just a minute or two before you picked me up?"

"Now, Bairny, dear," Adam reminded her, "you know the ground rules—ladies and gentlemen never implicate their friends."

"To anyone who would misuse the information," she interrupted, "which I most certainly would not. In any case, the last of their aura seems to have been expelled from the coach—if you want to turn the fan off now."

Back in the phone booth, Marcey got a dial tone then carefully pressed the unnumbered touch-dial button in the lower left-hand corner seven times, waited ten seconds by her wrist watch then pressed it three times, waited fifteen seconds and pressed the lower right button twelve more times. Looking at her watch she waited patiently for the minute of dead silence to pass. Then there was a click, and a taped voice instructed: "Please submit your report after the beep has sounded." Five more seconds, then a beep.

"This is BJ-69 reporting on field project A.T.L. dash four," she announced, and then proceeded crisply with her report. "Interim evaluation, on a scale of one hundred. Intelligence, one hundred. Candor—one hundred. Political dexterity and interactional gamesmanship—ninety-seven. Ambassadorial charm index—one hundred. Uncommon virtues index—somewhere in the top ten percent. Physical health—estimate low to mid-nineties. Relationship capacity: warm without melting and cool without freezing—index 98. Sexual capacity factored for age, time and energy availability is 100, though evidently hetero only. System savvy difficult to rate—he's so near and yet so far—rough approximate at 70%. Formidable gent, all considered. Field evaluation continues. Awaiting further instructions, if any. End of report. Over and out."

It was dinner time and almost dark when she stepped out of the booth. Glancing up and down the street, Marcey found it deserted. Smiling tenderly into the mirror of her sister's face, she drew her into a tight embrace and kissed her wetly on the mouth, flicking her tongue in and out, luxuriously stroking the firm, smooth and squirming rounds of her rear.

"The report is in, little sister, and we're on our own time. Come on, let's hurry home and finish what the good doctor didn't have time for."

Mesta giggled. "Or the equipment, for that matter."

They walked on down the street hand-in-hand, shoulders pressed together, touching cheeks and foreheads as they laughed and talked about the day's adventures, their hunger for each other mounting with every step.

Adam put his motor home into parking position then picked up the stack of mail he'd just collected from the little village post office twelve miles back and looked at it fixedly. "You know, sometimes I get the feeling that these great piles of mail are trying to tell me something—like there's some kind of secred code buried in there somewhere."

Bairny glanced at it. "That is one hell of a lot of mail. Mostly first class, or junk?"

"Both. It's really been on the increase over the past year or two." He looked at her, wondering. "Has yours—been increasing recently?"

"Not really. Same old bills, ads—stuff like that."

"Sometimes I wonder," Adam muttered suspiciously. "Questionnaires by the dozens—from the Union of Concerned Scientists, all the political parties, big pharmaceutical houses—all asking for my opinion—as if they really cared."

Walking around to the front entrance, Bairny marvelled at the house and the setting. "It truly is exquisite. Those stars—my god—they're five times brighter than in the city. It's all beautiful!"

Adam nodded. We're up about 6,000 feet. Solid desert and foothills all the way around—a pretty little piece of paradise on earth."

"Is someone else here?" Bairny asked as they passed a lighted window.

"My beautiful and brilliant and beloved daughter, Candide—Candy—precocious 12-year old pundit, prankster, scholar and probable latent nymphomaniac."

"Mmmm," Bairny play-protested, bumping him lightly with her shoulder, "I'm jealous already—will I get to meet the competition this evening?"

"I'm sure. She's into her books right now, but she'll be out to join us sometime later. Like a drink?"

"A little wine with dinner, thanks."

Adam took some food from the refrigerator and a bottle of good Rhine wine from the rack and put them in a pre-equipped hamper, then led her out to the deck overlooking the little lake and the endless expanse of desert around it, now bathed in moonlight.

"Here," he said, tossing her a big beach towel, "that's the customary dress around here." Then he slipped out of his clothing, threw another towel over his shoulder, picked up the hamper and loped down to the lake's edge. Bairny watched him for a moment and then, smiling at the cheery informality of it all, quickly disrobed and followed him down.

They sipped wine while Adam sliced up lean chunks of beef, and bite-size pieces of green pepper, tomato, onions, and mushrooms. "Instant shishkebob a la Solon," he explained. "And while the beef flavors up in the marinade, let's sharpen our appetite with a little swim."

Adam dove in and struck out for the far shore to finish off his twice-daily routine. He returned to find Bairny standing back against a smooth granite boulder that sloped almost vertically into the water, the surface of which reached her at breast level. He walked through the water toward her, the wet sand on the bottom, as always, a sensuous delight swirling around his feet and ankles. Putting both hands on her upper arms, he moved his front against hers and she looked up at him, smiling contentedly, and inquired of him quietly, "Are you getting ready to compromise my virtue?"

"If you don't resist me too sincerely, yes, I must confess it had occurred to me."

She draped her forearms loosely over his shoulders and sighed. "It's okay ... guess it doesn't matter to me one way or the other ... I just feel good, here in the water, with the spine of the galaxy shining over us ... "

"Well," Adam whispered philosophically into her ear, "none of us can turn on to everyone all the time, now can we?"

She nodded and looked at him serenely. "I guess it's sort of a problem with me, not turning on very well—as I was saying in conference this morning—just once in a blue moon, then all of a sudden—like out of nowhere."

Adam smiled. "And you're not excited now?"

"Not really ... " Her facile repression of the blatantly obvious in this hysterically pubertal mode was exciting to Adam. "Well, if you're not aroused upstairs, maybe you'd like to talk some about computer theory, because I'm having a heavenly time with the rest of you."

She patted his back affectionately, "It's very pleasant."

Adam smiled into her face. "I'm glad you find it comfortable, you flaming fraud."

She kissed his neck. "It'll be okay ... maybe someday when we know each other better you can find a way to really arouse my interest."

Adam laughed. "Heaven forbid ... any more and I ... "

She put her fingers over his mouth and changed the subject, pretending to reproach him. "Hey! Where do I stand in your day's activities—am I the third?"

"Only if you count the twins as one."

"Fourth? Jesus! Did you—you know—every time?"

Adam shook his head sadly. "Ah, would that I could," then with a nostalgic sigh, "Oh, to be fifty again."

A yelp of girlish laughter, a flash of speeding flesh overhead in the moonlight, momentarily eclipsing it, a cannon-ball splash and water surging up to their mouths and raining down on their heads.

"My god," Bairny exclaimed, "what was that?"

"My little Candide making her grand entrance."

"She scared the bejabbers out of me!"

"That's her style, I'm afraid. She's a joker."

A minute passed, then two, and still no sign of her above water. Bairny began to look about apprehensively but Adam reassured her. "Don't worry. She once stayed under for four minutes and twelve seconds. Her big brother can last over five minutes."

Another minute passed when Bairny asked, suspiciously, "Adam, is that your hand slipping up between our legs?"

Adam answered abruptly, "I thought it was yours," then quickly grasped and arrested Candy's wrist just as her hand was about to verify the intimate union he was still enjoying with Bairny. "Goddammit," he mumbled as Candy surfaced with a bound, "you have no couth at all, Patoot—haven't you ever heard of mutual consent?"

Candy, now standing close beside them, swept back her hair and laughed. "Yours was implied by the fact that you're still into it even knowing that I was somewhere down there swimming voyeuristically around you—and anyway you'd both have loved it." Then, smiling amiably at Bairny, "Hi. I'm Candy Solon."

Bairny returned the smile a little stiffly, at a glance taking in the girl's height, her large breasts glistening in the moonlight and seeming to be afloat in the dark water, her composed and very beautiful face, then answered hesitantly:

"Hi, there. I'm Bairny. Sheesh—you're twelve years old?"

"Going on a hundred," Adam added drily as he slowly withdrew from Bairny and turned to take both of Candy's hands in his own. "I'll just hang onto these wandering hands of yours until we're all safely ashore—you're simply not to be trusted."

Candy quickly put together a dancing fire of mesquite driftwood as Adam slid tender morsels of meat and vegetables onto their skewers. Bairny drew the huge, soft towel around her against the gentle night breeze, which Adam and Candy, through long exposure, found perfect for their temperature needs. As they sat around broiling their dinner Candy said:

"It was family day today—mom and Brian both called."

Bairny looked up, interested. "Oh? So there is a Mrs. Solon in the picture?"

Adam nodded. "Very much so. Livea's an actress, currently with a road company doing *Othello*. She's Desdemona."

Candy giggled. "She's doing Othello, all right—daytime, nighttime and in between the acts."

Adam smiled. "That would be good old Dust Hitwise," Adam explained to Bairny. "You know, that big, devilishly handsome black actor—he's been all over the tube the past few years. Good actor."

Bairny blinked her eyes and turned to Candy. "You mean she *told* you on the phone she's having a big affair with him?"

Candy bobbed her head, grinning. "Natch. I'd say it was inevitable."

"Quite so," Adam confirmed, picking a crisp tidbit from his skewer and popping it into his mouth.

Bairny studied him for a moment. "And that's all right with you, Adam?"

"All right?" He seemed puzzled. "Well, yes, if it's all right with her. She's a mature lady—it's not for me to say that's all right for her. Remember: There is no marriage in Heaven—we shall be as a band of angels. I'm concerned only that she's enjoying her life, and from the sound of things she really is. Is that hard for you to understand, Bairny?"

"A little I guess. I mean, you people are a tad on the, well, *unusual* side—wouldn't you say?"

Adam nodded matter-of-factly. "I should hope so, considering the rather sorry state of the usual. What the hell, Bairny, you didn't see me standing around waiting for her to approve the way I spent my day—which very much included a lovely interlude with you."

Candy grimaced. "Wow—that *would* be a drag. What a grim way of life."

"Okay—all right," Bairny conceded, "but aren't you just a teensy weensy little bit jealous, Adam?"

"Nope," he answered easily, "on the contrary. Hearing that she's having a good time gives me a lift. I can even enjoy her pleasure vicariously. I know it's hard to believe but it's true. I had myself pretty well cured of that old childhood malady by the time I was in my early forties—thank God. It's a bad, bad feeling. Nice to be shut of it."

Bairny persisted. "But what if they, say, took movies of themselves getting it on together—would you want to see them?"

"I sure would," Candy piped.

Adam was more selective. "If they were of good quality, dramatically and cinematically, yes."

Candy felt a need to explain her indiscriminate taste for unelaborated hard-core stuff "It's my age, Bairny. At my stage of life I don't want them wasting time on dialogue and characterization and all that arty stuff. I just want to see the straight action, in and out, back and forth—and up close. In time I suppose I'll get bored with it and want more refinements and tantalizing tricks and all, but not yet."

"What would really be nice," Adam mused, "would be a full scale Hollywood production of *Othello*, say, or *Romeo and Juliet*, with the bedroom scenes explicitly included, in context. Now *that* would be very exciting to me." Then to Candy, returning to the moment: "Will she be getting a break soon? And what about Brian?"

"Mom said they'll be taking a ten-day hiatus in the next month or two. She'll let us know when she knows. And my darling brother wil be arriving from the U. some time tonight for a long weekend—hot damn!"

Once in the big central room, Adam reached up and detached the communal pad from the ceiling and dropped it to the floor in the middle of the room. It was an ovoid piece of foam rubber, four inches thick, eight feet long and six feet wide, covered with a soft cotton imitation fur slip-on.

"One surprise after another," Bairny said. "I thought that was an integral part of the ceiling decor when I first saw it."

"It's handy this way," Adam replied, dropping to a cross-legged sit near the middle of it. The three of them sat there in a tight triangle, touching glasses and toasting the moon. Adam laughed. "If Telman Durst should see me doing this, he'd try to have me committed, the way he wanted to go with Roc Gonman for praising the sun."

Bairny quickly filled Candy in on the happenings of the two days before, including how and why she had come to meet Adam, the conference, their shared interest in computer theory and practice, right up to the present moment.

"I hope I'm not violating security, daddy, but does that mean that Bairny's, well—*in?*"

Their lovely guest was surprised again. "In? In what?"

"Almost certainly, Patoot, if she wants to be. Just a few formalities to take care of. I really need what she has to offer, to work with Gilth Ypres on computer strategy." Then turning to Bairny, "I don't mean to be talking past you—it's just that I haven't had a chance to discuss it with you."

"Mmm, interesting. Sounds like you're—like organized?"

He nodded. "Can't say too much about it until you've had your security clearance—if you agree to it, that is."

Bairny shrugged and smiled. "Sure. After all, you know what I was busted for. I really believe I have nothing to hide."

"Fair enough. This much I can tell you now, and you should know it as background for what I'd like you to do for The Cause tomorrow. We're quite an elite little group, still fewer than a hundred of us all told, but we *are* actively recruiting new talent—like yourself."

"Do you have a name?"

Adam smiled grimly. "Yes. For lack of a better one, we designate ourselves as the Group to Reveal Insiders' Plot to Exploit. A bit of wry humor there."

"I see," Bairny said, guessing ahead. "And may I safely assume that these 'Insiders' are the . . . ?"

"The ones you referred to this morning as the 'Overlords,' if I recall your wording. They're referred to variously as the 'Insiders,' the 'Illuminati' or simply as 'T.H.E.Y.,' which is an apt enough if somewhat unimaginative acronym for 'They Haven't Everything Yet.' "

"Great," Bairny laughed. "Right on. If you're out to unmask those money-grabbing, capitalist tycoons, I'm with you all the way. What's my first assignment?"

Pleased, Adam put it to her succinctly: "Paperwork. I need your professional know-how to check out both the theoretical and practical feasibility of my computer overpass theory."

Bairny nodded. "Okay, I know what you're talking about—long-circuiting systems that transcend the reach of lower level functionaries."

"Precisely, like corporation board chairmen, national leaders of whatever formal title, and so on."

Bairny laughed with delight. "Does the system really overpass that high up the network?"

"That's my best estimate to date, in accordance with Solon's first law: If they're visible and publicly identified, they're not of the Inner Circle. Lower level agents, maybe—like the Rothschilds, Roosevelts, and Rockefellers—but not really in the know."

"Okay," Bairny answered eagerly. "I'll check it out first thing in the morning, but I think I have a pretty good idea how it's going to turn out."

He stood up, offered both hands to his ladies and helped them to their feet, then slipped his arms around them as they stepped forward to cuddle in with him, and with each other.

"We're like the 800-pound gorilla around here," he explained to Bairny. "We sleep where we want to. At the far end of the hall on the right is our nicest guest room. You're welcome to sleep there, or out here with me if you'd like a warm friendly body next to you, or with Candy, if she's agreeable . . . "

Candy tilted her face upward toward Adam's hopefully. "May I sleep here with you, if I promise, *promise* not to molest you in any way?"

Adam was doubtful. "If you can keep that promise, okay. I can only endure so much."

Bairny snuggled in tighter and sighed softly, "You people are a bit much. Sometimes I'm cuddly, sometimes not. Guess I've had enough body contact for the time being so I'll go sleep in the guest room." She kissed them both lightly on the mouth, gathered up her clothes and walked down the hall.

Bairny, though close to exhaustion from her forty-eight-hour crisis, was too excited by it all to drop off. *These good people are all clearly crazy, and in just exactly the right way. Some different kind of shrink, thank heavens, and that beautiful girl . . . and brother Brian will be just like them, of course . . . and the Illuminati network should be fairly easy to fathom with a modified spatial analysis of known systems projected beyond . . . Daddy can get me lists of known systems with oceans of detail . . . Oh my god!"*

She stiffened, clutched the quilt around her and jerked to a sitting position, scooting back against the wall. A shadow had crossed the moon and a dark figure was outlined against the silvery desert backdrop through her window. Then it moved aside. Jumping to her feet she moved cautiously toward the window and peered out from behind the opaque drape. It was a man, or a person—or so it appeared—bounding down and across the gorge and now up the other side at an incredible speed—bionically. Now the racing figure approached the top, and Bairny started back in astonishment when she saw the faintly glowing apparition on top of the tor—and startled again as she watched it drift upwards and away toward the far horizon.

The glowing beamship vanished at warp speed in the direction of another, much larger discoid vessel off to the northwest, leaving a shimmering trail of light in its wake. Bairny rushed to the big telescope on the deck and watched the gigantic ship retreat at suprawarp velocity toward the Pleiades, five hundred earth years away, and it was going like a crosstown commuter!

"Good Lord!" she whispered to herself. "What is going on around this crazy pecan palace, anyway?"

Still wrapped in her quilt, she moved quietly to the front room. The moon had descended so there was now more light, and she could clearly see Candy stirring beneath her cover. Quickly, carefully, she crawled in between Candy and the lightly snoring Adam and turned excitedly toward the girl—*two heads!* "Candy, is that you?"

Dreamily, just audibly, "Mm hm . . . Bairny, this is my brother, Brian. He just got home."

Brian managed a courteous "Hi" and Bairny quickly apologized. "Hi there. God, I'm sorry to intrude like this but there was a strange looking dude outside my door checking me out . . . he ran across the gorge and up the hill like the Six Million Dollar Man and then took off in an honest-to-god mother of a UFO, and don't tell me I was dreaming, because I saw it . . . !"

In a rising whisper Candy answered, "Oh, Bairny, I'm sorry we forgot to tell you about that. He drops by now and then to look us over. We don't know what his mission is—probably an Illuminati agent of some sort . . . but he's made no hostile moves . . . should have warned you about him."

Bairny murmured back, "Oh, wow . . . he scared the liver out of me . . . guess I'll stay up here with you guys."

Turning onto her other side, she spoon-snuggled up to Adam's back and immediately felt warm and comfortable. She glanced at the pyramidal ceiling overhead, then out at the moonlit desert. There was a stirring of wind outside now, an orchestral background for the soft breathing of the patently unrivalrous siblings beside her. She sensed a tremendous energy in the room, and an air of supreme safety. With her eyes fixed on the peak whence the strange flying ship had departed just a few minutes earlier, she gradually dropped off into a soothing sleep.

Jasmyn's voice verged on petulance. "Why did you have to go down there in person, Sandol? You nearly frightened the poor lady to death."

Sandol yawned, took another sip of pilta and answered laconically, "This remote monitoring bores me at times—I need more personal involvement."

"You're playing awfully fast and loose with the rules these days. If you wanted a closer look at her you should have gone to her door as an insurance salesman, or filled in as her hairdresser."

"I was impatient."

"No more of that, though. We are absolutely *not* to frighten them— you *know* that."

Sandol could see that she was plainly put out with him, so went defensively on the offense. "I know, but how about you? You're not planning a personal meeting with your little pet?"

"I may," she replied, lifting her chin haughtily. "But only peripherally— perhaps during one of his dream states."

"And give him a nocturnal emission, I suppose," Sandol taunted.

"That would be none of your concern, my friend. Nor will I permit you to force me into a defensive mode."

Sandol stood up, stretched, and sauntered indifferently past the array of monitors, pointedly changing the subject.

"Reagan's going to run for the presidency again, as if it mattered in the least."

"It matters to them, and therefore it matters to us. And you will stay out of my personal business, Sandol."

He smiled faintly, averted his eyes and said nothing.

4

The Joy of Paranoia

Bairny started a double serving of espresso as Adam rolled the van down the hillside road and headed for the city. When it was finished, she brought two steaming cups to the forward seats and rejoined him.

"Well," she sighed, "these past two days have not been days like any other days, I must say."

"Can't tell whether that's good or bad," he answered. "Have you decided—would you care to join us?"

"Good, all considered. And, yes, I'm definitely in. I should have your Overpass Theory doped out by noon, if you'd like to get together then."

"Deal. We'll slip over to Kono Comusu's for some Nipponese viands and up-to-date intelligence on the oriental phase of the operation."

"Oh?" Bairny raised an eyebrow. "Your people are really worldwide?"

Grim at the thought of it, Adam nodded. "Has to be—T.H.E.Y.'re worldwide—all over the globe like ugly on a crocodile."

They arrived at his office moments later, where Kate Nay greeted him with an outthrust telephone. "It's for you Adam—the feds."

The voice at the other end was ominously polite. "This is Federal Bureau of Investigation agent Torunie, Dr. Solon. Agent Lashes and I received a phone call from headquarters in Washington this morning, directing us to, ah, *interview* you sometime today. A few routine questions y'know."

Adam glanced down at his appointment book and replied amiably, "Always glad to be of service—how about noon?"

"At your office, then?"

"Fine. I'm located at . . . "

Torunie's voice interrupted darkly. "Never mind, Dr. Solon—we know *exactly* where you are!"

Adam looked at Kate and shuddered. "Those guys give me the creeps. They must have a dossier on me a foot thick. Probably know to the minute the last time I peed, and how many cc's, and what its specific gravity was."

Kate was, as usual, sexily stoical. "No problem—peeing in the designated place is one of the few things that's still legal these days." Then nodding toward Bairny with a bright smile, she asked, "Who's your beautiful friend?"

Adam introduced them, briefly explained Bairny's mission in a lowered and confidential tone, then asked Kate to take her to the computer office and supply her with plenty of pens and paper. The two women left chatting friendly amenities.

Adam watched their retreating figures with amused appreciation, then turned and scanned his appointment book more carefully. A few new names, a few old, and also scheduled was Dan Winthrop, his good attorney friend. He suspected the rest of the day would be routine. Marrieds who didn't want to be married; unmarrieds who wanted to be married; gays who wanted to go straight; straights who wanted to loosen up and try bi; women who wanted to learn how to do it themselves; and others who wanted the will to resist the monstrously powerful impulse to myriad varied but rarely imaginative forms of kooky carnal self-indulgence—though to Adam none of them were in the least kooky. Patiently he would hear them out, helping them dissect one feeling from another, gently reassuring, carefully correcting crippling misconceptions, catalyzing thought, inducing self-acceptance, and always meticulously engineering the construction of what he privately thought of as "little solutions to little people puzzles—a puzzle-solver is what I am—anagrams—crosswords—Scrabble—word jumbles and people puzzles."

Ah well, he sighed philosophically, without it all he would be a mere neurologist. Our poor species: suggestible, gullible, dumb, hypnotizable and corruptible. The operation of the human brain's neocortex is notoriously disobedient to the tyrannical demands of its paleolithic understratum. Passion overwhelms reason, and as for our logic, be it Euclidean, Boolean or symbolic, it always came out the same: my logic is superior to yours—I'm right and you're wrong.—let's fight!

Adam pushed aside his dark ruminations as he shook hands with Dan Winthrop. Dan was a straight-looking, mild mannered attorney who specialized in international corporate law. Adam had talked with him many times, sizing him up—and he was still unsure about the man. But now the time for fencing was over; parry, thrust and *touche* or not *touche*.

After supplying the attentive attorney with a preliminary word of reassurance, Adam pressed his recruitment effort forward.

"I'm gathering together a few people who are agreed that the world is a complete mess—people who are very bright, dedicated to the cause of reform and absolutely trustworthy."

"Doesn't sound like your style, Adam. So grim, and, well—zealous."

"Not altogether," Adam smiled. "I'm not killing—but cultivating—two birds with one stone. When Freud was asked to define the good life, he went along with all the great men before him: the Good Life is Love and Work. My elite little coterie all accord with that. All of them are both political and pleasure activists, devoutly so. And from what I've seen of you so far, I'd say you're a very well-qualified candidate for membership. Interested?"

Dan eyed his friend thoughtfully. "Exactly what are you into politically—blowing up CIA buildings and all that?"

"Oh, no—that's not our thing. We like to talk about it but we're nonviolent by principle. Our thrust is investigation, research. Frankly, we're out to identify and expose those little gnomes of Zurich—the bastards who are engineering the mess—all the wars and the poverty and political corruption—and to have any kind of chance at success we need experts—experts in every field."

"All right, so far so good, although you'll understand that I still have many questions and a few misgivings."

"Quite understood. Introduction into the group takes place by stages because we do need to maintain very tight security. There will be a few tests to pass, in the course of which you will also naturally be testing us. And you are free to withdraw at any time—even after attaining full membership. The only hard condition is that whatever you do—even if you come to despise the whole venture and everyone in it—is that you *must* preserve secrecy. You must not, in other words, try to bust us under any conditions or for any reason."

"Well and good," Dan acknowledged, lightly drumming his fingers on the desk. "But what if someone does try to expose you—do you have them blown away or something?"

Adam laughed and shook his head. "Not at all—we really are nonviolent. Security is my problem, and be assured that it's really not much of a problem. We have a harmless little neutralization technique that will render any potential Judas instantly disinterested in acting on his traitorous impulse."

Dan pressed on in measured tones. "So, Adam, I gather you're serious about this venture of yours."

Adam nodded abruptly. "I am. I got tired of being a bloody hot-air-blowing armchair and cocktail-party revolutionary. Decided to do something about it."

"Admirable, I admit, and please understand that politically I'm very much in your camp—but are things really as bad as you paint them?"

"Worse," Adam grumbled. "I'm only beginning to uncover the garbage heap—or the charnel house—they've turned the world into."

Getting hotly into his indignation, Adam then proceeded to sketch a quick outline of T.H.E.I.R. ruthless and unbounded chicanery. Billions of consumer dollars being siphoned off every year by American Multinational Corporations. Billions of surplus dollars in the American insurance industry alone, with no thought of refunding one penny of it to the hapless suckers who had paid it all in. Good old Ike, whom Adam had truly liked, blandly signing over other billions of dollars in off-shore oil drilling rights to big American companies. Obscene!

"But it's their methods that really get me," he concluded, noting that it was nearly noon and the F.B.I. would soon be closing in on him. "They don't give one Holy Hell how they make it. They engineer wars between nations, tax the people to finance their own destruction, reap enormous profits from both sides selling arms and ships and food and uniforms *and* when the killing and maiming is over they even collect huge reparations for any damages done to their factories by misdirected bombs! They're totally without conscience!"

Dan was troubled. "But, if you do manage to put together a case against them, won't they just have you killed before you can publish it, the way they nailed Ian Fleming, the Kennedy brothers, Martin Luther King, and God knows how many others?"

"Maybe. They'll probably try—if I manage to get close enough. After all, others have tried before, like Teddy Roosevelt, and that marvelous muckraking journalist idol of mine, old Lincoln Steffens. Even Jack Kennedy, when he tangled with the big steel and oil people—but none of them ever got to first base. T.H.E.I.R. security is virtually perfect, and if it ever should be effectively penetrated—as I intend to do—then of course they can always fall back on force."

"Well, then," Dan argued, "if their security is so good how do you expect to write a book that will convince anyone of their guilt?"

"Good point," Adam conceded. "First off, presidents like Teddy and Jack rammed at them head-on at the Executive and Legislative levels of government. Very foolish, because T.H.E.Y. *own* the world's nations. Steffens was smarter. He went after them through the media, where there's still a vestige of freedom left. What he didn't realize, though, until maybe toward the end of his career, is that T.H.E.Y. also own the media. So, every time he'd make a score on them they'd simply load up their syndicated newspapers with a barrage of neutralizing lies that would wreck any impact he might have had on the public mind."

Dan nodded. "Okay so far—now how are you going to avoid the error of their ways?"

Adam's manner turned crafty. "Ah! By the only historically proven, tried-and-true way of reaching the people at the grass roots. Tom Paine pamphleteering—reaching the street people directly and *outside* of establishment media channels. I'll gather all the hard evidence I can, publish it on my own press, then peddle it on the streets and door-to-door. Gary Allen did it with his *None Dare Call It Conspiracy*—put out five million copies!"

Dan made no attempt to disguise his doubt. "To me it sounds like one helluva long shot, my friend—don't really see how you can possibly bring it off."

Adam shrugged, somewhat like Atlas. "Doesn't really matter. I have to try. Might say, really, that I'm just writing a book—convincing or not. It's a very personal thing with me. I just want those murderous, money-grubbing, power-lusting sonsabitches to know that I know they're up there—and what they're up to—and how—and to let them know exactly what I think of them. *They'll* read it, even if no one else does. They read everything, then file it away in that monstrously voracious Leviathan computer of theirs."

"Self-therapy, Adam?" Dan grinned. "Sounds like you're just out to get something off your chest—massive catharsis and abreaction."

Adam confirmed. "At *least* that. I'm nuts, of course, to even try. Me and my little dab of spare time, a few thousand measly dollars a year, a handful of helpful friends like you—against them and their trillions of dollars, their nations and armies, and that frigging omniscient-omnipotent smirking, snotty overbearing computer of theirs. Who knows—we might get lucky. But in any event, I do have to do it, just to let them have one expert's opinion—that their insatiable lust for money and power at the cost of all that human life, the pain and the suffering—is the foulest mental warp ever to corrupt and befoul our species."

"Okay, Adam," Dan sighed, "count me in. The whole thing sounds more than a little Quixotic, I fear, but you're right about one thing: someone has to do something about it, or at least try, and I don't know that I have anything better to do with my life."

Adam glanced at his watch again and his tone softened. "How about full-time flashing, maybe in a circus tent show?"

Dan laughed. "Don't tempt me. I could really relate to something like that, but, well . . . " he tapped his temple several times ". . . there is this other end to my body, and it also knows a pleasure of sorts—a pleasure sometimes as intense and real as the other."

"I know what you mean," Adam smiled, and then the phone rang. It was Agent Torunie. "Dr. Solon?" His voice was plaintive, almost whimpering, though it was striving nobly to sound self-righteously accusatory.

"I've been waiting here at my office for you gentlemen—it's 12:17 now."

"Where are you, anyway," Torunie whined. "We're over here on 36th Street and your office is empty!"

Adam winked at Dan. "Right. That's what I tried to tell you when you called earlier. I moved from there a month ago and the new phone books haven't come out yet." He gave Torunie his new address and turned thoughtfully to Dan again:

"Maybe I overestimated that dossier thing—the only address those F.B.I. agents have on me is from last year's phone book."

Dan affirmed. "It's very easy to get paranoid about the F.B.I. but I've never found them to be all that efficient. Same for the CIA and IRS and the other bureaus I've had dealings with. I think they trade heavily on old-fashioned bluff."

"Maybe," Adam answered hesitantly, "but they still scare the freedom-loving-feces out of me."

As Dan stood up to leave, Kate Nay came through the door a-bustling, her eyes bright. "Sorry I left you with the phone so long, Adam. I've been helping Bairny with her weird computations, though I haven't the foggiest what they're about. Wow, what a brain!"

Torunie and Lashes finally found their way to the office, and entered grumbling inarticulately about the unforgivable inefficiency of the Bell Telephone system and their outdated directories. Both displayed their neatly walleted badges, just like Efrem Zimbalist, Jr. and his cohorts did it on the tube. Their entire demeanor, for that matter, conformed very closely to the popular media image of the good G-Man. Privately tickled, Adam reflected that the tube did indeed provide clear identification models for a remarkable range of roles for good guys and bad guys, good parents and bad parents, even good bad guys and bad good guys—all in a running mix of baffling combinations.

Adam introduced them to Dan Winthrop and gestured for all to be seated. "If you're not in a hurry, Dan," Adam said with a teasing smile, "you might stick around and protect my interests—I have no idea what this little inquiry is all about."

Now it was their turn to be paranoid. The last thing they *ever* needed was *any* young, smart-ass, liberal left-wing fellow-travelling UCLA lawyer looking for legal loopholes to get killers and traitors and other hard-ass felons off the hook they should all be hanging on; but they realized there was nothing they could do about it and tried to handle Dan's presence by simply ignoring it.

In his very best, carefully courteous but official Zimbalistic voice, Torunie explained: "Dr. Solon, our superiors in Washington have directed us to ask you a few simple questions," whereupon he drew a folded sheet of paper from his inner coat pocket, unfolded it and commenced the interrogation.

"Dr. Solon: are you the owner of a certain piece of coastal property north of San Francisco, designated on county plat such-and-such as parcels A through et cetera?"

Adam nodded. "Sure—that's public-record information."

Torunie made a note on the paper and continued. "Is it further true that a certain portion of said land is ... " The agent hesitated, squinted at the paper in perplexity, and finished the question with a rising inflection, " ... detachable?"

"Well," Adam hesitated, "that isn't general knowledge but it is legal. Mr. Winthrop, here, cleared all that through the International Maritime Court several years ago. What's the F.B.I.'s interest in that?"

Torunie didn't even bother to look up. "We were only told what questions to ask—not the reason for asking them."

Adam was irritated. Those shit-eating Illuminati surely knew the rules better than that—they were deliberately out to taunt and harass him. He replied coldly, "It's conceivable that my attorney might advise me not to answer these questions until I know why they're being asked."

Both agents flushed and assumed forbidding expressions, finding it unthinkable that anyone would even consider resisting their right to probe at will. Dan passed a hand over his lower face to conceal a smile and said, "It's okay to answer, Adam. You're all covered legally."

"Okay," Adam said, "the answer is yes—part of my land is detachable."

Lashes, scratching his head, butted in. "Why? I mean, what the hell for—and how . . . ?"

"Is that question on your list?" Adam asked tersely.

Torunie elbowed his partner impatiently. "Dr. Solon, precisely what kind of activities are carried out on this property of yours?"

Adam started to object but Dan reassured him with a nod. "Well," Adam said, tight-lipped, "we do a lot of historical research."

Torunie, sensing that he was being put on, glowered briefly at his exasperating subject. "You anticipate the next question, Dr. Solon. On this property of yours, known as—Alpha Orion? [he pronounced it "ore-ee-yun"]—are you engaged in any form of political activity?"

Here Dan suddenly raised a staying hand toward Adam and replied for him. "Dr. Solon is and has always been a registered Republican. He is not and has never been a member of the Communist Party or any other anti-American group. He is engaged in a privately financed investigation of the world's supra-national political and economic structure. And that, gentlemen, is all you're entitled to know this side of an open Congressional investigation—which Dr. Solon would frankly welcome."

Looking a little insulted, Torunie refolded his sheet of paper and put it back in his pocket. "Those are all the questions we had anyway," he said sullenly. He and Lashes stood up with an air of forced dignity and moved toward the door.

The agents shook their heads disapprovingly and left, not at all pleased with the results of their interrogation. They knew enough about this odd-ball shrink to recognize him as a dangerous, Commie-loving extremist. "Republican, my ass," Torunie grumbled to his partner when they were out of earshot. "That's a goddamn front for his pinko sympathies—glad the Bureau's keeping a close eye on that one."

Dan was reassuring Adam: "That's all they knew, Adam—just that list of questions they got from Washington. Those two are just a couple of working cops."

Adam reflected, "Shrewd, those Insiders. Another example of the overpass principle. It's the old sealed-orders gimmick. Playing all sides against the middle. Divide and conquer, or divide and prevail. T.H.E.Y. are master puppeteers and we all—all of us—dance around at the ends of their five-billion strings—whatever way they want us to go."

"You're certainly not a very obedient marionette," Dan laughed, preparing to leave.

"Right," Adam asserted. "At least we at G.R.I.P.E. are straining at our leashes—we're *trying*."

"Okay, Adam. Should I arrange my schedule to be at the preliminary meeting?"

"Please. You'll be most welcome—and useful, frankly. I also think you'll enjoy the company, and the kind of leisure we enjoy on Alpha Orion."

The tentative agreement was sealed with a handshake and Dan left.

5

The Overpass Theory

They were greeted at the door by the Flower of the Orient herself,
the redoubtable Kono Comusu, businesswoman supreme, master of
the abacus, fifth-level black belt, lotus-loined repository of the wisdom
of the ages, and regional director for G.R.I.P.E.'s Personnel and
Operations Division. She took them to a secluded, candlelit corner in
the rear of the restaurant and seated them. Straightfaced, eyes dancing
with humor, she bowed formally to Adam.

"May humble servant make tiffen for white master?"

Adam patted Bairny's shoulder and said, "I'd rather make her myself,
Kono."

Bairny winced and Kono, affixing her most inscrutable smile,
withdrew to answer a customer's waving arm, then promptly returned
with two menus and delivered Adam a subtle facial signal as she
handed them across the table.

He turned to Bairny as he rose. "Be back in a couple of minutes—
need to talk with Kono. Find the lowest calorie item on the menu and
order me one, okay?"

Bairny bobbed her head agreeably and Adam followed the five-foot,
one-hundred pound Asian beauty down the corridor to her private

office, stunningly elegant—like Kono herself—in its classical Japanese simplicity. Inside, he stopped and encircled her tiny waist, lifted her a foot-and-a-half off the floor and, as her slender arms circled his neck, kissed her long and deeply on the mouth, to which she responded with true Gallic alacrity.

She nuzzled him knowingly. "Ah, well, east is east and west is west..."

"I know, I know," he interspersed impatiently, "but is the difference genetic or cultural?"

Kono smiled and extended her hand to him. "Come on, Adam—by now you've started to feel guilty, hung-up as you are on your brittle Western mores."

"Well," Adam lamely defended himself, "it is a little adulterous, isn't it? In here with you while my poor guest languishes alone in the midst of strangers."

Kono quickly kissed the middle of his chest, as high as she could reach on tiptoes, and giggled. "My god, Adam, your food won't be served for another six-and-a-half minutes. It'll only take about two to lay my report on you." She took a heavy, sealed manila envelope from her desk and handed it to him. "Here's the written version, coded for the K.I.D.—then you can have the lady all to yourself."

Then she went serious:

"Okay, here it is in a betel nut shell. Sue Fortret's cozily holed up in a little resort inn on the Tanega Coast, China Sea side, finishing up a cryptanalysis caper. From what I understand of it, an elite cadre of Illuminati semanticists based in Shikoku are resurrecting and modifying the old Hondo and Kinai dialects as the basis for a new international code. They'll have to move it to stay ahead of Sue, though. That beautiful Amazon knows more about oriental languages than all my ancestors together ever did."

Adam nodded approval and Kono's crisp, lilting voice continued. "We got Peter Newton's report in last night on our coded frequency. As you know, he's spent the last two weeks on good old 68th Street in New York, telephotographing the cast of characters frequenting the Council on Foreign Relations Building. What he's got so far sounds like a pictorial *Who's Who in International Skullduggery*." She interrupted herself. "By the way, Adam, have you seen his van since he refurbished it?"

"I saw it just as he was finishing it up," he confirmed. "Quite a layout."

"No kidding—like a fully equipped Hollywood studio. He has one lens as long as my arm. Could get a shot of the hair follicles in Henry Kissinger's nose, if you're interested in that particular view. Anyway, he's on his way back here now with a whole pot full of hard, graphic evidence on the local and international Gnomes of Enlightenment."

Pleased, Adam smiled. "Good, good."

As he and Kono moved toward the office door he suddenly brightened with the thought of Candy and her colleagues. "By the way—how's the Junior Auxiliary doing?"

Kono shared his pleasure in the matter. "Swimmingly," she smiled. "You already know about Candy . . . " she nudged him knowingly and added, " . . . just about all there is to know I suspect. And I've filled you in on Peter's latest—that boy is a scoptophilic photographic genius. Lemon Molsen is still working out of Alpha Orion base station, interviewing Hopi historians and trying to establish a connection between their national origins and the pre-Tut Egyptians, and—just a minute." She sidestepped away from Adam and drew a small pad from her desk drawer, opened it and read off the list of junior members and candidates for membership.

"Wanda Marple, Ruth Spainet, Lora Geldith, and Rhonda Vercot are all first-level black belts now, progressing well in their counterintelligence specialties—and they've all passed security clearance. Abby Murphe, Vida Worble, Page Solin, Rafie Watt and Vee Burber are all very close to black belt level and, coincidentally, to final security clearance as well."

"Fine," Adam said, then questioned, "Our juniors are all girls except for Peter—shouldn't we be beefing up their ranks with a few more boys?"

Kono laughed. "That doesn't sound like you, Adam—too many girls and not enough boys?"

He patted her arm. "I was thinking of business, not pleasure. What's the problem—no adolescent male talent around?"

Kono smiled at him laterally, impishly. "We can look harder, if you like, Adam, but do we really need them? The girls are handling things just fine."

Adam was pensive and vaguely troubled, though he did not confide it to Kono. He had long marvelled at the territoriality, instinctual xenophobia and group chauvinism of the human species—the extraordinarily powerful inborn need of the mortal individual to draw ego support from the company of others with whom he shared a certain number and kind of common characteristics, and his intense, innate fear of all others who differed from him in the slightest. Were The Illuminati elite also subject to such divisive frailties?

Time and again he had ruminated on the characterology of the Insiders themselves, postulating at one time that they were all women who had long ago capitalized upon their greater leisure and their chronic status as second-class citizens to silently, secretly usurp the world's money supply and all the power that goes with it, using the "Great and Famous Men of History" only as fronts.

Or was it the ancient clan of the Hopi with their unbroken trimillennial history, masquerading as underprivileged social outcasts in their private nation around Oraibi in northern Arizona?

Then again, might not they all be blacks, who were by all available evidence the very first humans to appear in the African cradle of civilization?

In his wilder moments of free running speculation, he had even chastised himself for daring to entertain the Daniken thesis of extraterrestrial infiltration.

Beyond that outlandish improbability he had, in the rarest moments of unfettered fancy, envisioned a world-wide coalition of highly intelligent chimps, porpoises, baboons, whales and orangutans, meeting in the dark of night on distant ocean shores where human feet had never walked, communicating with each other in ways known only to them, plotting out their newest campaign to delude their Johnny-come-lately evolutionary cousin—the baldest, most vicious, eternally jabbering and symbol-worshipping species ever known—into believing that he reigned supreme over them all. Perhaps he would never know, but his curiosity burned constantly within, and he never tired of battering his head against the seemingly impregnable walls of this monolithic conundrum.

He replied pleasantly to Kono. "Maybe you're right. Anyway, we do seem to be in good shape for the time being. Now, back to Bairny and my starvation lunch."

Bairny, who had already hungrily moved in on the perimeter of her steaming bowl of chow mein, greeted him with a wink and a smirk. "Adam, your iron self-discipline and single-minded devotion to business leave me in awe."

Adam apologized. "Sorry it took longer than expected—we had more to deal with than I realized."

"I guess so," she giggled. "If I'm going to be around you much, I'll just have to accustom myself to the telling scent of women in heat, yes?"

Adam's face registered a disclaimer. "Believe it or not, these last several days have not been typical. Most of the time I just talk and work. But, well, there's a sort of excitement in the air among our people. Anticipation of the quarterly meeting, I suspect—we're all getting pretty excited about it. A generalized aphrodisiacal effect, you might say."

"Wonderful—I hope it gets to me soon. I need something to light my fire."

Adam shot her the indulgent skeptic's arched brow. "Sure, sure— and I still say you're a fraud and a fakir on that score."

She deftly ducked the issue with her usual secret smile and change of subject. "Eat your oyster beef, white master, while I fill you in on my morning's work."

Adam watched and listened intently as she excitedly discoursed over a sheaf of papers spread out on the table between them—papers covered with mathematical symbols that were all but foreign to his eye.

"Your overpass theory is no theory—it's as real as granite, grass and grinding groins. Look here . . . "

"Don't hit me with too much theoretical math, Bairny—I never got beyond college algebra. That's some kind of spatial array analysis, isn't it?"

"Well, my modification of it," she answered, her hands trembling finely with excitement. "I'd never thought about it this way until you mentioned it at rounds yesterday morning. What it adds up to, if I may oversimplify the thing, is that all around the world there are more computer circuits operating than can be accounted for by those presently in the service of *visible* business, government, universities and so on."

"Any estimate as to how many more?"

She slipped another sheet onto the top of the pile. "Yes. Very close to eight or nine percent by my calculations. I'm really quite sure of it."

Adam sat back, a thin smile both proud and thoughtful stealing across his face. "That means, then," he thought aloud, fingering his chin slowly, "that we may safely assume the active existence of what amounts to a transglobal wire tap—a strictly covert wire tap—on every computer (or more properly, 'computer component,' " he amended) "operating with public knowledge."

Bairny confirmed with a quick, eager nod of the head.

"So-o-o," he continued slowly, sketching a crude diagram on the blank back of an overturned page, "that means, for example, that any or all data coming from, say, federal office buildings here and there around the country into Washington Central . . . or, say, from the various Sears retail stores into Sears' central headquarters—wherever that may be—is being ever so silently and secretly skimmed off, siphoned off at the top, and fed into that Great Console in the Sky . . .

above the clouds around old Olympus' towering top . . . "

Bairny shivered. "Now *that* excites me," she murmured.

" . . . where the invisible Gods sit in sumptuous splendor," he went on dreamily, "reading our innermost thoughts and darkest desires, regulating our lives, playing with us as a girl child plays with her dolls, laughing at us, peeking through our keyholes, all-knowing and all-powerful—the master of us all . . . "

Bairny, only nodding her head dimly, slid farther forward and let her head fall back, mouth parted and eyes now drooping and veiled.

" . . . and all of it over the heads of the peons and the presidents, the kings and the great scholars, the chairmen of the boards—*fantastic*. The loathesome bastards!"

Bairny half-turned a deliciously tortured face to his, her voice barely audible. "Adam, please—is there anything you can do for me, like *now*? I mean, when it *does* hit me it's like . . . like an inferno . . . a medical emergency."

"No, m'dear. Not a thing," he replied quietly, maddeningly, cheerfully into playing her little game.

6

Assassination Plot

Back at the office, Kate was waiting for him with the neatly typed letter to Clarence Kelley. He read it over quickly:

Clarence Kelley
Director, Federal Bureau of Investigation
Washington, D.C. 20535

Dear Sir:

Pursuant to the Freedom of Information Act, Title 5, United States Code, Section 552, I hereby request access to any information you might have on file about me.

Enclosed you will find my Social Security number, place and date of birth and my United States Marine Corps serial number.

I trust this is sufficient identifying information for you to retrieve the desired material without too much difficulty.

With appreciation in advance for your assistance I remain,

Very truly yours,

Adam Trasy Solon, M.D.

He then patted Kate on the shoulder and signed it. "Not sure it'll do any good—they don't have to send me anything they don't want to."

Inside his office, he ran his finger down the automatic dialing system. After his call was transferred through several different extensions at Police Headquarters, Lieutenant Geneva Spear finally came on the line, her mellow black voice friendly but efficient. "Sure, Adam—a meeting with you is high on my official agenda," and then with a little laugh, "and right up there on my social one, too."

"Splendid on both counts," he answered briskly. "The more immediate issue, as you might guess, is the somewhat unearthly business with Slaide Armstrong and his seedy band of uncultivated barbarians . . . if you could bring along the files."

"We're on the same wavelength, Adam, but no need to bring any files—every grimy detail about those lowly bastards is impressed indelibly and forever into my personal memory bank. But I will bring their mug shots."

"Great. We're waiting for you."

"Hold a sec, Adam." She delayed a moment, quickly organizing her plan of attack. "I know it's short notice, but it would help my program if you could get Dr. Bels to join us, and bring along that thingamajig you and she designed. I think we're ready to go into the field with it."

"I'll try to get her in, Geneva."

"And, last but by no means least," she continued, her voice lowering, "I do have some updated information on that little matter we discussed last month—and it's blowing my mind."

She screeched to a halt in front of Adam's office just a few minutes later and spun into the office like a twister on a rampage. Lt. Geneva Spear, thirty-two years old, head of the Police Department's Rape Control Unit, and close to perfect for the job. Only two inches short of an even six feet in height, and built like the fabled masonry outbuilding, bright as a new penny, pure ebony in epidermal hue, sporting a gleaming wild Afro that was downright intimidating in its mass and surrealistic lines—altogether a living, breathing model of the black-is-beautiful chestnut. She and Deb Suners lived together in a sinfully plush downtown apartment, where Adam was a frequent visitor.

Adam motioned her into an easy chair. "I got hold of Ina before she left her office. She'll be here in a few minutes. Some wine, Geneva?"

The stunning lieutenant nodded her head and drew a thick manila folder from her briefcase, her dark eyes aglow. "Last week I was able to log in some time on the computer at State Police Headquarters, which has some intriguing federal and even a few international connections that we don't enjoy downtown. I also cadged a copy of their top secret personnel T.O., showing their administrative relationship to various Federal policing agencies and to Interpol. Certain of their movements and connections, but especially some of the activities of Interpol's National Central Bureau, lead me to only one conclusion. To sum it up, Adam, your hypothesis that the Insiders exercise undue influence over the world's police network is a near-miss. Of course, I can't really prove it yet, but after going over the paperwork with some trustworthy lady chums in the C.I.A., there's just no doubt at all left in my mind: our dear friends, the Enlightened Ones, don't just influence it—they fuckin'-A *own* it!"

She accepted the wine from Adam and lit up a long, slender, rich brown cigar. Adam smiled at her. "Guess I'm not really surprised. Much as I despise and respect those goddamn rich bitch elitists, I'm forever underestimating their reach. As for proof, don't lose any sleep over it. So far we've not yet succeeded in actually *proving* so much as an overtime parking violation against them, let alone an age-old conspiracy to establish total, oligarchic world rulership."

Geneva nodded. "True, but I will keep on poking around, doing my Sherlock bit. Meanwhile, the latest details are there on your desk—a tasty little tray of canapes for the K.I.D. to savor, digest and metabolize—if I do say so myself!"

Adam saluted. "Right on, pal. G.R.I.P.E. and I are in your debt. Thank you."

There was a quiet tapping on his door. Excusing himself, Adam strode into his outer office and admitted his dear friend of many years, Dr. Ina Bels, whom he had known since her medical school days. He took her hands fondly and kissed her lightly on the forehead, then stepped back to survey her. Shaking his head in a pantomime of despair he said softly, "Ina, you are still the sorriest excuse for a butch bull dyke I have *ever* seen." It was true, in a way, as she was definitely not his physical type, even though the intellectual and emotional rapport between them was hand-in-glove.

Just five feet tall and a scant ninety-eight pounds, she came very close to emulating a slightly grown-up Shirley Temple, complete with dimples, bright eyes, golden curls, and a girlish purring geewhillikers voice. She looked at least ten years younger than her actual age of forty-two and seemed to radiate acquiescent, late-adolescent femininity from every pore.

Smiling, she tiptoed up to her tallest and kissed his cheek. "You should see me in my pinstripe Hart, Schaffner, and Marx suit, button-down shirt, old school tie, and Derby hat. You know, I just come to work in drag like this to keep from horrifying my colleagues."

"That's your story," he chuckled. "You still look eminently molestable to a dyed-in-the-wool D.O.M. like me."

The two women exchanged quick touch, pat, and howdy greetings with each other, then went directly to business with Geneva taking the floor first.

"When this thing started coming down," she said, drawing rakishly on the cigar and streaming a billow of smoke toward the ceiling, "I thought we were just facing an unusually heavy bit of traffic in the usual spring rape epidemic, but then I began to pick up on some distinctive patterns that didn't fit the supposition. First, the victims: all of them are dedicated activists in the women's movement and all are far to the left politically—our kind of people. Could be coincidence, of course, but the possibility piqued my curiosity enough to inspire me to feed a few names and faces into our computer—all the way to D.C. and back."

She tossed some mug shots on Adam's desk. "These dudes are not just lone-wolf, Saturday night, hit-or-miss rapists—they all know each other from way back and seem to be working in concert. Graduates of the same reform schools, jails, prisons and so on. Next point: they've all been repeatedly charged and/or convicted for crimes of violence other than rape—assault with a deadly weapon, mayhem, manslaughter, suspected murder and many others. The worst of them is that scumbag on the top there, Slaide Armstrong, probably their ringleader."

Adam studied the photo for a moment then passed it on to Ina.

"It gets worse," Geneva continued. "He's been arrested seventeen times and gone to trial nine times on charges of first-degree murder—contract hits, no doubt—but no convictions. He is one cold-blooded, sadistic *m-u-uth-a-a-a*, believe you me. He likes to hurt the ladies bad when he rapes them, but when he shoots turkeys for profit he does it clean through the head."

Adam asked, "Are you suggesting that they're organized for purposes other than recreational beating and raping?"

"So it seems to me. Looks like some kind of purposeful terrorist tactic directed at activist women liberals. And, so-o-o," she drawled, "I dug a little deeper and found a strong professional tie between Slaide here, and a group of right-wing extremists known as God's Thunder."

"Damn," Adam fretted, "they're far to the right of the John Birch Society—could easily be a muscular arm hired by the tycoons to stomp on us lefties."

Geneva turned to him, her face drawn with concern, "Yeah, kind of looks that way. Here's the part that really bothers me, Adam—brace yourself."

"Oh—bad news?"

"Not good. Yesterday I had Slaide hauled downtown for questioning on suspicion of everything, partly just to let him know we care, but mostly to get him out of his pad—which I then handily and unlawfully entered with the help of my trusty little all-purpose hatpin. What I found was a porno collection worthy of the Pope's, a kitchen full of dirty dishes, any good mechanic's tools-of-the-trade—a disassembled high-powered rifle with scope and silencer and an assortment of small arms, dirks and garrots—and this, taped to the bottom of a bureau drawer."

She took another envelope from her case and handed it to him. He withdrew the contents and examined them, his poker face breaking slightly when his eyes fell on a photo portrait of himself. There were also pictures of him entering and leaving the hospital and his office— even an up-to-date shot of him beside his Landau with the Sapinet twins. Another one of his home appeared to be a telephoto taken either from a chopper or from the high tor across the valley, and a chill of apprehension ran through him in sudden fear for Candy and Brian. Along with the photos was one of his business cards, an extensive personal biography, a thorough log of his movements and activities for the past month, and a one-page cryptogram.

Adam whistled softly. "You're right, Geneva—this doesn't exactly warm my cockles. What do you make of it?"

"Enough that I decided not to pussy-foot around with him any longer. I zapped right downtown and confronted the slimy prick with the goods—he was in no position to squawk about my B and E."

"Get anything from him?" Adam asked nervously.

"A bunch of crap—pure adulterated garbage in my opinion."

Adam cleared his throat and tapped the pilfered pile of evidence gingerly, as if it were poison ivy or the furry back of a petulant tarantula. "So, is this what I sorely fear it appears to be?"

She sighed in solemn regret. "That's all I can make of it, Adam. It's the well-laid groundwork for a contract hit—on you."

Paling slightly, he objected a little irrationally: "I don't get it—what's the Mafia got against me? I'm not into gambling, girls or dope, except for my own consumption, of course."

"Oh," Geneva quickly assured him, "Slaide and his pals have no link with the syndicate—I confirmed that through several of my well-placed contacts in the mob. The Mafia honchos know Slaide and his slaymates and agree that they're on some organization's payroll, but not even they know just who or what that organization might be."

Adam leaned forward, hands clasped between his knees and thought aloud: "The money-bag magnates, eh? The Insiders . . . So they've finally decided to do it." He paused for a moment then looked up brightly. "It's quite a tribute in a way, y'know? Didn't realize I was getting that close to them."

"They're our best bet," Geneva agreed, then pointed at the cryptogram. "We're already working on this, Adam. Thought your expertise on their cryptographic M.O. might help. Can you make anything of it?"

Adam had barely glanced at the sheet earlier. Now, scrutinizing it carefully, he recognized it almost at once. "Yes. Yes, indeed. But this is very odd—extremely so."

Geneva's brow went up. "Oh?"

"It's Illuminati code, all right, but it's as hoary and obsolete as the chastity belt—over a century old. Weishaupt's lower echelon boys used it for a short time in their various European scams but it's worthless now—any kid could break it down with a Little Orphan Annie Secret Code Disc. Here—look."

He took a pen and commenced scribbling rapidly. "It's a plain, old-fashioned circular alphabetical transposition—child's play. Start with the common articles, prepositions, pronouns and conjunctions . . . and . . . we find that ah, yes, a five letter displacement forward. E is A, F is B and so on. Give me a couple of more minutes here."

Transposing quickly, he soon completed the decoding and began reading it aloud: "The prevalence and solidarity of Ingolstadt must be recovered and the latter day usurpers deposed and eliminated. All power to the cultural, political and ideological heirs of Weishaupt, Zwack and St. Germaine . . . " His voice trailed off and he speed-read the remainder of the page as he dropped it to the desk, then shrugged, " . . . it's just a lot of hyped-up, political cultist rhetoric—significant content zilch. This is a put on! I'll have Gilth run it through the K.I.D. and discrypt the code within the code."

Ina wondered absently, "Who is the statement attacking? Who are the usurpers? The visible Establishment, or the Communists, or some new branch of the Illuminati who stole a base on the Old Guard and managed to take over the reins of power?"

Adam shook his head. "Don't know—any of those I guess. We'll just have to keep digging. And I'll have to keep a sharp eye on my rear view mirror, 'twould appear."

"You do that, Adam," Geneva said, "and I'll have someone covering your tail as much as possible." She bit her lip thoughtfully. "I'm sure we can cure him of his raping ways but it's going to take special genius to find out exactly who is picking up the tab for this hit. Anyway, rape isn't the issue here—world supremacy *is*."

Then, turning to Adam, "I doubt there's any immediate cause for alarm. I spiked all his artillery so it'll take him a few days to replace it, and that"—she turned to Ina with a cheery smile—"will give me time to deal this bastard a blow that should give us the info we need and then waft him right out of town. Do you have my turnip trap ready, Ina? Whatever it is?"

Ina dipped into her purse and came up with it, then held it out. Geneva leaned forward, inquisitive, and touched it cautiously, asking, "How does it work, Doc?"

Ina jerked it back reflexively. "Careful—don't put your finger inside of it. It's a little device Adam and I dreamed up in the hope of combating this rape festival we're having. It's a specially designed, intricately interwoven, plastic vaginal insert—a version of the old Chinese finger-trap. Inside here, you see, are five-hundred tiny barbed and recurved needle tips, super sharp."

Geneva grinned and Adam crossed his legs uneasily. "All right," she said, "I get the picture. Once it's glommed onto its prey, though, is there any way to get it off?"

Ina produced another instrument and held it up for inspection. "Only with this specially designed, diamond edged cutting tool, and they're available only at our hospital emergency rooms. So, our local rapists either go there and get themselves apprehended, or they live with it the rest of their lives, or they very messily amputate themselves trying to remove it."

"Ghastly, but ingenious," Geneva observed, eagerly extending her hand for it. "Is it ready for me?"

After deftly rubbing a thin coat of lubricant over the device's outer surface, Ina passed it over to her gloating black sister. "I hope it fits all right, Geneva. I just used the figures Adam gave me."

Geneva took it with a nod of thanks and stood up, smiling confidently. "It'll fit fine." Then, discreetly turning her back to the others, she planted her left foot on the arm of the easy chair, bent forward, and began the insertion as Ina hastily reminded her,

"Remember, press only on that smooth post-pubic retainer at the top, then push in slowly until you feel your cervix pop into that receptacle at the back, then lift the retainer upward and snug it behind your pubic bone."

Geneva acknowledged the instructions, then a moment later said, "There—a perfect fit." On both feet again, she smoothed down the front of her mid-thigh skirt and flopped back in the chair with a satisfied smile. "I'm all loaded for ol' Slaide-baby tonight—gonna pare his spud for him, all right."

Ina tilted her head and asked uncertainly, "I've done plenty of circumcisions but this is too much . . . I mean, I'm sure he deserves it, but . . . isn't this a bit retaliatory? Talion motive and all that?"

Geneva was philosophical. "Maybe, baby, but it's first and foremost to neutralize his act. It wouldn't bother you if you could see a few of the nice young ladies he's worked over."

Adam chimed in. "One thing, Geneva—just how can you be so sure he's going to come onto you tonight?"

"He will," she answered knowingly. "You should have seen his face when I was hot-boxing him down at headquarters—rape and revenge written all over it. He looked me up, down, side to side, in and out, with pure jungle threat in his eye-balls! He's been tailin' me ever since—right now he's sitting across the street in that dark green sedan. From here I'll drive straight home and park at the back end of that big supermarket lot next to our place—nice and dark and isolated. Irresistible. He'll move on me then."

Ina fretted about the good lieutenant's safety but Adam was not concerned. "Don't worry. He's one mean, tough monkey, all right, but he's no match for Geneva. Anyway," he grinned, "Deb Suners will be looking on from the bedroom window with my twelve-guage Browning automatic shotgun ready to blaze—just in case."

Geneva had anticipated correctly. The gorilla-sized Slaide Armstrong now approached her under the dim light at the rear of the supermarket parking lot, his head jutting warily forward and arms held out from his sides in a grappling position.

"Well, if it ain't King Kong hise'f," she hissed in her best black jivery. "Now, jes' what the hell you think you doin'?"

"Little change o' luck, Topsy," the brute snarled, glancing quickly around to make sure they were unobserved. "You just hold that big, black ass of yours still and maybe you won't get hurt—not *too* bad anyway."

Geneva backed off slowly, acting frightened and brave, raising her arms as if to defend herself. "Jes' 'cause you smells like ape shit don' mean yo' Tarzan, honkey. You back on off now—heah?"

When he lunged for her she managed to generate a little terror, and to put up a believable though really token resistance. Soon they were both down on the asphalt, with Slaide slapping her face back and forth, then ripping off her panties as he hovered over her, clumsily fumbling to extricate his own hardware for executing Operation Humiliation against the territory's most celebrated cop. "A sow—that's what! Goddamn black sow—this's your lucky night, not mine. You gonna have the privilege of gettin' the special treatment from ole Slaide himself. So, take it, bitch pig—like this!"

Feigning helpless resignation, Geneva relaxed at the last moment so that his first plunge would go all the way—which it did. Groaning with pleasure, Slaide paused briefly, buried in completely, and glared down at her in triumph. "Take it and love it, you black sow!"

Then, as he started to withdraw, his face transformed instantaneously, first to blank astonishment and then to shrieking pain as the hundreds of little hooks bit into place. Then he was on his feet, babbling in confused agony and clawing wildly at his crotch in a vain attempt to dislodge the demon that seemed to be devouring his most cherished parts.

Springing to her feet, Geneva looked on with quiet satisfaction, and dropping her phony jive talk—mocked him: "Well, baby—you got your change of luck all right. Now stop messin' with that thing and I'll take you on down to the hospital to have it removed—before I press charges against you."

Standing there spraddle-legged, the first blood beginning to ooze over the brim of the satanic contraption, Slaide glared at her in homicidal rage. "Not while you're still alive, you castrating black bitch." Whipping a six-inch switchblade from his pocket he snapped it open, toward her face, and advanced on her.

In their bedroom overlooking the parking lot, Deb Suners aimed the Browning at the middle of his chest and prepared to squeeze off a saving shot, but there was no need for it. With the speed of a lashing whip, Geneva's leg fired forward and the shaggy brute collapsed to the ground screaming, his right femur snapped cleanly through just above the knee. Looking up toward Deb with a happy grin, Geneva signalled for an ambulance to be summoned before returning her attention to the wretched ogre now writhing at her feet. "Baby," she instructed him matter-of-factly, "your raping days are over."

A short time later, in the emergency room, with Slaide Armstrong screaming in the background as a half-sickened surgical resident struggled to remove the contraption from him, an assistant D.A. took Geneva aside and explained in a hushed, urgent whisper, "Nice try, Geneva—but there's no way we can make it stick—it's entrapment!"

Geneva was floored. "En-*trap*-ment!? Oh, man, don't say that. He *raped* me!"

Standing nearby was Detective Sergeant Ruben Gamez, a recovering alcoholic with sixteen years of sobriety behind him and one of the city's truly finest. Smiling amiably, he confirmed the A.D.A.'s assessment of the situation in a gentle singsong: "Cruel and unusual, torture and mayhem, sadistic coercion, extortion, entrapment—ah Geneva!— these are a few of our favorite things—but they're all illegal! Everything you got against this *cula* is purely inadmissible."

The A.D.A. went on excitedly. "You obviously set him up for it, and that's entrapment. If that ghastly gadget isn't entrapment then there's no such thing. Worse yet, if the court should buy that, then that howling sonofabitch in there could charge you with assault and mayhem."

"Oh, my God," Geneva moaned, the air dropping from her sails. "There it goes all shot to bits."

"The best thing you can do now is try the old blufferino—scare the living hell out of him and get him out of town, dig?"

Geneva hesitated, thinking hard. "Not so fast. As long as we have him on the rack let's pump him for all he's got."

With six hard-faced cops flanking her, Geneva gnarled at the pain-racked figure on the ER table with icy certainty. "Here's the deal, punk. You name your contractor and you walk. Otherwise . . . "

Slaide Armstrong, believing he had nothing to bargain with, capitulated without a struggle. "It was a correspondence contract, that's all I know. We got our orders by mail and a cool grand for every hit. Whoever it is paid and paid good."

"Keep talking, turkey. Why? Why all those rapes?"

"I already told ya—I dunno!"

"Then guess! Or start packing your personals for the Big Slam!"

"A'right a'ready! Someone's jerkin' ya around, keepin' ya busy with little stuff while they make the big one!"

"Big one? Bank job?"

"Nah—white collar stuff. Graft, embezzlement—crap like that."

Geneva's eyes blinked in surprise. "The tycoons," she murmured, but no one heard her. Then loudly again, threatening: "You got orders to do a number on Dr. Solon!"

"Nah—just keep an eye on 'im—I swear!"

"Okay. We're gonna let you go, turkey—on the condition that you get the hell out of town and take all your little playmates with you. All of us here know your faces and names and haunts and everything else there is worth knowing about you. We catch any of you in town after noon tomorrow—you'll be walking capons by dinner time. You got that straight?"

She could tell by the look on his face that he'd given up the fight. Nodding weakly he said, "I'll go. So will the others."

Then she turned to the surgery resident and snapped gaily: "Okay, Doc, plaster the leg and slap a king-size Bandaid on that mangled noodle and get him out of here—the man has some heavy travelling to do!"

7

Marvels of the Media

At home in his inner sanctum, Adam was busily monitoring network television for subliminal signals when Candy and Brian walked in, just back from their desert outing. He glanced up at them, nodded and smiled, then turned back to the monitor.

Glancing over at Adam's shoulder, Brian asked, "Have you picked up any more, dad? I haven't been around much the last couple of weeks."

"Lots of class-one stuff, all the time—flickers too brief to pick up on—I'd guess in the range of one-tenth to one-twentieth of a second. I did get a good Class-III though: another naked arm, male, dead-looking, dropping down from the top of the screen on the left side—about a fifth of a second."

"That's your third arm, isn't it?"

"Yep, in three months. All swinging down in the same place, all looking lifeless, two naked and one covered with a coat sleeve."

"What's with all the arms, anyway? I thought subliminals were to get movie watchers hungry and thirsty so they'd spend their money on candy and Coke. Doesn't seem to me there's much of a market for dead arms."

Adam shrugged. "I have no idea. Teeny parts of the total program.

Subliminal reminders of the imminence and reality of death, maybe. Fear of death is a powerful conditioning stimulus—aversive. Charlie Manson would agree, I'm sure."

"Any class fours?"

"Quite a few, actually, but they're hard to classify, you know. It would be very difficult to sell a non-believer on there being what—to me—they obviously are."

Brian rolled on his side toward Adam, now more interested. "What are your criteria again for the class four subliminals?"

Adam's brow creased thoughtfully. "Well, they're not actually subliminal. They last from one to ten seconds, usually on the shorter side—two to four seconds. You see and hear them, and the scenery and the actors fit all right, but the scene itself is totally out of context. It adds nothing to the story continuity, it adds no humor, no theme, no character development. It's just dropped in there for some obscure purpose."

"Couldn't it be just sloppy writing?"

"Not as far as I'm concerned. I know those writers and directors and producers. They're bloody perfectionists. If a scene is in there, it's in for a purpose. And it all makes sense somewhere—to *someone*," Adam added with an amused smile, "if you don't mind thinking a tad schizophrenically."

Candy leaned forward earnestly. "Listen pappy, you can forget that schizophrenia jazz. If you think you're delusional, you should hear what Brian and I came up with."

"Oh? Try me."

She and Brian looked at each other, smiling but clearly in sincere agreement with one another. Brian took over. "We think that thing"—he pointed to the tube—"is a transmitter as well as a receiver. We think our conversations are bugged, like right now."

Adam thought about it a moment. "Hmmm. Yes, that is a little more paranoid than my paranoia, but . . . "

He paused a moment, thinking back on his three years of training in the U.S. Marine Corps' radar engineering school. "Well, technically it would be a cinch. Basically, a transmitter is just a receiver in reverse, and vice versa."

"It really could work?" Candy asked.

"Easy," Adam mused aloud. "And if you had a little relay amplifier every few miles, you could transmit the signal to anywhere on earth—or to outer space, if you like them apples."

Both of the kids were impressed. Brian asked, "No kidding—you mean it wouldn't even take any secret, advanced technology?"

"None whatsoever. Our known electronic technology has had that capability for years."

On the tube, an old Clark Gable movie ended and a second or so of scribbly black and white script, supposedly the movie's trailer, flashed on the screen.

Adam laughed. "Good lord—a Clark Gable movie, on a national network during prime time, and we're supposed to believe that the film editor doesn't have sense enough to clip out that ugly trailer. Those guys must think we'll believe anything—which of course we will."

"It's really awesome," Candy murmured. "All those millions of people out there who think they're just watching sitcoms and dumb commercials for poo paper and cunny clouts."

"Awesome is right," Adam agreed quietly. "A video subliminal as brief as one three-thousandth of a second can be perceived and integrated by the human brain—enough to actually influence thinking and behavior."

"One three-thousandth!" Brian exploded. "How can you possibly keep up with that?"

Adam waved lazily at the rows of neatly stacked video tapes on the surrounding walls. "We're doing the best we can, but it isn't easy." Then he added thoughtfully, "The horizontal sweep signal on the tube is roughly three hundred cycles per second, which means that theoretically a single sweep could encode as many as 10-12 imperceptible yet psychoeffective signals per second, or 36,000 per hour."

"Oh, wow," Candy groaned. "How can you possibly fathom it?"

"Can't, Adam smiled. "We'll have to delegate that problem to the K.I.D.—it's just too much for the human mind to grasp."

After a moment of reflective silence, Brian said, "I have a confession. I'm impressed with all this. I mean, I believe you guys—that something's going on—but I've never seen any of it myself."

Adam shrugged. "Fair enough. But you have to be looking to see it. They run them in when you're most susceptible. Like at the fade-outs before a commercial, when you automatically lose interest, or during a lull in the action. And especially, I think, later at night, after you're beginning to get sleepy. The class two subliminals, especially, would have easier access to the unconscious, completely bypassing conscious awareness of the percept."

Brian smiled at his father. "Well, you're the shrink—I'll take your word for it."

Adam shook his head. "No need for that—you can see the class two's and three's easily—but you have to be looking for them. Let's all watch awhile—see if we can pick any up."

Ten minutes went by, then Brian reluctantly observed, "I guess I see what you mean by class ones'—those fast, bright flicks that are too quick to grab consciously."

"Right. You'd have to tape the whole thing and do a slow motion inspection to get them. Gilth is doing that now, on Alpha Orion—all networks. That, or you'd need tacyhstoscopic training, like they gave us in the service during WW II, camouflaged as 'aircraft identification.'"

"Like how?" Brian wondered.

"Oh, they'd sit us all down in a dark room and flash these airplane silhouettes up on the screen, for a fifth or tenth of a second, and we were supposed to identify them. About every tenth picture would be a pinup girl—to keep us awake."

Candy asked, "Were you good at it?"

"Lousy. About the only one I ever got was the Marine Corps' P-38—because it had a twin fuselage. Hard to miss. But what I have to ask myself now," he went on, "is why the Insiders were giving us that kind of training at all, since there's reason to believe there wasn't really much of a war going on. Could have been to prepare us for this stuff—give us a chance to glom onto clues we might otherwise miss."

They were watching a mediocre shoot-em-uppa-tony western yarn, with an abundance of the usual fistfights, showdowns on Main Street, threats of homicide and the rest. Then a scene flashed. Adam picked it up but remained silent as the story rolled on. Candy looked entranced and Brian's face was forming into an incredulous scowl. Ten seconds passed, fifteen, and suddenly Brian bolted upright.

"Hey! What the . . . ! I saw that! Did you all see that?"

Adam jumped from his chair, switched off the set and said, "Okay—science time."

Handing them both pencil and note pads he instructed, "Don't say a word yet. Just write down what you saw, then we'll all compare notes. Go!"

Candy murmured, "I think I saw it."

"Just start writing about what you *think* you saw," Adam said reassuringly.

In less than two minutes they were all finished.

"Okay," Adam said, "that one was about a tenth of a second, I'd guess. Candy—what did you get?"

She shook her head in brief distaste and read from her note: "I wasn't paying close attention, dammit, so I missed some of it. I got the impression of a man's arm laying across the tube. It was bare. I think there was something on it, like dirt, or some yucky bugs. I don't think it moved. I guess the man it belonged to was in deep trouble—maybe dead. That's all."

"Oka-a-ay," Brian said approvingly. "That's about what I got. Listen: A man's arm, naked and motionless, bent at the elbow. Looked like some kind of insects all over the arm. The arm was still—man dead or unconscious."

"Right on," Adam said, "here's mine. Male right arm, shoulder at lower left hand corner of the screen, flexed at elbow about ninety degrees in center of screen, with dorsum of arm and hand showing and fingers clenched. Well-muscled, no movement, glistening—as with sweat—and swarming with what seemed to be a mixture of cockroaches, maggots, and one or two scorpions—all in motion. The arm appeared lifeless, its owner freshly dead."

"Jesus," Brian muttered to Candy, "you can tell who's the clinician in this house. All that in a tenth of a second?"

Adam grinned proudly. "I must be improving with age—I didn't do that well with the P-38's or even with the pinup girls."

Candy spun around on her bottom and flopped back, resting her head on Brian's bare thigh, then smiled up at him provocatively. "How about it, brother—are you a believer now?"

Nodding his head slowly, "What else? I saw it with my own eyes—but what does it mean?"

Adam laughed. "Only T.H.E.Y. know for sure, and T.H.E.Y. ain't sayin'. The overt information—the macromessage—is pretty much what it appears to be. I've now been around enough years to identify some unmistakable trends. The ads are mental and emotional conditioning stimuli as well as moneymakers: there's a blatantly disproportionate representation of products. The system is currently pushing health foods, adding more and more vegetables and less meat to fast food burgers. There are no hard liquor ads and the beer is getting weaker *and* more macho. Cleanliness preparations in wide variety. There's an amusingly skewed emphasis on personal body parts: toilet paper, hemorrhoid preparations, vaginal douches and maxipads. It looks like we're being gradually weaned from our carnivorous ways to vegetarianism—a good move? And we're also being stepped down on our alcohol intake, while undergoing desensitization to body parts that have been irrationally sacralized in the popular mind. More specifically, the standard, ambivalent masculine fascinated abhorrence toward female genitals is being steadily resolved, softened."

Candy was visibly shocked. "You're kidding!"

"Nope," Adam answered with a reluctant grin, "Doctor Freud wasn't wrong about everything. Several years ago I had a stopover in the Dallas airport when the giant TV in the terminal showed one of the first commercials for sanitary napkins, 'cunny clouts,' I believe you so irreverently dubbed them. An hour later the announcer came on the tube to give the results of the station's telephone survey of how their audience had been affected by the ad. Over 70% of the respondents had found it disgusting and revolting. Today those ads are just a slightly embarrassing commonplace.

"It would appear that we are being ever so gently weaned from our worst vices, everything from red meat to booze to cigarettes and all such. We are repeatedly exposed to ads of 'light beer' (watered down, that is) being heartily hawked by muscular bearded jocks who are the very essence of *machismo*. This refreshing message is very clear: *real* men do not drink whiskey, rum, or vodka—they drink fresh water faintly contaminated by alcohol. They even promote chewing gum with the beefcake guys. Query: will *Big Red* chewing gum ever replace booze?"

Brian was skeptical. "You make it sound like, well, a total program. They're all just a big bunch of hucksters, right?"

"If so, they spend money like it was going out of style. A million bucks a minute for prime time on a national network is just the beginning. A single McDonald's commercial is equivalent to one Broadway production, complete with band, dancers, a hallelujah chorus, and a broadside of bright patter, all for *our* benefit—to convince us that one egg McMuffin and a full day at hard labor constitute a fair measure of paradise on earth."

Now Adam was on a roll. Pacing restlessly around the room, he gestured and declaimed. "Yes, the national commercials are as much a part of the program as the entertainment. The days of the large, lovable, all-anglo family—*The Brady Bunch* and such—are past. Today, a proper sitcom has to have at least one black, one oriental, and maybe a Mexican or a Greek. Same for the commercials—smiling foreigners all over the place."

He stopped, paused, and shook his head wonderingly. "And then there's the regular rhythmical beat of the big news breaks—a fact of our carefully designed, largely synthetic, psychological environment. Nuclear accidents, hostage seizures, assassinations, mass murders, Ted

Kennedy, and Profumo scandals-in-high-places, which we love to hear about, all break at an evenly paced tempo—two to three biggies a year. They're designed to entertain, stimulate thought, teach object lessons, apparently by just the right dosage and schedule: enough to keep us alert and on our toes but not too much to inundate us and leave us catatonic with over-stimulation, swamped. We're being brainwashed!

"Then again, these are not flat lies. The System simply makes the most of authentic tragedies, and we *homo non-sapiens* certainly create enough of these. When news is short and some attractive event must be created or enormously amplified, we find the reporting thereof replete with transparent journalistic 'outs': 'casualties may have been as high as 2,000' (later amended to two slight injuries), 'it has been reported that,' 'it is purported,' 'according to unconfirmed reports,' 'allegations have been made,' 'according to eyewitnesses present at the scene,' and so on. How to impact the mass mind without actually lying! And our friends are not actual liars—they are just extremely selective in what they report."

By now he was rambling poetically, inspired, and getting a little wild-eyed, while Candy and Brian exchanged uneasy glances.

"Local and State news is as trustworthy as it is dull. At the national level the distance between newsworthy principals and citizen-observers increases, and our reliance on The Media for accurate information increases accordingly. If something of significance happens in Flagstaff or Phoenix, I can drive to the source and check it out myself. If it happens in Los Angeles, I can telephone a friend. If it happens in Beirut, well, I don't know anyone there and do not have the time nor money to go see for myself. So I read about in *Time* or *Newsweek*, and their version of events—being virtually identical—I am mightily inclined to accept as valid. What we do not allow for is that *their* information emanates from a common source. In the timely and reassuring words of WKRP's Les Nessman: 'The wire service never lies!' Oh?"

Adam caught the doubt on the faces of his captive audience. "Ah! You doubting Thomases! Just watch the tube with your third eye! The United Press, Associated Press, *Time, Newsweek*, NBC, CBS and ABC all convey virtually identical information at any given time. Switch channels from *Good Morning America* to the *Today Show* and the change is scarcely noticeable as far as national and world news was concerned. The explanation for this is absurdly obvious: it all derives from a common source—it is all part of the same Program. Oh sure, independent presses are started, most fail and some succeed—but the successful ones are soon legally bought up and their control thus insured!

"What's more," he went on, waving his arms helplessly, "They're forcing us to behave well! When America went ape in the 1920s on booze, drugs, rampant sexual activity, and a confetti storm of paper money, a few buttons were pushed on high to create the Great Depression, whereupon our milling herd suddenly found economic religion, settled down, and went back to work. Moral: we are simply unable to handle too much prosperity. Beyond a certain point of affluence, the playful primate in us takes over and progress comes to a halt. The sociologists have long since established that relative poverty is associated with *lowered* crime and delinquency rates, contrary to popular belief.

"Hell," Adam ranted on, "they even advertise themselves!"

Shuffling through a stack of notes, he retrieved a scrap and read it aloud. "Look at this! October 18, 1986, national television, a half-second flash of the Eye In the Pyramid—three of them side-by-side—subtitled 'Persistence of Vision,' followed by a distracting, utterly infantile commercial for fresh veggie snacks!

"Just take a close look at it, you guys! In popular fiction and in one guise or another, the *Illuminati* theme recurs time and again, though not usually by that name. They are invariably depicted as conspiratorial villains, enormously wealthy, with vast though concealed political power, and they are viewed as devious to the utmost. Here and there, however, there is the faintest of suggestions that they may not be of foul purpose altogether. In R.A. Wilson's *The Golden Apple*, one character, a reporter, intimates that they may be of benevolent purpose. Ha! In the novelization of the popular movie *Network*, Hedrin alludes not only to their power but to their integral association with Big Business. Remember it? The Peter Finch character, Howard Beale, is getting the once-over from his television superior, Jensen, who sternly reminds him that there is *no* America, *no* democracy, but 'only IBM and ITT and AT&T and DuPont, Dow, Union Carbide, and Exxon.' He describes the world as a nationless business that has been exactly that since our poor species crawled out of the primal ooze! And when a chastened Howard asks humbly why he was elected to carry this thunderous message to the world, Jensen drily replies, 'Because you're on television, dummy. Sixty million people watch you every night of the week. . . ' Struck dumb, Howard manages to murmur, 'I have seen the face of God!' and Jensen wryly confirms, 'You just might be right, Mr. Beale.' "

Adam paused for a moment, then forged ahead. "Do you two remember that third-rate, low-budget movie, *The Monitors?* It dramatized the very genuine need for their preserving their anonymity. In the film, the extraterrestrial governors of the world community are utterly benevolent in every way, yet the earthlings—outraged at the thought of being governed by anyone but themselves—rise up in armed rebellion. It is essential, then, that their program be conducted from behind the scenes; we would not have it otherwise. After all, the great Socrates was given the hemlock because, in his later years, he affirmed openly that our species is neither bright enough nor good enough to govern ourselves.

"T.H.E.I.R. chicanery knows no limits! In the Robert Mitchum movie, *Agency*, their villainy is boundless. Using diabolically clever subliminal signals in their manifestly commercial television ads, they manage to unhorse noble political candidates while bringing their own scoundrelous puppets into high office. They cheat, deceive and murder at will—which is pretty much typical of the treatment they receive in the media—and the *Illuminati* themselves like it just that way. It is, in fact, their favorite inside joke. But is it a joke?"

Now Candy was smiling again. "Brilliant analysis, Pappy, but consummately paranoid."

Adam was unfazed. "You think so, eh? In the late '70s I flew to San Francisco and pored through the microfilms of the *Examiner* to check out the great earthquake of 1906. What I found rated little more than a lingering yawn. Front page coverage of the great catastrophe lasted about one week, and even that much was oversell. Several associated deaths were recorded but none of these were the direct result of the quake—heart attacks that would probably have happened anyway, old age, heat stroke, and so on.

"One front page panoramic photograph of the city revealed several wisps of smoke in the distance, not a raging inferno.

"There were abundant shots of the Hearst syndicate emergency tent city, but it was unoccupied. There was one small picture of a quake fissure somewhere out in the boonies but even it was narrow enough for a child to jump across. Compare this with the total catastrophe depicted in the Clark Gable movie, *San Francisco*, and we begin to see their underhanded trickery!

"No falsification was required in the whole operation. The movie was rightly represented as fiction—and yet that's about all any of us really saw of it—and that's what sticks in our minds: Great San

Francisco Earthquake = Holocaust. We are left with that image. I've no doubt that a record review of the Great Chicago Fire (started by Mrs. O'Leary's cow, if you can buy that one) would yield the same. A couple of old Southside tenements went up in flames and became a citywide conflagration in the media!"

Adam suddenly sat down, relaxed and smiled. "I guess I'm making myself abundantly clear. T.H.E.I.R. media is our monster. Here, watch this—a randomly selected national network channel."

The three of them watched, amused but thoughtful, as a merry band of M and M candies danced and sang over a computer keyboard. "Still another meaningful mental/emotional association. If candy tastes good, then computers are fun. It is the infallible logic of the gut—how can one argue with it? And the message reaches millions of young minds many times a day. I tell you—we all are being programmed for some kind of slave labor!"

Reluctantly fascinated, Brian pressed on with his next question. "Do they play around with the audio signals too—by your interpretation?"

"Very much so," Adam replied, reaching for an older cassette. "Here's a good example from the Montreal Olympics. Listen carefully while the international jocks do their thing."

As they sat watching the Olympic boxers cave each other's heads in at the Montreal meeting, Adam listened intently, then nodded his head knowingly.

"Yes—definitely. They're using the same aversive audio conditioning technique here that they use during scenes of violence and other naughty behavior in the TV dramas. Listen carefully to the roar of the crowd."

Candy and Brian sat quietly listening for several moments, then Candy broke the silence: "I hear it. It goes up and down, like undulating."

Brian confirmed: "That's weird. It's sure not what a real crowd sounds like—I've heard enough of them from the arena to know that. Maybe some kind of transmission problem."

"No. It's too consistent. Check out any cops-and-robbers show and you're apt to hear the same thing. The sound of street traffic, or of a big piece of power equipment, amplitude modulated to give that irritating hum—roughly thirty to the minute, or one cycle every two seconds."

Candy chirped, "It's true, okay. I've checked it out. It has to be deliberate."

They returned to the Olympic boxing. At the end of one of the matches a little comedy special was inserted, showing one boxer after another being belted to the mat in Keystone-Cops rapid motion.

Brian stared quizzically at the display while Candy and Adam laughed, then Candy turned and asked, "There they go again. What's this one all about—more aversive conditioning?"

"Hardly aversive, I think. That little show isn't likely to persuade many people of the idiocy of bashing each other to a pulp. No, this one has all the earmarks of characteristic Illuminati humor—they put this one together for themselves. I can almost hear them laughing now, like the old Greek Gods on Mount Olympus, privately relishing the Human Comedy from their own box seats. Same for movies like *Those Magnificent Men in Their Flying Machines* and *The Great Race* and *Around the World in Eighty Days* and *Mad, Mad World . . .*"

Then Howard Cosell came on with a nauseating eulogy for American boxers, and was all but drowned out by the same irritating, undulant roar in the background—courtesy of the Illuminati sound engineers, no doubt.

"I'm going to check that one right now," he grunted, reaching for the telephone extension.

He called his old friend Dub Limon, a top Hollywood film editor, for more information about the background audio modulation maneuver.

"I don't know about that, Adam. A film editor does the basics right near the set, but his output then goes to the main studio in Los Angeles for the finishing touches. Same for the audio background. I know the effect you're talking about though—it drives me nuts. Hell, an amateur could get it out of there—no excuse for it."

"I won't take your time to explain my little theory to you right now, Dub, but I have a hunch that considerable effort goes into putting it there. Tell you all about it next time I see you."

8

The Attack

He polished off Saturday morning hospital rounds as swiftly as conscience would permit, then had a brief but fiery stand-up session with the Sapinet twins in the pantry off the patients' dining room, and then began mental preparations for the desert meeting with his G.R.I.P.E. locals. Marcey, teasing as usual, smoothed down the front of her uniform and complained good-naturedly. "You have real potential, Adam. Just wish you weren't always in such a hurry."

And Mesta extended the complaint, subtlely searching. "What's the big hurry, boss—got another date?"

Adam explained absently, "With a lot of people, yes. Going to mix some heavy business with a little light pleasure out among the agaves and the ironwood trees."

When they heard the exit door from the ward slam behind him, Marcey grinned at her sister and said in a lowered voice, "Guess we'd better upgrade him on sexual gymnastics and drop him a few positions for political indiscretion."

Mesta nodded thoughtfully. "He does tend to be a little sloppy about security—announcing a G.R.I.P.E. meeting to a couple of perfect strangers. Well—almost perfect. Shall we tail him with the big ear and see what they're up to?"

127

Marcey vetoed the notion. "Not without specific orders—we'd be exceeding our actual assignment. Others will be picking up on him, I'm sure."

Coursing along the narrowing desert highway in his van, Adam listened with a mellow sense of gratification as Bairny excitedly filled him in on her further work with his Overpass Theory.

"It's a gas, Adam—I'm having the time of my life with it—and I owe it all to you!"

"You're a happy lady, then?"

"Completely," she beamed. "I feel like a different person—free at last! And I'm in your debt forever, Adam. Have anyone you'd like me to blow away for you? Or unspeakable perversions you'd like to engage in? Just say the word."

"I'll have plenty of favors to ask, Bairny, but they're practically all legit. Like writing up a detailed report on Overpass for the Alpha Orion meeting."

The rendezvous was at the foot of Roc Gonman's mountain. Standing with his arm around Bairny, in knee high desert foliage, Adam pointed to the thin trail leading upward to the concealed entrance of the old man's lair. "Nice little hideaway, that. And can you believe, that kindly old liberal is a bloody capitalist? I looked him up in the county recorder's office—he outright owns that whole damn mountain."

"He's a groove," she said, snuggling up. "Fits right into my father complex."

Adam laughed. "More like a great-great-grandfather complex."

All the local members were present. Dan Winthrop, Brian and Candy were on tap. Kono and Kate were there. Also Geneva, looking sober and fretful from her recent disappointment in the Slaide Armstrong affair. And young Peter Newton, in his studio van, had been accompanied by the other eligible members of the adolescent cadre. For the next four hours they labored intently on the agenda for the quarterly meeting, each presenting his own report, then quietly debating, proposing, amending, clarifying and detailing. Morale was high, and as they worked it mounted with enthusiasm and excitement. Finally Adam stood up and stretched luxuriously.

"Well, I guess that does it for now. We seem to be in pretty good shape. Kate will get it all in report form and send it off to Gilth for integration with the other regional agenda proposals. The K.I.D. will establish priorities before we assemble, so we can get right down to business."

Brian raised a hand and said, "I think you forgot something, chief. What about your book—is it together yet?"

Adam groaned with pain. "All but, Brian—*all* but. There's a clincher to it that I've been searching for desperately—a missing link—a secret key—that I feel would really wrap it up and make the case. But so far I haven't been able to dredge it up. I'm just about frantic enough with it all to start dropping Peyote."

Kono, who knew his ways well, volunteered: "Adam, if you're going to have it ready for Alpha Orion you'd better go into retreat for a few days. Just go hole up with Goldy Sulo and get it over with."

A wave of dread swept over him. Go into retreat, eh? How easy it was to say. Go shave a Kodiak bear, Adam. Go punch Muhamad Ali in the nose, Adam. Go have yourself a little holiday in hell, Adam. And yet he had known for some time that it was coming to that. A marathon race of the mind, free-associating from the bowels of earth to the farthest galaxy, from the unknown beginning of time to that invisible Omega point toward which all futures inexorably roll, and all the while skirting madness, tempting lunacy, scourging himself through the labyrinthine maze of his own memory—of all that he had ever read, heard, experienced, thought or dreamed. Yes, all that and more. To the missing tie, the buried gem—The Answer.

He sighed, a faint tremor in it, and sent Kono his very best wan-little-smile. "I know, Kono. I know. It's just that I've been hoping to make it, somehow, short of that dire extreme."

The remainder of the afternoon was devoted to restrained revelry and capped with a succulent barbecue of lean beef over a roaring fire, after which most of the company made preparations to leave. Geneva and several of the others gathered together with Adam for a quick, last-minute conference, with Geneva taking the lead.

"Kono's right, Adam—you'll have to go into retreat."

Adam resisted. "Isn't there any other way?"

"Don't fight it, Adam," Geneva admonished him. The whole mission depends on you. Think it out!"

Within a few minutes the area was cleared, leaving behind only Adam, Bairny, Candy and Brian, who had decided to spend the night in the Landau right where they were. After another leisurely spell of spritely conversation around the campfire they went into the Landau to retire. Taking Bairny by the arms, Adam locked gazes with her and said with a straight and very earnest face, "I'm bushed, Bairny, and knowing how frigid you are, well, I guess it's safe for us to sleep together tonight. If you're agreeable, that is."

She yawned and leaned against him comfortably. "Sounds good to me. But if you'd care to molest me indecently while I'm asleep, or anything like that, I'll hold still for it."

"I shall keep that in mind."

The side window suddenly exploded, spraying glass fragments around like grenade shrapnel, and the unmistakable sound of rifle fire filled their ears.

"Holy Jesus," Adam growled, lunging for the light switch. "Everybody down—hit the deck!"

They were no sooner on the floor than another bullet crashed through the window and thunked into the opposite wall.

"Stay down!" Adam hissed to the others.

Brian whispered, "Pappy, I know you're strictly nonviolent and all that, but you wouldn't happen to have a little artillery around, now would you?"

"Matter of fact, I do," Adam answered reluctantly, "but the burning philosophical issue to be dealt with here is whether or not we are morally justified in striking back, as aggression does naught but beget further aggression. And Seth has reminded us repeatedly, as you know, that violence is *never* justified."

"Would you mind cutting the bullshit, dad, and tell me where the hardware is—I'm not about to turn my cheek to this business."

Adam went on, maddeningly. "The admirable Christian ideal of cheek-turning in response to violence has always created for me an insoluble moral dilemma. By baring one's breast to the aggressor's blade, you see, one is not only needlessly sacrificing his own life, but helping his assailant to become a murder . . . "

Brian cut in urgently, his voice rising: "Dad! Would you please cram that noise, and . . . "

A third shot came crashing into the vehicle.

Adam said, mildly, "The Marlin is in the closet behind you, and I now have my trusty Charter Arms .44 revolver in my hand."

As Brian groped around in the closet for the rifle, Adam raised slowly, cautiously, to peer out the window, and soon picked up the silhouette of head and shoulders—then a glint of metal—against the moonlit sky.

"Ah—I see him. Now remember, Brian, it is not our purpose to generate violence, but only to neutralize it, for our own spiritual welfare as well as for that of our assailant."

"Speak for yourself, sir," Brian whispered back furiously. "Given the chance I'll blow his ass off him."

"Temper, temper, lad," Adam chided him. Then a fourth shot came slamming into the side of the vehicle. "Okay," he went on evenly, "I'll pin him down with this so you can get good cover outside and put him on the run with the Marlin."

Using Kentucky windage, Adam aimed the revolver a foot or so above the shadowy figure and squeezed off a deafening shot, the revolver recoiling painfully against the heel of his hand. Scanning carefully, he saw that their attacker had dropped out of sight.

"Okay—take off!" and he fired off the remaining bullets at three second intervals as Brian scrambled outside and took a position of good advantage behind a low-lying boulder. After a minute or two of waiting, the outline of a head slowly appeared above the rock, and Brian's first shot struck sparks from the boulder just to the left of it. Then Adam saw the figure leap from behind his cover and head at top speed, broken-field running, down the slope to the west—with Brian full-tilt in pursuit.

"Oh damn," Adam swore softly, "that impetuous boy doesn't know when to leave well enough alone." Leaping from the door he took off after the running figures, catching up with Brian—prone on the top of a flat rock—just as he was about to squeeze off another shot at the retreating figure.

"I'm gonna cut that fucker in two," he cackled, but Adam pressed down the barrel of the rifle and said, "No, Brian, dammit—we've got him on the run."

Brian protested, "Aw, Pappy—not even one little old pellet in the leg?"

"Overkill, m'boy—overkill. Remember: no more force than is necessary to achieve a socially desirable end. However," he added as a concessionary afterthought, "please feel free to blow the living hell out of that beautiful new four-wheel buggy of his . . . but don't flatten his tires—we want him to be able to get away so we won't be up all night swapping shots at one another."

"Hot hooey!" Brian exulted, unleashing a volley of shots in quick succession that reduced the alien vehicle's superstructure to a shambles in a matter of seconds.

"Well done, m'boy," Adam congratulated him as they lay there watching their chastened assailant spin up a cloud of dust in his headlong flight down the rocky desert road. "That should put a crimp in their homicidal ambitions."

"Jesus, but that felt good," Brian exclaimed, standing up and shaking his rifle aloft like Geronimo signalling an attack against the U.S. Cavalry. "But I still think you should have let me bust his legs for him."

It took them an hour to get the van cleaned up and livable again, and to restore Adam to reasonable equanimity, though Bairny and Candy were laughing and chattering excitedly at the thrill of their unexpected adventure. Adam looked at them dourly.

"Glad you two enjoyed that little scam, but has it occurred to you that someone out there was trying to ace me out?"

Bairny patted his leg maternally. "Oh, Adam, you take life too seriously—what will be will be."

"Sure," he retorted grimly, "*que sera* and all that; but where would we have been without weapons to fight back with—I mean to protect ourselves with?"

"Probably down on the floor still," Bairny said laughing, "waiting for him to finish his little outing and go away. Just some beer'd up cowboy out on a toot."

Brian shook his head. "I'm not sure, Bairny. I think he was out to kill. And he could come back with reinforcements. Maybe we should head for home."

"That would be the better part of valor," Adam agreed, "but I've been thinking seriously of trekking up to see Roc tomorrow morning—hoping that a little consultation with him might save me the ordeal of a marathon retreat."

"Okay," Brian said, glowing happily at the thought of another engagement with the enemy, "but I'm standing watch while you all sleep."

Picking up the box of cartridges, he headed for the door with Candy right behind him. "I'll keep you company, Brian. Then we can sleep tomorrow morning while Pappy goes up the mountain—and Bairny can stand watch."

9

Secular HQ

Slumbering gently with Bairny cradled in his arms, Adam had another dream—more vivid and detailed than average but with no accompanying sense of self-projection. In it, he found himself lounging comfortably in Roc Gonman's palatial cavern atop the nearby mountain, where he found the gigantic old gentleman in a congenial mood.

"You accord me too much, Adam. I do odd jobs here and there, by assignment—like my visit to you and your psychiatric ward—but mostly I'm just a sort of doorman around here. My boss is, uh, nearby."

Nodding toward the huge, intricately carved boulder against the back wall of the cave, Adam said, "I noticed your magnificent monolith back there. Is that the entrance to headquarters?"

"It's a sort of local HQ, you might say."

"I'm curious—might I be permitted to see inside?"

Roc stroked his chin thoughtfully. "It's not out of the question, but our security measures being what they are, well, you would have to die afterwards."

"Rather a steep condition I'd say. Would it be painless?"

"Quite a delicious way to transit, as a matter of fact," the old man smiled suggestively.

"All right, it's a deal—I'm that curious."

Roc code-activated a button on his desk and the great boulder slid smoothly to the side. Then he explained to Adam, "The elevator will take us down to the main hall."

"What a layout," Adam whistled softly when the elevator door opened.

"Well, Adam—how do you like it?" Roc asked.

It was a great, circular laboratory and office, with a domed ceiling through which full-spectrum light poured as if from the sun—even though Adam had the feeling that they had descended several hundred feet below Roc's quarters. The walls were lined with computer-related electronic equipment, and handsomely attired workers ambled about the hall tearing off printout sheets, comparing notes, and refeeding information back into the system via one of the hundred or so lesser consoles.

In the center of the hall, on a raised but open dais, attentively working at the Central Console, was a woman with flowing blonde hair that contrasted for an oddly pleasing effect with a black velvet patch over her right eye. She was wearing a matching velvet bikini that revealed (Adam could not help but note) an intriguingly youthful body of indeterminate color. That is to say, her smooth flesh was multi-hued, and Adam reflected with veiled amusement on the gross incongruities—the outrageous violations of logical realities—that could be so handily tolerated—perhaps even deliberately spawned—by the sleeping dream life. "It's incredible," he murmured in genuine awe.

"It's the Ultimate Multinational Headquarters," Roc explained with just a touch of forgivable pride. "Here on this planet, that is."

Adam was then introduced to the remarkable looking lady at the Central Console, who greeted him amiably but without undue ceremony.

"Forgive my directness," Adam said with a slight but gracious bow, "might I ask, though—are you God?"

She shot him a twinkly smile and answered curtly, "Such impertinence! Gracious me, but you folks are such incorrigible hustlers—always on the make for God. What's the big hurry to know everything all at once, anyway? But no, to answer your question, I'm not. Just a local representative."

"I see," Adam said politely, though he realized he was far from seeing much of anything. A glimmering of appreciation, however, stirred in his mind, and he went boldly on. "So this is where you run it all from, eh? All those bloody wars and famines and earthquakes and all the other calamities and catastrophes that blight the world of man."

"Tush," she interrupted curtly, "you make us sound like such scoundrels—how little you understand."

Fearing he had overstepped himself, Adam retreated discreetly. "In any case, it looks like a dreadfully complex operation—amazing how you manage to keep track of it all."

This observation pleased her. "Matter of fact, Adam, it's simple as pie. Nothing to it. Watch. I tap the National Temperament button for Mexico and we find them getting a bit restless—the killer mood is mounting. Then we take the index number you see on the video display screen there, 14.073, and feed it back into the Therapeutic Program Synthesizer, and in a moment it will deliver us a tasty little recipe for restoring our Mexican friends to an optimal frame of mind and mood. Ah—there we are: Inflate the peso 3%, legalize hardcore flicks in Mexico City and Guadalajara, cut the retail price of tequila by 7%, broadcast news of a terrible wave of terrorist activity in Palestine, headline street riots in Chicago and Hong Kong, increase TV violence by 14%, and stage a wildly sexy mass-killing in the desert twelve miles south of Hermosillo. Then, you see, I have only to touch this key to translate the program into the efferent—or outflowing—side of the system, which leads directly to the appropriate components of our regional Media and Street Theater offices for implementation. All of Mexico will be in judicious balance again by late tomorrow morning, working and enjoying life at the greatest possible levels of efficiency."

"Truly remarkable," Adam said with undisguised admiration, "And all too believable. But how, may I ask, do you keep running tabs on national leaders and other influential world personages?"

"Television, of course," his host person said.

"You mean you have hidden cameras mounted in their offices?"

"Good Lord no!—you should pardon the expression—that's been obsolete hereabouts for ages. We just punch the proper time-space coordinates here, and presto!—here we are in the Oval Office itself. You see—the prexy is zipping up—just took a leak. Now he's yawning. Ah, time for a little nap, I see. And as a matter of common courtesy we naturally leave him to his privacy while he changes into his jammies. He's no spring chicken, y'know."

The screen went blank and Adam clucked his tongue in continuing astonishment. "Exactly how, may I ask, do you go about influencing a man like that?"

"Oh," she said airily, "good presidents always listen to their special advisers—good men like Bernard Baruch, Harry Hopkins, Dan Moynihan. Right, Bernie? Hank? Dan?"

The three men lounging in nearby easy chairs looked up, and the thin one with the receding hairline said candidly, "Frank never gave trouble—always very open to suggestion—a realist, he was." The older gentleman with the bag of popcorn, from which he was feeding pigeons on the window ledge (which from the outside appeared to be solid stone), smiled and nodded in agreement. The third, *Handsome Irish devil,* Adam thought, replied with uncharacteristic economy of expression, "Oh, sure, most cooperative."

Taking Adam easily by the arm, Roc smiled and said, "So, that is essentially how it works, Adam. It was good having you call on us."

Recognizing the import of the words, Adam asked uneasily, "Oh—is it dying time already?"

"Here in the lounge, if you will, and do put yourself at ease."

The spectacle awaiting him in the lounge took his breath and fixed him motionless in his tracks. She was, he knew instantly, the most radiantly beautiful creature he had ever beheld in his whole life—awake or asleep. With a gallant sweep of his great arm, Roc introduced them: "Adam, this is the incomparable Jasmyn."

Adam laughed, shook his head and muttered to himself, "This dream is getting ridiculous, but, what the hell—might as well go along with the gag." Then to Jasmyn: "I only regret that we meet under such, well, strained circumstances."

Allowing her billowing white gown to slip slowly to the floor, the beautiful woman stood naked before him, her eyes warm and inviting. "Please believe me, Adam. You won't be sorry in the least."

Eagerly commencing to disrobe, Adam turned to his towering white host, who was preparing to leave them together. "Please convey my regards to The Boss, and my most heartfelt gratitude to her for taking the time and effort to show me . . . "

Suddenly and quite unexpectedly the sleeping dreamer shifted to a C-8, and the dream faded as he felt himself accelerating swiftly up the mountainside, over the sleeping coyotes and past the aerie of the great eagle. Realizing that he had projected, he entered Roc's cavern cautiously, apologetic for arriving unannounced.

"Quite all right, Adam," the old gentleman reassured him. "You were expected—though I'm afraid I'll not be able to help you in the way you're hoping."

Adam glanced around the interior of the cavern, concluding at once that the Taj Mahal could not possibly be more skillfully appointed. It was simple but in perfect taste, similar but not identical to the picture of it he had just dreamed—but the carved monolith in the rear was exactly as he had envisioned it. It dominated the decor, for that matter, with the neolithic wallpaintings, the costly oriental tapestries and the Persian rug patterns serving chiefly to emphasize its centrality.

"My sincere apologies for intruding on you, Roc."

"Think nothing of it—I am pleased to see you. Would you care for a little Napoleon?"

"Not in my present state, thank you. Afraid it would be a waste of good brandy."

"You seem troubled."

Adam nodded. "About several things. First off, someone tried to kill me this evening, and well—I didn't exactly turn the other cheek." He described the occurrence in fine detail.

"Your response seems reasonable enough to us, Adam," the old man said, stroking his cheek reflectively. "There was once another civilization, another people, highly developed morally and intellectually, but so terrified of violence that they withdrew from it instead of remaining to deal with it constructively, creatively."

Adam smiled wanly. "Oh—you mean the Lumanians?"

Roc remained quietly noncommittal so Adam went on: "In any case, I can't see blowing apart a dude's expensive set of wheels as being all that creative."

"Far more so than destroying his life," Roc concluded easily. "You created circumstances that put an end to the promise of violence toward all concerned. The term 'violence' is quite relative, of course—a violent word, a violent thought, a violent storm. . . . "

Again Adam felt easier. "My next nettle, Roc . . . "

"I think I anticipate you accurately, my friend," he interposed, grinning broadly, "and that is the one, I fear, that I cannot possibly help you with."

Adam was persistent. "Then you do know what I'm looking for, and you could tell it to me outright?"

"That I could," Roc confirmed, still smiling.

" . . . but you won't tell me because I wouldn't believe it—I'd argue with you, wave my arms and spew fine rhetoric, assault your logic and dismiss you as a false prophet!"

"Precisely—well said indeed."

Half-nauseous at the thought of going into retreat, Adam persisted half-heartedly, though with only the faintest of hope that he might find an easy way out. "You could *explain* it to me, Roc—I'd promise to receive it with a wide-open mind!"

Now the old man laughed aloud, then addressed him as a good teacher might good-naturedly reproach a recalcitrant school boy: "Now, friend, you don't even believe your own words. In this matter you cannot possibly accept anything but that which you get to on your own. Is that not true?"

Adam slowly exhaled a groaning sigh. "I know, I know. You're right, of course, but I had to try. So, it's off to my forty days in the desert, my hair shirt, my autoflagellator and all that."

"You're fighting it too hard, Adam. Relax. My guess is that you're up for the greatest excitement—the most stunning adventure—of your entire life."

"Hard to imagine that, but I'll keep it in mind." He started to leave but hesitated with a lingering afterthought. "You were recently in a dream of mine, Roc, or vice versa. Was that really Atlantis we were standing on? Jacques Cousteau dove for it and couldn't find it."

"Perhaps he was looking in the wrong place. Yes, there's no harm in my answering that one for you. It was Atlantis."

"Then, whatever became of it—volcanic destruction or the like?"

"Not at all," the old man assured him. "It is, by prior plan, safely ice-locked in the mass you know as the South Pole. When the time is right, it will be on the move again."

"On the move!" Adam exclaimed. "You mean it's mobile—like my Alpha Orion?"

"Sorry to deflate you, Adam, but there really is nothing new under the sun—except our perception of it."

Adam nodded in reluctant agreement. "I'm beginning to see that. In fact, I'm beginning to see and understand a lot of things I've never even dreamed of before."

"Speaking of dreaming, Adam, the Council is very much looking forward to your next visit."

"My *next* visit? I backed out on the last meeting, and before that . . . I don't remember."

Roc pish-toshed him genially. "That's because of where your consciousness is presently concentrated, my friend. You'll be directing it elsewhere soon, and the Council is eager for your views on implementing the illusion of *nonexistence* as a sort of ultimate aversive conditioning stimulus into the mind of the human herd."

"Nonexistence?"

"Yes. A majority bloc of the Council is resisting it as much too cruel a measure, but an articulate minority consider it a regrettable necessity."

"And they want *my* opinion? I mean, as far as I know, nonexistence does exist . . . but . . . " he finished lamely, " . . . that doesn't make much sense, does it?"

Roc smiled. "They want you to meet with them when you are ready, Adam. Everything, everyone—all in their own good time."

"They're ready when I am, eh?"

"Precisely."

Over a breakfast of scrambled onions, eggs and potatoes, Adam told the others about his dream and the subsequent projection. Bairny remained skeptical but interested, though Candy and Brian, droopy-eyed from their sleepless night, accepted it without question. Candy said, "I guess that means you won't have to climb up there this morning—you can get right into your retreat instead."

"Just as soon as this whole shooting affair is settled," he answered.

"I should think you'd have to settle that," Brian added anxiously, "before T.H.E.Y. settle *you* for good."

Sandol's nose was painfully out of joint. Sulking quietly on the dais, he deliberately ignored Jasmyn when she danced happily into their domed quarters.

"Good morning Sunshine."

"You were gone awfully long."

"Don't be such a cloud, Sandol. I simply will not allow you to spoil my happiness."

"Nor would I care to. You saw him?"

"Yes, and he was a barbarous delight. I'd almost forgotten how much fun bodies can be."

Sandol snorted softly and glanced at her. "Barbarous indeed. And of course that would mean I'm too genteel for you."

"Oh, must you always compare? You forget yourself, my friend. Each encounter is a triumph in itself, uniquely incomparable to all others. Remember?"

"My rational mind remembers—my thalamus is doggedly recalcitrant."

"Reprogram it then—it's your task to do."

She slipped down beside him and tousled his hair playfully. "Don't be so glum. I'll take you sailing this afternoon. Where would you like to go? Tahoe? Sea of Cortez? Indian Ocean?"

Sandol forced on a conciliatory smile. "Wherever you say, and I am not jealous—only slightly envious."

"Even that much is a symptom, you know. As usual, our technology outstrips our emotional development by several thousand years."

"Perhaps your heathen witch doctor could cure me, eh?"

"Heathen, you say? He's managed to cure himself!"

"So," Sandol murmured darkly, "perhaps they're not altogether inferior."

10

Master Blueprint in the Sky

Adam knew it was time to make his move. An invisible, ghostly infant was gestating in the fertile womb of his mind, swelling and pressing it, kicking and stretching and straining for release. *Yes, good analogy,* he decided. *My cranium feels like a fully pregnant uterus gone into heavy labor. Strong, powerful, painful contractions, with the baby in some kind of a transverse lie—totally hung-up at the pelvic inlet. Must get over to Goldy's place, put on my version gloves, reach boldly in and haul its ass out, somehow, alive and kicking.* There was no excuse for postponing it any longer.

Back at the office, he explained his plans briefly to Kate Nay. "Do your very best not to interrupt me, Kate, but if you *must* contact me then call me on Alpha Orion, where I'm planning to head for when I finish my little retreat. Okay?"

"Sure. And good luck with that." There was another pause, an uncertain one. "Adam, are you sure you're not deluding yourself, or are you absolutely certain you've got some kind of tiger by the tail?"

Adam laughed. "I know I have, Kate. Don't quite understand what it is yet, but it's big—on the order of earth-shaking and all that. It's just that I'm too stupid to see it."

"Don't be so hard on yourself, Adam. Remember, you're only human."

"I know. That's my problem. But as mere mortals go, I'm really brilliant."

"I see," she teased. "Then tell me this, as the old lady said, 'If you're so smart, why ain't you rich?' "

"Lots of geniuses are lousy money managers," he shot back. "Look at Socrates. Jesus. Balzac. And I'm not making much money either. See you, Kate!"

"Good luck, sweetie," she waved cheerfully.

There was no need to pack anything, as his sequestered quarters at Goldy's were fully stocked with clothing, toilet articles, tobacco, bourbon, and the essential nucleus of his brainstorming research library. On the way in he made a single, three-hour stop at his favorite bookstore, which he spent speed-reading book titles, authors and publishers, and pulling down an occasional selection for purchase as much by instinct as conscious reason. A new biography of his old idol, that hard-nosed, clear-thinking, plain-writing old muckraker, Lincoln Steffens—a volume that might add something to his oft-read copy of the great man's famous autobiography.

He also pulled out several new interpretations of American history, including the massive *Tragedy and Hope* by Carroll Quigley which, as luck would have it, had just that morning arrived. (He gulped at the $25.00 price tag on the 1,300-page, three-and-a-half pound book, which the John Birch authors had erroneously weighed in at a ludicrous eight pounds—surely an unnecessary exaggeration of the volume's cumbersome reality.)

He also selected a couple of B.F. Skinner books. The latest report on the earth's troubled ecological status from the exclusive Club of Rome. A copy of that odd-ball but intriguing little Gary Allen book, *None Dare Call It Conspiracy*, all loaded down with names, facts, figures, curiously cogent and persuasive arguments and more than enough of the grand old John Birch point-of-view—their seething hatred of the infamous Insiders (but Nelson A. Rockefeller a *Communist?*—now, *really!*).

To the growing stack on the cashier's counter he also added some recent books on banks and banking, a programmed self-instruction refresher book on Fortran computer language, and others on the dossier system in the American bureaucracy, a brightly written little pop paperback on *The Screwing of the Average Man* by one David Hapgood, and, finally, for good measure, a copy of the very curious and equally popular *People's Almanac* of Wallace and Wallechinsky, the freshest version of American history he'd come across in a coon's age.

He paid for them with his Master Charge card, carefully printing on the slip—"for IRS deduction purposes—Research for expose book on the Illuminati."

Adequately forewarned by the efficient Kate Nay, Goldy was waiting for him in her sumptuous little downtown bungalow, discreetly lodged behind tall shrubs and a wrought-iron fence between two ultra-modern office buldings, with ever so private walkways from the front, side, and back to the alley in the rear. It was also her place of business, and it looked like a fancy brothel because it was one: strictly a high-class, one-lady whorehouse catering exclusively to the best-known names in the whole state—politicians, businessmen, judges and bishops—a blue chip clientele altogether.

In anticipation of his arrival she had arranged to be alone, and she greeted him now with a happy shout, and with open arms. Laughing, he held her back from him at arm's length and explained: "It's not your cosmic body I'm after, Goldy—it's your mind."

Turning her serene, uncluttered face up to his she made a pshaw sound and reproved him. "You're just kiddin' around with me, Adam. You know I'm a dummy. I ain't got the smarts like you and your classy uptown friends got."

True, in a way, Adam thought, kissing her again, affectionately and with a reassuring hug—*and in a way quite untrue.* Goldy was a gem. Physically, she was almost a caricature of an easy woman, with her *Playboy* pretty face and figure, generous outpointing breasts, wide hips and beautiful columnar thighs—right down to the country-western blonde hairdo she was a stunning symphony of feminine contours, sounds and smells. Mentally, he had estimated her formal I.Q. as hovering pretty close to the 50 mark—for whatever that meant. Because, no matter the explanation, she had exactly what he needed at times like these, when the brilliantly convoluted semantrobatics of self-conscious intellectuals did far more to confuse issues than to clarify them.

Feigning strictness, he shook her gently by the shoulders several times and reminded her: "How many times must I tell you, Goldy— you're *not* a dummy. You're just not an intellectual type, and thank God for that. We don't know anything either, but we don't realize that we don't know—as you do—which gives you an edge over us. You see?" (And he meant it. Lincoln Steffens had also learned that we self-professed intellectuals are the very first to be taken in, which is the bloody truth; because of our much reading, our own little mutual admiration society and our festoons of degrees and academic honors,

we truly believe we already know everything knowable—which makes
us pushovers. We're the fools' fools.)

"I guess so, Adam," she laughed softly. "You're so funny. Hey, now."
she said, moving on to him with breasts and belly, anxious to get away
from the embarrassing subject of intelligence, "You wanna screw
around some, Adam, or you just wanna get ta work?"

He scratched his head. Good question. "It's hard to explain, Goldy. I
feel funny—like I've never felt before in my whole life; totally horny,
yet totally disinterested in doing anything about it."

"Gee, honey," she said with a sudden show of concern, "you ain't sick
are ya?"

That tickled him. "No," he laughed, "it's just that I happen to be in a
different frame of mind than usual. I'll get to work now. You know, the
usual routine. Squat in the center of my room and go crazy. Come out
here every now and then, rant and rave weird ideas at you, lay a few
questions on you, and hear what you have to say. Okay?"

"Oh, sure, hon—any time. If I'm asleep just wake me up. But . . . " she
hesitated, nervous, " . . . if I'm workin'—ya know?"

He held up his hands, palms forward: "No sweat. Just remember to
push the signal button. Wouldn't think of intruding on anyone who's
into making an honest buck or two."

"His room" was exactly that; his very own, inviolate. A monastic
retreat. A fifteen-by-twenty-foot rectangle. Soft beige carpet over two
inches of foam rubber. Low-standing shelves, loaded with books,
circling the room, and the walls above them starkly blank. One draped
window looking out over a bustling city street. At the far end was the
door to a small bathroom, and just before it, concealed behind a sliding
panel, a studio kitchenette. Above the door was the signal light, and on
a shelf next to it was a closed circuit television monitor for making sure
the coast was clear before barging into Goldy's territory.

Stripping down, he hung his clothes neatly in the bathroom closet
and took a long and luxurious shower. Then he dried off carefully,
poured himself an enormous mug of thick black coffee, dumped his
carton of newly purchased books in the middle of the carpet and sat
down among them, naked and cross-legged.

He fixed his focus on the blank wall across the room, drew a deep
breath, exhaled slowly, took a sip of the steaming hot coffee and said
aloud: "Here goes nothing, my friend. Be good to yourself. Start out
easy—relax. It's in there somewhere—just make like you've got all the
time in the world. Your books are all around you. Philosophy. At least

eighteen different copies, one version or another, of the *Holy Bible*—a great clue book. And physics. Astronomy. Archaeology. Education. Mathematics. A whole goddamn shelf full of history references. The *Encyclopaedia Britannica*. Computer technology.

Taking another deep, slow breath, he set about to shore up his self-esteem—to brace his confidence—with some further reminders. Yes, he was a Charter Fellow of the American College of Psychiatrists. Sigma Xi. New York Academy of Science. The AAAS. Guest lecturer at Johns Hopkins, U.S.D., Georgetown, University of Edinburgh, and scads of other biggies. The author of beaucoups books and articles. Up to his ears in credentials, golden credentials. And, over the years, those hundreds—no, thousands of patients—literally thousands—an enormous body of raw data on the experience and behavior of the human animal. An expert—ha! Officially, yes—but in fact a tyro—a very rank amateur. *But it will suffice,* he insisted grimly: *it must.*

The answer was in there somewhere amongst all those people and all those books, and in the dark depths of his own mind. It was only a matter of setting his head up properly, like the good little computer it was. Feed prepared data through the input media device of the frontal lobes, to on-line input, relay on to high speed internal storage banks of the temporal lobes for interchange auxiliary storage and symbolic logical processing and then to on-line output. Go, baby, go—let 'er rip!

Okay, take the creationist version first. "In the beginning God created the heaven and the earth. And the earth was without form, and void; and darkness was upon the face of the deep. And the spirit of God moved upon the face of the waters. And God said, Let there be light: and there was light. . . . " Yes, a gorgeously brilliant Big Bang light some ten billion years ago, the echoings of which were still faintly resounding in the straining ears of our electronic telescopes. Then cooling and contraction, and primordial lightning crackling amid the elemental vapors, dropping myriad molecules into the rolling waves of the ancient earthly sea. Life, first in single cells and then in many branching and growing, surviving and dying out—or transforming?

Then man, another experimental form, another species among the millions that have come and gone. Some kind of experimental process—an infinitesimal flash of existence in some gargantuan test tube of the Gods. We are being played with, tampered with, poured cavalierly from one vessel to another in some divine graduate student's doctoral dissertation problem. But what have we to go on? Nothing but our wretched science and miserly history—and how far, really, are they to be trusted?

Sure, a study of history should reveal some clues, but these seem as rare as they are unreliable. Sedentary farming and the formation of cities were well-established institutions by five to ten thousand years ago, in old Sumeria. With this came the invention of money, and with money came political power. By four to five thousand years ago there was a goodly concentration of people, cities, commerce and money-power in the eastern Mediterranean area. This force quickly spread both east and west, generally lodging—or perhaps creating—the largest cities in various geographical areas around which boundaries were drawn and named as nations: Babylon, Akkadia, Athens, Peking, Shanghai and Tokyo to the east, and Rome, Madrid, Vienna, Paris, Morocco and London to the west.

All movements were motivated and spearheaded by commerce, by expeditions which were usually led by well-financed adventurers—and missionaries—but certainly far more impelled by well-planned quests for money, territory and political control than for reasons of religious idealism. We are told that Christopher Columbus's westward probe was financed by Spain's executive office, but we also know that executive power at this level must have financial backing to create and maintain such power. But from where? Who put up the bread?

That, he reminded himself unhappily, is the granddaddy question of them all—who has all the money? And how do I set about answering that impossible question?

11

Human History's Manuscript

Science tells us little and history tells us lies, yet they are all we have—save faith. But faith in what? Order, pattern, and purpose?

Certainly not in our recorded history, which is naught but a string of fairy tales, of dead facts linked one to the other and strung out in tons of unreadable tomes by withered little scholars who don't even know why they're doing it. It could very well be that just last night the entire human race underwent a uniform memory erasure which was then electronically replaced by a new "phylogenetic" store, which would mean only that our collective remembrance of all things past is only an illusion. But that, clearly, is an absolutely unworkable and dead-end thesis, so ditch it, my friend, and go from the assumption that there is at least a kernel of truth in the great, tall-tale of history as we have received it.

Now then, has it been accident or chance? Has it just happened, will-ye, nill-ye, or has it been formed and programmed, somehow, in a way we have never really conceived of?

Picking up the John Birch "conspiracy" book, he riffled through it and pondered gloomily on their little-known and richly scorned theory of the human pilgrim's progress. Yes, the Birchers put it well enough, he reflected. There really are only two schools of history. Either everything has just happened willy-nilly, by more or less accidental happenstance, or it's all been planned out on a gigantic hidden blueprint, drawn up and executed by those ancient masters of social architecture, The Illuminati—the Enlightened Ones. FDR evidently subscribed to the conspiratorial theory of history to have remarked, as he once did, "In politics, nothing happens by accident. If it happens, you can bet it was planned that way." And, yet, as far as anyone knows, every blessed university, institute, high school, and grammar school in the world buys and peddles the willy-nilly brand of historical interpretation—it all just happened at random.

Score one for the Birchers, he added reluctantly. By all rights we should still be back in the jungle, murdering and raping on impulse, clawing each other to death over a scrap of food and dying at an average age of about eight years. Could it be that someone, somehow, some very long time ago, sold us on guilt and seduced us into sublimating our baser impulses into productive cerebral work? And, if so, what has been the upshot of it all? Who is really better off, the happy savage or strife-torn and work-worn modern man? Montaigne and Rousseau, both confirmed comfort addicts themselves, exalted the unspoiled savage, but Adam, after some soul-searching, found that he personally had very little trouble disputing their venerable authority.

He did not relish the thought of squatting in his own offal at the mouth of a cold, dark cave, club in hand, waiting in terror for those hairy brutes down the gorge to come charging in after his meager stash of vittles, his mind filled only with fleeting and simple-minded, kaleidoscopic images of the immediate moment, with maybe a few occasional flashes from yesterday and the day before and no notion whatever of tomorrow.

No, he admitted, he was fully addicted to his local grocery store, Howard Johnson's, organized government (though not inordinately so, of course) and—for all their bewildering prolixities and complexities— even to language and mathematics. And medicine. And his Posturepedic mattress. His FDA-regulated hundred-proof bourbon. Yes, he had once made it very clear to the physically more venturesome Livea that he would join her on that ten-day cruise down the Colorado River as soon as they put a Hilton Hotel on pontoons.

And yet there it was—plain as the nose on his face. Every respectable academic historian in the world spoke, wrote and thought in accord with the primal horde school of history. Out of the jungle and onto the farms, then off the farms and into the cities; struggling, destroying, building, inventing, exploring—all a sort of frenzied, randomized and unplanned accident. Tragic—but hopeful?

No, that wasn't quite true. Not all qualified historians bought the "accidentalist" theory of history. His mind surging erratically in his mounting search for his "missing link," he followed up hastily on the Bircher's accusations against noted historian, economist and sociologist Professor Carroll Quigley, lately of Georgetown, Harvard, Princeton and the U.S. Navy's Post-graduate School in Monterey, California (as a consultant to Project Seabed—a futuristic weapons systems analysis project).

Tragedy and Hope: A History of the World In Our Time. Hefting it first, then riffling and speed-scanning it, he grimaced and shook his head. Good God, he marvelled, it's even longer than my big one—and almost as wordy. But scholarly, thorough, methodical, massively researched and beautifully written ("also like mine," he cheerfully congratulated himself). And revealing! *Very* revealing.

Just as the Birch book claimed, Professor Quigley coolly, candidly revealed the factual existence of this conspiratorial network, just as calmly disclosing that he had investigated it for twenty years and, for two years in the early 1960s, had even been allowed to peruse its papers and secret records.

Quigley was quoted on his own attitude toward the conspiratorial agency: "I have no aversion to it or to most of its aims and have, for much of my life, been close to it and to many of its instruments. I have objected, both in the past and recently, to a few of its policies—but in general my chief difference of opinion is that it wishes to remain unknown, and I believe its role in history is significant enough to be known."[1]

Interesting, Adam mused, very interesting indeed. Moving on, he read Professor Quigley's interpretation and description of the conspirators' prime objective as "nothing less than to create a world system of financial control in private hands able to dominate the political system of each country and the economy of the world as a whole." This, in turn, the Birch author construed as "this power mad clique wants to control and rule the world. Even more frightening, they want total control over all individual actions," or, as Professor Quigley puts it, the individual world citizen's " . . . freedom and choice will be controlled within very narrow alternatives by the fact that he will be numbered from birth and followed, as a number, through his educational training, his required military or other public service, his tax contributions, his health and medical requirements, and his final retirement and death benefits."

"A paranoiac's paradise. And that, according to the Birch expose, means that T.H.E.Y. want absolute control over everything—all natural and man-made resources: the money, banks and insurance companies, all business, governments and nations, and the media! And they cheerfully hop about firing up wars, manipulating money values and consumer goods prices to create economic depressions at will, spreading hatred among nations and races, between men and women, children and parents. They would eliminate all competition and totally eradicate the free enterprise system that made America great."

1. Quigley, Carroll, *Tragedy and Hope* (New York: Macmillan, 1974), p. 950.

12

The Horrors of Free Enterprise

Adam scratched his head and silently cursed the exquisitely exacting nature of his own disciplined sense of logic. "Goddammit," he swore suddenly at the unflinching wall across the room, "if the conspiracy is that strong, what makes us think they haven't *already* achieved their objectives—maybe a long, long time ago?" And yet, as a dabbler in systems theory and a reasonably fairminded thinker, he had to concede at once that there *are* systems within systems, and the conspiratorial arrangement the Birchers were so acidly assailing could just as easily *foster* as eliminate free enterprise.

After all, he reasoned, the purest free enterprise that ever was exists in the primeval jungle setting. Put all the wealth of the world atop one hill, then give every man, woman and child in the territory a spiked club or a spear and let them batter the guts and brains out of each other until one of them—the strongest, the most vicious, the fastest and the luckiest—maims or kills everyone else on his way up the hill to collect it all! Yes, he went on (though he didn't particularly like the way his line of reasoning kept colliding head-on with his chronic and deeply entrenched, even socially obligatory liberalism) that's *one* kind of freedom.

Another is the kind we supposedly enjoy in the civilized nations of

Western Europe, and especially in Amerika. Or, is it America? With a c? I am free to enterprise? Maybe not, he laughed to himself, but I seem to have done one hell of a lot of it whether I'm free to or not—which would seem to lead inevitably to the conclusion that I have been more or less free to do so—by definition. Why, it's downright syllogistic.

If I were king, he murmured tentatively to himself. All right, let's skip on down that lane a way. If I were king, all powerful, say, like the colorful lady I dreamed of in Roc's mountain, just how would it be? Not difficult at all, according to her, and I suppose that really could be—if you knew how to do it. We people are, after all, utterly suggestible, vulnerable, gullible. There's one of us born every minute. We do try to understand, no doubt of that, but we have only the meagerest of clues to go on. As Goldy had just reminded him, "My daddy didn't have much smarts either, but he understood lots of things. He used to tell me not to believe anything I read in the newspapers. Then he'd laugh and say that he didn't know nothin'—'cept what he read in the newspapers." And Mr. Sulo's plain-minded observation had been resoundingly confirmed for him that very morning by New Zealand's Prime Minister Lange, on the *Today Show*: "You must remember, Bryant, all we know of the world is what we see through the eye of your camera."

That is, sure as hell, just about the size of it. We seem to live immersed in a sea of whimsical—perhaps utterly contrived—clues—all handsomely spawned and promulgated by the ever-lovin' media.

That is one way to look at it, he concluded, if you can stand the view. We live in a seething sea of clues, clues to the greatest puzzle that ever was—the puzzle of life itself. Are you planning to solve that one, Adam, you grandiose, paranoid, mentally retarded knothead you? Going to improve on Dante and Kant and Neibuhr and the rest? Of course—why not? You'll solve it the same day that Goldy Sulo derives $E=Mc^2$.

But Mr. Sulo was entirely right about "the news," which by definition is anything that gets into the newspapers or on the tube— and anything that doesn't is automatically *not* news. Headline, "Joe Doaks Gets a Speck In His Eye" and it's news. But a resurrected Jesus could walk right down Main Street without making news if the papers decided they just weren't interested in the story. Lincoln Steffens and his fellow reporters once created an ersatz "crime wave" in New York that way, by writing up a lot of routine police chores and then calling it a "crime wave." Given ownership of the media, you could create a moonshot like that, or an invasion from Mars (which Orson Welles actually did) or even a war. The distance between the events reported and the gullible consumer is so great that . . . A war? Wars?

So? If I were king. If I owned all the money, the media and the nations—the power and the glory . . . His thinking, still rambling from here to there in this phase of his analysis, rushed on at a good clip. Okay. Given control of the Federal Reserve Board, the Nation's banks and the consumer's wage-price ratio, it would be simplicity itself to create economic prosperity, depressions, recessions, panics or paradise by punching a few of the right buttons. And the media, the college course work, and the big brainy books on economics and history—all under control and sensitively responsive to my will.

He promptly argued himself into a muddle then backed off quickly and cleared his head. Addressing himself once more to his good friend, the blank wall across the room, he suddenly jettisoned all history, all theoretical ruminations about economics and philosophy from his thinking and waxed rigidly pragmatic: man, you were in the middle of it—the Big Depression of the Thirties, WW II—now what did you actually see with your own eyes? Block-long lines of hungry people standing in soup lines? No, you didn't. You saw some pictures of that in the newspapers—plenty of pictures. People starving in the streets? Nope—not a one. Tycoons diving out of Manhattan skyscrapers after the bust of 1929? Not a one—just a batch of stories about them. My God, fewer than one percent of the American people had so much as a penny in the stock market when it went under—so what did it really have to do with them?

He pressed on with his pointed reminiscences. My family, my friends, we did okay. Low-budget casseroles for dinner, and chicken— or beef or pork or lamb—every Sunday. Eggs for breakfast, with bacon—sometimes even steak. I still love all that good garbage, we all loved it, just as we loved school—and as much as we loved bitching about it. We had sports, girl friends, beer, movies, picnics, campouts, the Boy Scouts (which he resigned after two weeks as a Tenderfoot because he couldn't stand the bloody regimentation) and even a couple of unavoidable fist-fights.

On the way to high school, though, I did see some sad things with my own eyes. Poor men, "not as fortunate as we," sitting in the streets chipping old mortar from old street bricks, WPA workers, eyeing us vacantly as we trooped off to our fancy public school, working for pennies-an-hour to feed themselves and their families on some day-old bread and a little thin bean soup. Sad, sad. . . .

Adam caught himself up short on that one. How do I know it's sad? I don't even know where they came from! I was spending my precious Saturdays working for fifty cents a day, slaving my ass off sweeping floors and chipping carbon off old piston cylinders . . . And wasn't that why pappy had me doing it—so I could learn at my tender years that I didn't want to spend the rest of my life doing that kind of work? Honorable work, certainly, but not for me. The whole experience was downright inspirational—inspired me to get my tail in gear and move it onward and upward to something more congenial—for me!

However distasteful though, he had to admit it. In his own practice he had long since learned that economic disaster is not always what it appears to be—if ever. To the casual newspaper buff, the periodic shutting down of Arizona's copper mines looks catastrophic, with "thousands out of work." But what happens to the newly unemployed? One of his clients, a copper miner, cheerfully reported that his $900/month in unemployment benefits gave him a chance to prove himself another Kurt Vonnegut. Eighteen months later, satisfied that he was not Kurt Vonnegut, he sauntered back down into the reopened copper mine. Most of the miners followed suit, but a few did not. They took this "unfortunate economic calamity" for what it was: a hiatus, a breather, a chance to get some additional training and get out of the mines. The choice, the opportunity, are always there.

His brow furrowed. The big question, though, is how did I ever latch onto all that power and control in the first place? Of course, I do understand about the incestuous, triangular affair between bankers, kings, and warfare that's been going on for many a century. Two Florentine banking houses backed Edward III in the fourteenth century and the Medici went to the financial aid of Charles the Bold of Burgundy at about the same time—although these were two of the few transactions in which the bankers lost (or so it has been told). But the loans *were* made to support the enormous cost of waging war. Elaborate plate armor was far more expensive than the chain-mail garb it replaced, and the costs of designing and building fortresses and warships was also rising. The warring princes needed their bankers as much as the bankers needed them—and both needed war to preserve the power of the king and the wealth of the banker.

And behind them both, I suppose for the moment, were the infamous Illuminati, invisibly pulling strings, aggravating old wounds and enmities, provoking and inciting—then reaping enormous profits from the fruits of their loathesome machinations. Blood money. The battlefields of England and Europe awash with human blood for centuries, perhaps millennia, and all of it—or surely most of it—craftily engineered by a mere handful of cruelly ambitious psychopathic manipulators, sacrificing countless lives and working whatever anguish and destruction was necessary to the harvesting of their gold.

Adam bumped his temple several times, hard, as if attempting the inexpert repair of a malfunctioning radio or toaster. "Something is missing," he told himself. "I've read about all that blood and savagery in books but I—I never saw it myself. Remember, I'm from Missouri. Jarring his right temporal lobe with another bump, he loosened a vague recollection of an account he had once read in one of Professor Durant's stories of civilization. During the age of chivalry, on a battlefield in Normandy, an army of mounted Frenchmen met an army of mounted Englishmen at dawn, and they assaulted each other with lance and broadsword until nightfall. The casualty box score by the day's end. Dead: none. Wounded: none.

A bloodless, fractureless battle? What the hell kind of war is that, he wondered? It sounded more like a game of lacrosse—a bunch of rowdy ruffians getting together to joust off a pent-up head of steam . . . as if someone had simply promoted a strenuous athletic competition that had been resoundingly enjoyed by all concerned. Adam decided he wouldn't feel at all guilty over promoting such a venture for fun and profit. But that was just one battle in one war, and he shuddered at the thought of the ghastly and almost endless chain of ravaging wars that had blighted his poor species in the centuries thereafter, right down to the two great World Wars, Korea, and Vietnam. "Bloodsuckers," he muttered. "Peddlers of butchered human meat."

He sat back against the wall and took another gulp of hundred-proof, anxiously dissatisfied and dimly hoping that if he couldn't jar the missing link—the elusive connection—up to the forefront of consciousness, perhaps he could float it up with a sufficiency of good bourbon.

13

A Necessary Evil

One thing was very certain—money was—is the key to it all. "Money makes the world go around," as it were once again reminded by a lavish musical production number of the same title on the Carol Burnett Christmas Show. And that boastful sign at the local Valley National Bank: "We've Got What It Takes to Get Things Done—Money!" Come and get it is their message—like their big, taunting billboard in downtown Phoenix: "We're Ready When You Are!" But ready for what? They must know something, those bankers—they've sure been around and making out in a grand way for one helluva long time. Think about that, my friend—just think about it. Where did they start, and when—and why?

What do we really know about money? First, it makes the world go 'round. Second, the love of it is the root of all evil. Third, it is a *necessary* evil—and all of the above are correct. Is it a finite amount, guaranteed by hoards of gold and crown jewels in the Fort Knox's of the world, or is the supply infinite—always enough to get the job done—whatever the job may be?

He scratched his head and began mulling that one over. The banking industry was flourishing in Florence by the thirteenth century. There

157

were already some seventy to eighty houses in operation, and the towering giant of them all was the Mother Church, whose "camera," or treasury, was bursting with revenues donated by and collected from every nation and province in the widening circle of Christendom. Adam recalled having recently heard that the Catholic Church, at last tally, was the third largest corporation in the modern world. So, if money truly buys power, as surely it must, then the much publicized break between the Church and the European Kingdoms of the Renaissance could have been one great charade—a camouflage to conceal from the eyes of the world that the true power of the Western world was still with the Pope. The Vatican—stronghold of the Illuminati? Or just another front?

Grimacing with the strain of his torrential ruminations, he forged ahead. Now, back up arf a mo', he admonished himself. As the books have it the *modern* banking system got rolling in southern Europe in about the 12th century. Modern? Does that make sense? Not a hell of a lot. Our nearly hairless and somewhat-brighter-than-your-average-ape species has been around for probably one to three million years, maybe longer, depending on the Leakeys' next find. And where the naked ape goes, so goes commerce, haggling, swapping, moneymaking and moneylending. We do know that loans were made from the temples of Babylon, and the Babylonian Igibi bank was going strong by the 6th century B.C.—with the Greeks, Egyptians and Romans not far behind.

But Adam groaned to himself—all of that is still current events . . . two thousand years is exactly 0.2 percent of one million—so what happened with people during the first 99.8 percent chunk of all that historical time? Milling around in the jungle tossing coconuts at each other? Not likely. Somewhere along the line—and I suppose only they and God know just when—T.H.E.Y. went underground and began running things by remote control—eventually becoming completely invisible while remaining, in fact, all-powerful and wealthier than Croesus to the umpteenth power.

Not a bad box score at all for our supposedly shaggy, slant-browed and slack-jawed ancestors. For a moment he pictured a gorilla in a $300 double-breasted, pinstripe suit, white shirt and cravat, sitting behind a big mahogany desk at the headquarters of the World Bank, smoking a cigar and going over the ledgers, the latest computer print-out on current assets, debits, accounts receivable, etc. Stupid. Amusing but stupid—a child's image.

Somewhere in the crescentic, Palestinian cradle of civilization had come Cro Magnon man; tall, upright, and proud, with a cranial vault larger than that of modern man—a thinker and an artist of the first order—over 30,000 years ago! The pride of Sumeria! That much was public knowledge and had been for more than a hundred years. In 1867, the Universal Exhibition in Paris demonstrated convincingly that man, man the thinker and the doer—the creature of commerce and connivery and arts and sciences—had lived and flourished long, long before the "historical" eras of Greece and Rome, of Abraham, Moses, Pericles, the Pharaohs, and the Hopi.

And one way or another—by hook or by crook—they had created the incomprehensibly complex world monetary and business system.

Adam found himself taking a closer look at the word "business," which he saw as a derived contraction of "busy-ness." Yes, our natural appetite for housing, fancy food, classy cars, and other material goods—most of which are purchasable only by money—render us beautifully susceptible to the carrot-on-a-stick inducements that only money can offer. And money, as most of us well know, is not easily come by. We must think, scheme, and work for it, which means that we are kept *busy*, and this in turn stimulates thinking as a strenuous physical exercise stimulates the growth and strength of skeletal muscle. It also promotes the sublimation of our aggressive energies from physical combat to mental competition, and admirably occupies the time and energy we might otherwise squander on the basic and mindless mammalian pursuits of food-gathering, drinking, sexing, fighting, and loafing on the nearest clump of grass.

The money system is indeed, as the old chestnut goes, a necessary evil—compelled by our inherently indolent and combative nature. Theoretically and in fact, it would not be needed to lure us on to greater things were we inherently capable of loftier pursuits on our own initiative. The contemporary Pleiadean cosmonauts credibly report that the people of their home planet have not had a monetary system for centuries (earth time). And this, presumably, is because they have become innately self-actuating.

But until that utopian hallelujah day on this planet, we are driven by the money-carrot, he mused somberly. There are some 15,000,000 corporations in this country and they are indeed privately owned, but compared to the *Fortune 500* they are small potatoes. This latter aggregate of wealth, in turn, far surpasses the wealth of nations (or more properly, the poverty of nations). The principal distinction between these monetary mastodons and the nations of the world is that the former operate at a profit, the latter at a deficit. Once again, the nations are clearly and outright owned, or at least controlled by the Big Money.

Even worse is the little-known fact that the megacorporations do not compete with each other. They cooperate together in a mutual support and admiration society. Today, a substantial three-quarters of the non-Communist world's productivity is controlled by 200 megacorps, and with that kind of money behind them, there can be little doubt that they are the *de facto* governors of whole nations and cultures of the entire planet!

And the system was complexly stratified, layer upon layer, pursuing a relentless and endless pattern of amalgamation.

Which might also explain, he reflected, the gobbling up of smaller business groups by larger ones as a continued and utterly ruthless process. Several years ago, Little, Brown publishing company, baldly indicted by the Birchers as part of the Great Conspiracy, was taken over by Time/Life, and more recently Sperry was bought up by Burroughs, and so on and on and on. But the executives of these companies are aware of the amalgamation *only at this level*. From direct experience Adam knew, for example, that the executives of Little, Brown do not know who owns Time/Life. These increasingly complex strata of organization are carefully buffered, one from the other, ultimately leading upward to an *Organizational Ceiling Zero* beyond which we field peons simply cannot see.

Which might also explain, he reflected, the seemingly miraculous rise of insurgent new megacorps. Another master stroke of social engineering? What a ruse! *Sprint, MCI, U.S. Telecom,* and the other boldly rebellious long-distance telephone services could never have flown without the blessings of Ma Bell, but the oppositional television commercials deliver a picture of intense competition, when in fact there is none whatever? All is chaos—masterfully organized and deftly delivered!

The system is covert and many-veiled, strewn hither and yon with enough red herrings to sate a whale. The inclusion of the world's megacorporations in *The People's Almanac* listing of the nations, based on their dollar assets, is utterly misleading by way of gross understatement. These massed corporations are vastly wealthier than the nations. Once again he grinned thinly at remembering that the United States of America, the wealthiest nation in the world, is plainly bankrupt—but thriving nicely. And the American National Debt, now in the trillions, was owed not to the people but to those all-but-invisible international money combines.

And so it has been with New York City, Cleveland, and other major metropoli the world around—broke but booming. These carefully engineered financial catastrophes create a convincing facade of fiscal frailty, instability, and impending economic collapse—all of it meticulously devised by those cleverly shy *incognito* masters of the human herd—the Enlightened Ones—*The Illuminati.*

Yes, it was all controlled from on top, far beyond our range of vision. But why, and how? Adam suddenly recalled that famed Scottish economist and philosopher Adam Smith, best-known for his epic *An Inquiry into the Nature and Causes of the Wealth of Nations,* made frequent reference to the "invisible hand" reaching down to favor self-interest, an influence that seemed to secretly assist people or groups of people who were intent on garnering large sums of money. "The invisible helping hand," deigning to assist the leaders in life's ongoing intelligence test. Here he was reminded once more of Steffen's curious conclusion after a lifetime quest for a rational morality: "Don't be ethical—be intelligent." Make money! Think!

Still struggling to think it through, and for the moment concentrating only on what he himself had actually seen, he anxiously perceived the international automobile industry hype as a mass exercise in peaceful interculturation. In our era, the first phase was the American running joke of fifty years ago, when "Made in Japan" was synonymous with "cheap and silly," and regularly occasioned scornful giggles. The contemporary phase includes a continuous but benign debate over the comparative merits and prices of foreign versus domestic cars. With this, there is inevitably an associated consideration of the people and cultures who have produced the cars in question. Like it or not, we now think of the Japanese as substantial moderns, and not just brightly kimono'd comic characters from a Gilbert and Sullivan operetta, as was the case until very recent years.

"Great!" he suddenly stormed, "but T.H.E.Y. pitted America and Japan against one another in the costliest and most brutal war in all of history! Pure evil, garbed in benevolence!"

14

The Galactic Sires

Lost in thought, Adam absently scalded his gullet with too generous a gulp of steaming hot coffee, swore eloquently, then recovered and rummaged through his books for the dog-eared copy of Zecharia Sitchin's *The 12th Planet* and focussed his mind to a fine point.

Yes, Sitchin, Van Daniken, Seth and other interested discarnates were in very close concert on the import theory of human origins on planet earth. Sitchin's own scholarly, impressively documented analysis had it that we are the direct descendants of the *Nefilim*, the people of a far advanced civilization from the twelfth planet, Marduk. Before them, lowly Neanderthal man had grubbed about his caves for a couple of million years without making an inch of progress. Then came the *Nifilim*, all heart and loins, inseminating the cavern-bound Neanderthal ladies and so producing a superior breed of anthropoid—our ancestors and the sires of our prophets.

And these then would have given rise to Seth's Lumanians and the geniuses of Atlantis. Dedicated to science, law, medicine, education—to the pursuit of any knowledge in any form—they were innately peaceful and inherently repelled by the least hint of violence. They looked in horror upon the assaultive, the murderous ways of the ignorant brutes around them. Some of them abandoned the problem as hopeless and took to their beamships and set off for more congenial places. But a few of them, with remarkable scientific detachment, remained behind, silently withdrew from the public domain and devised the ingenious system of mass brainwashing that operates throughout the world even today.

Consistent with this were the findings and conclusions of Erich Van Daniken. Shocking and incredible when first published in 1970, Adam now realized they were no longer seen as esoteric or even startling. Through his publications, the widely publicized (by whom?) television documentaries and movies, and thousands of corridor and cocktail conversations about them, it had all become deeply imbedded in the public mind.

Adam knew this to be true; he had talked with the people. Imperatively, he commanded the blank wall across the room: "You don't believe me? Ask anyone under the age of forty, and a great many people older than that, and you will find a solid majority who firmly, matter-of-factly believe that our planet has been visited by extraterrestrial cosmonauts in the past and that we are still being actively monitored by them even today!"

For the most part, he reflected sourly, the belief is rejected only by our self-declared intellectuals, who reflexly dismiss anything not originated by themselves.

Yes, it is all rapidly becoming a reality in the mass mind. If we still find a few recalcitrants in the over-forty bracket, then move down to the under-twenty-five bracket. This is the generation that will receive our galactic masters peacefully? They will be traveling to the stars, but in their vessels—not ours. And as slaves in a brave new world?

And we, with our characteristic anthrocentricism, have naively assumed that our vast array of electronic telescopic transmissions have simply been lost in the silent void of space, unheard by anyone. Far more likely, Adam speculated, that we are raining a cacophony of electronic racket on the quietly contemplative ears of the many who do not respond to us because we are not yet ready to hear what they have to tell us. That is, *they* are ready for us, but *we* are not quite ready for them.

He smiled to himself, finding additional support for this view of things in the media, especially television. There he had personally witnessed the steady transition of the depiction of ET's in pop drama from sadistic, demagogic villains, as in H.G. Wells's *War of the Worlds*, to the sympathetic little ET character on the Special Olympics commercial, and to the hip but homely ALF (Alien Life Form). Yes, our cosmic neighbors are methodically softening the public mind toward their imminent *coming out*. This ever so gentle, systematic propagandizing is pointedly directed toward our children, who in turn are remarkably sanguine—even eagerly anticipatory—anent the approach of our galactic invaders. This particular part of the program, Adam reflected, was indeed a slow, admirably diplomatic and carefully calculated remedy for our innate xenophobia.

Fair enough, he thought, but is the mass of mankind really ready for this benevolent incursion in our still myth-bound horde? How many of us can really accept this version of Moses, Jesus, Ezekiel, Socrates and Plato as the offspring of Star "gods," all of them gloriously mortal but not so immaculately conceived. Their theification has been masterfully accomplished by the greatest PR talent the world has ever known, from Paul onward.

But, under the Law of our land, we are all entitled to the adored if mindless superstitions and pointless rituals that still distinguish us from the monkeys and the chimps. Our protohistory, though admittedly apocryphal, is probably no more so than the one we have received. We are all quite free to believe as we will, as narrowly or as broadly. In our much vaunted literate societies the oral traditions of the "primitives" have been overwhelmed by our beloved written history. Why would anyone believe the orally transmitted account of the great Hopi migrations—all guided by space vessels—when our "infallible" written texts tell us otherwise?

Finding himself in a thin sweat from his mental exertion, as if he'd been toiling physically, Adam indulged himself in another cold shower, but the pelting water did not brake his thinking. Van Daniken has asked a question that can not be ignored. The texts cited by him date back thousands of years, in times when there were no special messengers or other means to spread such "fables." These persistent, independent accounts of visiting space vessels are almost identical. Had they all hallucinated the same ghosts? Is it possible that the "chroniclers of the Mahabharata, the Bible, the Epic of Gilgamesh, the texts of the Eskimos, the American Indians, the Scandinavians, the Tibetans" should all speak with quiet certainty of "flying gods?" Were they not, like the good Ezekiel, simply reporting what they had actually seen?

This abrupt, panoramic review of the history of a species was strangely altering Adam's sense of time. Parts of the marvelous Epic of the valorous Gilgamesh dated back to about 3,000 B.C., and Gilgamesh himself was probably a flesh-and-blood local ruler (of Uruk) where he is said to have reigned for 126 years. Yet another missionary from outer space, like the commander of Ezekiel's beamship—the "god" of the Old Testament? On that time-table, Socrates, Plato and company suddenly became very, very modern. And why, Adam suddenly found himself capriciously bemused, had not some bright Hollywood producer ever made a movie of the heroic Gilgamesh—the very stuff of which great synthetic drama is made?

He dried himself and donned his working clothes, then turned his thoughts to the more conventional historians of the modern era. In twelve turgid, scholarly volumes, noted historian Arnold Toynbee had struggled to distill some sense from human history, and he had. Man is a lazy mammal who will not stir his bones until compelled to do so by a hostile and demanding environment. Left to the sunshine and the figs and other free fruits of Eden he simply squats in one place, feeds his face and transmits entertaining stories to his progeny. It is only in the cold and flinty temperate zones that he is forced to move off his haunches and invent, create, think and produce.

But it would be crediting Toynbee too far to suggest that, even with that rich insight, he ever really made sense of it. None of our great historians have ever been able to respond satisfactorily to the battery of adverbial interrogatives that constantly harass our minds. *Who* are we? *Why* are we here? *What* is our purpose on this alien shore? *Where* are we going—if anywhere at all?

Adam untethered his mind and let it run afield. No professional historian has ever considered our orbiting mudball as an open air prison colony, even though we readily enough accept that Australia and America were both settled for that very purpose. Nor had they considered that we might simply have been established as a therapeutic community for the chronically mentally ill, or as an interplanetary grade school for marginally educable fledglings of the galaxy. We *are* isolated, technologically incapable of communication with others in the universe, unable to travel to their places. We are alone!

And historian Will Durant had reached only one conclusion after his lifetime appraisal of our received history: we are here to learn. And we do learn, however slowly. We learn in our schools, from life experience, and in one other way of which we are almost totally unaware—that great academy in the sky—the one that operates in deepest secrecy and in a contrived, systematically manufactured psychological environment largely created by our anonymous teachers.

Adam stiffened his back and his mind, then stretched them both. "I can only believe what I myself have experienced—and even that is to be gravely doubted." Three months earlier he had flown to North Carolina to lecture at Duke U. He had flown TWA, and somewhere over northern Arizona the pilot had come on the intercom and smilingly announced, "Folks, I'm gonna cut a few miles to the west and show you a little American history. Now down there on the left is the Third Mesa, where the Indians used to line up to watch our frontiersman going west, and to see our cavalry go galloping by. The Indians would stare down at them, and they'd stare back at the Indians. And that's about all that ever happened out here folks—they just stared at each other."

So that's how The West Was Won? So much for John Wayne and company. There was no doubt in Adam's mind that his good, wayfaring captain had received the script for his apparently impromptu little travelogue from TWA's front office, who got it from...? Who got it from...?

But why, he wondered—why the systematic spoofing of our Founding Fathers in the animated cartoons, the comic strips and in the television parodies—especially during our fabulous bicentennial year? What is the message? Are we now mature enough to be let in on the gag, or is it T.H.E.I.R. private little inside joke? Are we to be allowed at last to participate in the Great American real estate development for what it really is, without all the Madison Avenue ballyhoo of "history" so sorely needed earlier in the game?

The American Revolution. "Taxation without representation is tyranny." The tax in question had been exactly fifty cents per year per person. The Boston Massacre was a piddling street corner donnybrook. The Shot Heard Round the World resounded only through the Media—T.H.E.I.R. exclusively owned and regulated Media.

And so, Adam tentatively decided, let the Darwinists and the Creationists carry their debate forward, with one faction making as much or as little sense as the other. So be it and amen.

But not so for the import theory—and as a real and continuing activity. He knew that at earth level the fanciful science fiction of this scenario was rapidly drawing to an end. The fantasy is now becoming a reality, as is always the case?

Riffling through the Elders testimony[1] he looked for some believable indication of who or what our E.T. neighbors might be—and what their possible interest in us. Here, at last, was a believable place to start—or at the very least a sane model for what the future might hold.

Freshly fascinated, Adam read on, critically reviewing the age-old human fantasy that was now becoming fact. The Pleiadean cosmonauts calmly identified themselves as "men" (human) and were accordingly found to be quite human in physical appearance but inclining to the Nordic habitus. They do not claim to be superhuman at all, but modestly acknowledge that their fund of information substantially exceeds our own, especially in technology. They commend our faltering entrance into space but realistically deem it "primitive." Our space propulsion methods have not yet enabled us to enter what they call "hyperspace," where our measured time is all but extinguished. Their vessels exceed the speed of light many times over. By our present methods it would take us approximately 500 years to reach their native Pleiades, whereas they can make a round-trip commute to earth in about five minutes. Hence the diminutive size of their interplanetary vessels: about twenty-one feet in diameter and usually handled by a crew of three.

They volunteer little about their law, medicine, government, manners and morals. But heaven help me, Adam suddenly prayed with arms aloft, may no marriage counseling ever be required of me there or anywhere! That aside, he ruminated on just how this kind of information might be received by today's earthly community—by those who sincerely believe we have already learned all that is knowable. The average earthling regards his leading scientists, physicists and astronomers included, with a degree of all-accepting awe that the scientists themselves do not harbor. Advanced though it may seem to us the untutored, our physics is still primitive, with far more remaining to be learned than has been learned. Ptaah, the Pleiadean cosmonaut, remarks plainly enough: "A single second in the timeless, amounts to many million years in normal space." From their home planet of Erra in the Pleiades, which is but one of a union of planets inhabited by some 127 billion people, they must look upon us as poor and ignorant country cousins at best, but it could well be that they are doing what they can to help us—or to govern us?

Knowing us as they do, Adam mused, they would of course be quite familiar with our predictable mammalian pattern of approach—avoidance behavior. Whatever we do not understand we first withdraw from fearfully, cautiously. Then curiosity overcomes fear and we tentatively approach, and again withdraw. If we find ourselves uninjured we approach again until we have mustered enough trust to more closely investigate the source of our alarm.

This would surely be one of the two obvious reasons for their quite deliberate, graduated and intermittent demonstrations in our skies. From time to time they show themselves to us conspicuously and then deliberately retreat. The human witnesses spread word of their appearance—including the fact that no harm ensued—and the word gradually spreads. Thus we are being systematically, *emotionally titrated*— given an opportunity to accustom ourselves to their amiable and harmless, even helpful presence? Or is it the strategy of the Trojan Horse all over again?

The second reason for their tactful, standoffish approach was distressingly obvious. If I were a member of an advanced, rational and non-violent civilization, Adam inquired of himself, would I want to step into this earthly sump directly? Would you, he asked his friendly wall? No, not unless you want to be mugged, shot, raped, kidnapped or broad-sided with a salvo of foul names—or forced to defend yourself by violent means when violence is anathema to you. Then again, perhaps they simply intend to take us alive.

That we may well have been quite literally "created in His image" squares nicely with the historical reflections of Semjase, a contemporary Pleiadean astronaut and recent earth visitor: "We feel duty-bound to citizens of Earth, because our forebearers were their forebearers." (February 8, 1975.) She further explains the reluctance of her fellow Pleiadeans to make themselves fully known to the mass of humankind because "they would merely revere us as gods, as in ages past, or go off in hysteria."

Hence, they limit their personal contacts to a few select individuals, at least for the present, by way of making themselves know to us gradually and at a rate we can accept equably—and to inform our notoriously paranoid species that they come here with entirely peaceful intentions.

Ptaah, a fellow cosmonaut, advises cryptically that "we extraterrestrial living forms have no authority yet to interfere by force with terrestrial concerns." Adam laughed aloud. This would not necessarily preclude, however, their instituting our international monetary system and subsequently controlling the behavior modification program enabled by it.

Just how long they have been skirting our turf is another question. Wilgus referred to the "legends of prehistoric civilizations, implying that surviving supermen from those times may continue to act as our secret masters." And once again, Adam chuckled softly, we come head on with Seth's brilliant, devoutly pacifistic, pre-Sumerian Lumanians, who withdrew in revulsion to the earth's deepest caverns and thence to the very viscus of the planet. Have they headquartered there ever since, and even now? The Hollow Earth theory is not without its insistent and persuasive exponents.[2] After all, the Enlightened Ones do enjoy playing with our fluctuant hash of language, layering meanings within meanings, and hence another meaning to the whimsical sobriquet—"The Insiders."

Once again pacing the room, distraught but with mounting excitement, Adam reflected further on the import theory of human origins. Perhaps our earth people of today could at least consider this possibility, as there are heartening signs that the popular mind is slowly coming into harmony with it. The great U.F.O. controversy is hardly that at this late date. Approximately one in ten Americans have personally seen the beamships, and even allowing for a generous craziness-quotient, enough sane and reliable witnesses have reported them to satisfy any reasonable requirements for proof. The U.S. military's Operation Squelch is probably well-intended. Like the visitors themselves, they are afraid of mass hysteria reaction in the earthly community, in which they may well be justified. That the E.T. sojourners have left little or no physical evidence of their junkets to earth is easily explained. Unlike ourselves, they are not polluters.

1. Elders, L.J. and B.N., Welch, T.K. **UFO** . . . Contact from the Pleiades, Genesis III Productions, Ltd., Phoenix, Arizona, 1979.

2. Trench, B.L., *Secret of the Ages*, Pinnacle Books, New York, 1977. Bernard, R., *The Hollow Earth*, Dell, Secaucus, N.J., 1969.

15

Utopia When We're Ready

Allowing his mind to stray briefly from prose to poetry Adam found himself wondering what life might be on some distant planetary Utopia. Having spent a lifetime in psychiatric clinics, and in the *soirees* of the sane, he could only hope for a cheerier environment than this one.

We might wistfully surmise that there would be no more obligatory labor. There, all "work" would be happily voluntary and experienced as recreational, which would spell the end to the need for any kind of monetary system.

Learning would be equally voluntary—a much cherished option.

There would be no more negative affects—no anger, boredom, envy, jealousy, vengefulness, depression, fear, anxiety or power-madness.

Law would have become a natural way of life, reduced to what we now know here on earth as "common courtesy."

Hopefully, all physical, medical diseases would have been eliminated. Or, if necessary at all, treatment would require no mutilating surgery or other intrusive, painful or incapacitating measures.

The sexual drive would be decisively divorced from the welter of rapturously agonizing emotions to which it is so commonly attached here in our sphere, and thus put an end to romantic love, which he had

171

once heretically described elsewhere as a confused olio of infantile
dependence and adolescent hot pants. Soap Opera and Shakespeare, all
drama from *Pagliacci* to *Porky's*—banished forever to the archives of
human folly.

Staring pensively upward at the starlit sky he found it almost
impossible to imagine that our species would ever be able to enjoy
conflict-free drama. It did, in fact, seem to be an essential metabolite for
the proper nurturance of the human's emotional metabolism. Instead,
might we relish a grand variety of music, graphic arts and strictly
upbeat drama, with leisure in abundance but little used?

Surely there would be no government as we know it, but only the
generous counsel of wise elders, freely offered and readily accepted.

Major mental illness would be virtually unknown. The occasionally
addled or retarded person would be transported to earth or a similar
outpost, where he would be accepted as normal or even superior.
Adam stopped and jotted a quick note reminding him to once again
review Gore Vidal's *Visit to a Small Planet*. Better yet, he decided, check
out Gore Vidal himself.

There, the individual's right to privacy would be held in the highest
regard, and "people who need people" would be pitied as the unluckiest
people on the planet. Instead of clinging desperately to one another
they would come together only when they wanted to—never because
they *needed* to. They would "work," study, socialize, dance, sing,
converse and enjoy whatever pleasures are customary there, but only
when all concerned were in clear concurrence. Their children, and with
127 billion people occupying the system we can assume that there
would be children, are thus genetically disposed and accordingly reared.

Easy cooperation would have replaced bitter competition. An
attitude of "your success is my pleasure—it is an honor to know one of
your accomplishments" would have replaced the earthly staple, "lucky
bastard—I'll top you yet!"

Adam grimaced at the thought. People who need people! It extols a
pathological emotional state that is blithely accepted as "normal" in the
human community. The very word "need" flags a painful, child-like
dependency inevitably conducive to clinging, demanding, possessive,
controlling, jealous behavior between people that inevitably leads to
emotional disaster, one regressing in time to a heart-rending dissolution
of the relationship—which then becomes a cold, loveless emotional
standoff—a desolate counterfeit of love.

Emotionally independent, self-reliant and confident, now assured of our immortality, we can be alone without suffering the awful hunger of loneliness. We can enjoy our solitude and avail ourselves of the company of others as only another of many pleasure options, and not from an aching, cloying yen for a love-fix from some other person. We have no thought of "rejection" because we are unrejectable. The fondness we feel for others is authentic such that we find pleasure in their pleasure, whatever or whomever its source. We esteem ourselves highly enough to recognize the availability of countless others who would find pleasure in our company.

Adam shook his head and smiled sadly. Great, now all we need is a change of species. Are we, by definition, capable of interbreeding with these extraplanetary others? Have they in fact attained the degree of emotional maturity I envision? He decided they must have achieved it, or something very close to it. And yet their sense of humor borders on the childish at times, though it always carries a meaning beyond mere humor. Consider their routine burlesquing of our Great American Presidents in the media: George Washington's idiotic cherry tree and clacking wooden teeth. Teddy Roosevelt's "bully" tic. Woodrow Wilson's aching feet. Eisenhower's "nucular." Unbridled sex in the White House under our lovable and favorite Hyannis sport, J.F.K. Gerald Ford's klutziness, Nixon's jowls and Reagan's jelly beans. The message behind the joke is that any jester can be president—Eddie Cantor or Pat Paulsen would be just fine.

If they control it all, then, how are we to resist, Adam wondered? He supposed that if their purposes were to prove truly benevolent there would be no need to rebel, nor would there be any effective way to do so in any case. When they do make themselves known to us, he decided uneasily, we would probably be well-advised to cooperate and learn, though he knew his supposition placed him at some risk of being denounced as an interplanetary Quisling.

No! he suddenly shouted softly, resolutely. *Sic semper tyrannis!* We shall not endure Big Brother in any guise!

Then he sat down again, dropped his head, and slowly turned his thoughts to the second of their mightiest weapons against us. After Money came the Media.

Jasmyn was at the tiller, a soft and steady breeze wafting her long, blonde hair behind her.

"It's lovely out here," she said to Sandol, wanting to engage him in amiable conversation and lift his spirits.

"Considering the general state of the planet, yes—it is."

"I'm going to come about to a port tack. Would you do the jib for me, please?"

He looked aft, then forward. "Jib. That's the one up front, right?"

"Oh, don't play the fool, Sandol. You know it is."

Hauling in the starboard jibline he said, "I'm not playing. It's been so long I've really forgotten most of this business."

"Well," she consoled him lightly, "you're a master at electronic control systems, so I'll handle the more prehistoric modes of transportation."

"Speaking of prehistoric," Sandol replied, glancing at the arrayed monitors down in the midship salon, "your favorite earthling is now struggling over the origin of his species."

"Is he making any progress?"

"A little, I'd say, but he's having a terrible time shaking the paranoid stance. It's instinctual with them, y'know; brain-based and hereditary. Their paranoia, xenophobia, and their ungodly hunger for disaster."

"Ah, but they are capable of rudimentary love, and surprisingly often they display a finely edged sense of humor."

"True enough," Sandol grudgingly agreed. "Your psychiatrist friend is a real giggle at times—especially when he's serious."

An unsmiling Jasmyn reproached him quietly but firmly. "Reset your thalamus, Sandol. You're being a boor."

16

The Great Wars That Never Were

Adam tossed down *Time* and picked up a recent issue of *New Yorker* magazine. Oh, they're cute all right. He stared at a Manufacturers Hanover ad. Such modesty! T.H.E.Y. call themselves *the* financial source. Worldwide, yet. They lend a billion-and-a-half to underwrite our heat, light and communications and advertise the boast in a beautiful two-page color spread, and they need to advertise to *New Yorker* readers like Elvis had to pass out handbills to get people to his concerts. And what's at the bottom of the second page? Just two words: *The Illuminators*—in Second Coming type! Why not the heaters? Communicators? Shrewd, those *Illuminati*—it's like confessing to something so loudly, so openly and so often that no one will believe you, *especially* if you're telling the truth.

Looking quickly through the rest of the magazine, he came to a Save-the-Starving-Children-of-the-World ad and studied it carefully for a moment. Odd. The little girl pictured in it was obviously not starving; a smudge on her cheek, hair a bit tangled, unsmiling, but otherwise chubby-cheeked, bright-eyed and altogether healthy-looking. So what's that one all about, he wondered. Messages, messages, all over the place—but how to divine their meanings.

Disgruntled and perplexed he posed the question to himself again. Why? Why the need for all those mock wars and other spectacular— and contrived—street theater shenanigans? Try Goldy's line again. It could be, he tentatively supposed, that our very human needs and limitations have long been understood—and perhaps even provided for?— by those dastardly Insiders, the malevolent Illuminati. Our need to rage and have revenge, to achieve self-righteousness through indignation and denunciation of the wickedness of others—the need to hate, envy and fear.

Yes, we do have an inborn drive to experience the pleasure of fear, like little children ecstatically relishing the exquisite terror of a gruesome horror movie or a spine-chilling ghost story. Paranoia is also an inborn drive—a survival mechanism lingering from our jungle days no doubt.

It is possible then, he wondered (marveling at the mere suspicion of this insane possibility), that these loathsome Illuminati have long since discovered ways of harmlessly detonating and discharging these irrational animal needs? Vicariously? Satisfying from time to time our collective blood lust and our craving for the morbid by producing these marvelous performances in the artificial "reality" of the media?

Then forget the media! he commanded himself. He knew how the movies did it for WW II. In your local neighborhood theater, on came the news in black-and-white, showing our thousands of troops— smiling and waving—boarding the great ships to stirring martial music, all glory-bound to save democracy on foreign shores. End newsreel, and on with the feature film. *Bataan, The Sands of Iwo Jima* and so on, replete with mutual mass murder, blood and guts, thousands killed in battle—but all fiction! The newsreel was fact, the feature fiction, but they fell together amorphously in the public mind. It was *made* to seem real.

Discount the movies and the newsreels, then. Forget what we were told by *Life, Time* and the other instruments of the diabolically ingenious Insiders. What did you experience, Adam? What did you see with your own eyes, hear with your own ears? What were the Great Wars to you, and in the hundreds of interviews you've conducted with people you've known and can believe?

He slid down to a sitting position, leaned back against the wall and commenced a deliberate reminiscence. Yes, that dialogue with the nice Nazi lady. His chat with the bloodthirsty Chicano killer. A most telling exchange with an affable bombardier from the Viet Nam fiasco. His recent heated encounter with an old friend and colleague, now a famous psychiatrist, about the whole ersatz scenario. Or was it?

He had met the nice Nazi lady for wine and cheese on a late Spring afternoon, at a peaceful sidewalk cafe in La Jolla. After concluding their business (a small real estate transaction) Margot mentioned that she had been born in Bremen and had spent her childhood and adolescence in that major German industrial City during the wonderful War to End All Wars, WW II. She had answered his questions quietly, willingly, her voice and eyes soft, intensely sincere, as she replied to his pointed probing.

"What was it like, your daily life during the war?"

"Not too bad, really. Every morning the air raid alarm would sound and we'd all go down into the shelters and wait."

"And then?"

"We'd wait for the all-clear, twenty or thirty minutes later, then go back up and be about our business."

"And this went on for four or five years, the Allied bombings?"

"Yes. Almost every day. We would listen to the bombs exploding in the distance."

"And during that time did you personally see anyone killed?"

"Well—no."

"Did you see anyone wounded?"

"Not really. I guess it was a miracle."

"I'm curious about the pattern of the bombings. Did you notice any definite pattern? Arsenals? Industrial plants? Utility plants? Old warehouses and railroad yards? Historical landmarks? Like that."

"No-o-o. Yes. There was a pattern—funny thing you should ask it. At the time, well, I had the strangest feeling, well, that someone up there was controlling where the bombs were dropped. They hit where you just said, in the old part of the city—the old warehouses and railroad tracks . . . strange."

"And you've been back there since coming to America. How is the city now? Bombed out? Gutted?"

"Oh no! It's beautiful! More beautiful than I'd ever seen it!"

Urban renewal on a grand scale? According to Margot, it apparently was. No wounded, no dead, and a major European industrial city rebuilt, all of which makes for a very interesting war. But with an outcome that does not square at all with the media coverage we received in this country. We were given the clear impression of a Germany destroyed, ravaged, reduced to rubble. We remember all that, and marvel that Germany today is thriving, prosperous and a major influence in world affairs.

Adam had several more questions for Margot.

"After your coffee break in the bomb shelter, then, what was your day like?"

"Oh, the usual. I went to school, my father to work. Once or twice a year my mother and I would take a holiday in the Netherlands."

"Did you ever see a concentration camp on your travels? You know, Dachau or Auschwitz—any of those?"

"Yes, we went past them. We saw the fences, and prisoners in uniform. But they weren't starving—just ordinary people. We never found out about all the terrible things that happened there until after the war was over. It was dreadful . . . dreadful."

Adam next turned his thoughts to a late morning stroll several years earlier, when the first glimmerings of the *Sapiens System* heresy had started twinkling at the darker edges of his mind. He was doing a case consultation with Pablo Matado, formerly a dedicated Chicano killer and now a fully trained and licensed psychiatric social worker.

With the consult completed, Adam had tactfully inquired about the Viet Nam experience, and Pablo had answered with grace and candor.

Pablo looked the part. Dark skin, heavy black eyebrows, broad shoulders and powerfully muscled.

"Were you drafted into the army?" Adam had asked.

"Drafted? Oh, no. I couldn't wait to get in—get into the action."

"How old were you then?"

"Eighteen, and full of fury."

"Fury? About what?"

"Nothing—and everything. I was eighteen, and, well, I grew up a certain way, fighting and all. No, I can do better than that. I was born that way—a *macho* fighter."

"You're saying that you really enjoyed fighting—got a kick out of it."

"Loved it! My parents, they were good Catholics. When I was a kid they would tell me to respect the dignity of my fellow man. Hell, how could I respect anyone's dignity when, if he looked cross-eyed at me, I'd punch out his lights?"

"So you were ready for Viet Nam, then. Did you see any action?"

"Front-lines, a foot soldier. We had a blast."

"What kind of action? Hand-to-hand? Bayonets and that sort of thing?"

"No, not like that. Our guys, we'd be on one hill with the Cong on a hill opposite. We'd get behind trees and shoot at each other. It was a lot of fun—at the time."

"Did you kill anyone?"

"Maybe. I don't know. Whenever we saw something moving over there we'd shoot at it. Don't know if I killed anyone. Hope not."

"Any killed on your side? Any wounded?"

"Some. A couple. One of my buddies got hit in the shoulder and another one committed suicide. That was about it."

"So you're saying the whole thing was a really good experience for you, or a bad one?"

"Both. It was good at the time, but never again. As the saying goes, I wouldn't take a million dollars for it, but I wouldn't do it again for a million. It gave me a chance to get some bad things out of my system—a chance to grow up a little."

"What if there'd been no war for you to go to? What then?"

"Who knows? The way I was, my buddies and I, we'd likely have cut each other up in bar fights. Or knocked over any dudes on the street who happened to get in our way. Matter of fact, one of my old war buddies was shot to death in a bar fight just last month."

"Why psychiatric social work? That's a rough course to go."

"I knew my parents were right—that I was headed for big trouble if I didn't clean up my act. I wanted to learn more about people, and about myself—why we all behave the way we do. It's quite a zoo, isn't it?"

"You like your work?"

"Love it. I'm working with the neighborhood Highriders now, getting them to turn in their zipguns and knives. And we're setting up an amateur boxing tournament to help them let off steam. We should have some good Golden Gloves material around here."

Then had come the intriguing and remarkably revealing cocktail chat with the affable, former U.S. Air Force bombardier, also of the Viet Nam charade. Through growing experience, Adam had honed his interviewing technique with veterans to a nice cutting edge. The first step was to wait through the customary opening defenses, which ranged from "it was hell" to "I'd rather not talk about it." The next step was to make the questions as specific and concrete as possible. It was not enough to ask, "Did you see any action?" or "Much damage done?" as these invariably elicited equally general responses: "It was a bloody mess," or "There were a lot of people killed out there." These latter replies were not outright falsifications, as Adam gradually came to realize, but were pickups from official reports, newspaper and other media accounts, and not from first-hand observation.

The dialogue with the bombardier slowly revealed the incredible ingenuity exercised in creating the illusion of vast damage done where little actually existed, and it was all done above the heads of the fighting men themselves—and of their commanding generals.

"Did you fly many missions?"

"More than I care to remember."

"What were your main targets? Military? Airfields, munitions stockpiles, troop concentrations?"

"Anywhere they sent us. We weren't running the war—just working there."

"Were you able to see where your bombs hit? Whether you were on target?"

"Of course. Naturally."

"Were you close enough to tell if the bombs killed many people?"

"No. The photographs wouldn't show anything like that."

"Photographs? I don't understand."

"Right—aerial reconnaissance. That's how we found out about our results from any given mission."

"Then you didn't see where the bombs dropped with your own eyes? Just the reconnaissance photos?"

"Sure. We only flew night missions, for defensive purposes, so we wouldn't have seen our results anyway. We flew by instrument, bombed by instrument."

"How long did you have to wait for the recon photos?"

"Usually three days. Why are you asking?"

"Just wondering. Was there ever any question in your mind, well, about the authenticity of the photographs?"

At this question the beleaguered bombardier suddenly turned red, was visibly annoyed and started to walk away. Then he turned abruptly and snapped what could well be the most telling retort of the century:

"Hey! Get off my case, okay? We knew damn well we were bombing cow tracks out in the boonies—I'm just glad we weren't killing real people!"

He then walked away, probably wondering what asylum Adam had escaped from.

Adam's first awareness of this kind of exquisitely refined manipulation of human affairs in high places began to come through to him just a few short weeks after his initial realization that All Is Not What It Appears To Be. The other principal in this warm, staccato exchange was an old friend and colleague, now an important figure in American psychiatry, and it took place quite spontaneously at his friend's home following a meeting of the American College of Psychiatrists in February, 1976.

Still stunned by his growing awareness, and utterly preoccupied with its import, Adam had sent up a small trial balloon.

"I spent almost four years in the Marine Corps in World War II and, looking back on it, I'd have to say well, not much happened but a lot of media hoopla."

Fixing Adam with his cold, blue, Irish eyes, his friend shot back warily, "What do you mean?"

Still guileless and tentative, Adam replied, "Well, just that. I mean, I really don't know anyone personally who was killed in the war."

He fired back without a moment's hesitation. "You're talking foolishly! My whole company was wiped out in one day of action in France."

This was Adam's first and probably most instructive lesson in the fine art of interviewing veterans. He resisted the temptation to apologize for his heartlessness and pressed on.

"Oh. Bad. Did you see it happen? You were there?"

"What do you mean, did I see it happen? I didn't have to see it happen. The report came back from the front the day after they went into action—all of them dead."

"Why weren't you there? What happened?"

Getting huffier by the moment his friend snapped back, "I was transferred out the day before they went into the field. Convenience of the Service—that's why!"

"Oh. Well then, did you ever have a chance to follow up on any of them? You know, contact their families—anything like that?"

"No reason to. I didn't know them that well. They were from all parts of the country and our outfit had only been formed a few weeks before. What are you driving at, anyway?"

Adam saw it now. Stunning. Magnificent. All but incredible. Just picture it: a hundred different troops scattered to a dozen or more different, widely separated outposts, all for "the Convenience of the Service," and all of the unwitting players later receiving the horrifying news that their comrades had just been killed in battle. And this in an era when most of us had never heard the word "computer"—but it was obviously there and hard at work. Nothing else could have handled such a staggering logistical problem. Ah, those Insiders, Adam marvelled—they would cheerfully dupe a million bumpkins to make an extra buck or two.

Adam reflected that the maneuver was consistent with his own experience in the Great War. Thinking back, he remembered that he and his wartime buddies were never in the same place long enough, with the same kind of people and involved in the sort of intensely emotional events that would lead to military reunions. Those reunions happened routinely in fictional war movies, but not in real life.

Systematic dispersal would be an appropriate name for that gambit. At the hoary old age of seventeen Adam had volunteered for the Marine Corps in Columbus, Ohio, but by the time he reached boot camp in San Diego he was among strangers. His platoon-mates hailed from almost every State in the Union. A couple of ivy league undergrads, farm boys from the corn belt, a sprinkling of good-old-boys from the deep South who were still—to young Adam's amazement and considerable consternation—fighting the Civil War.

Carefully calculated *interculturation* in the field? They had all remained together long enough to become friendly, to squabble good-naturedly about their diverse boyish philosophies, and to recognize and even begin to appreciate the differences among them. When the manly rigors of boot training were completed they were then methodically scattered to the winds: Cooks and Bakers School, Fleet Marine Force, Special Services, Radar School and so on. Several of them had gone the radar route together and became good friends, but because of geographical and a diversity of career interests there had never been occasion for them to reunite after the "war" was over. And all of that had been known *before* the whole operation was set into motion. How handily handled!

Nor was that the only astonishment at hand. Adam next found himself marveling at the miraculous preservation of the world's major historical landmarks throughout the two Great World Wars: Westminster Abbey, London Bridge, Big Ben, the Eiffel Tower, the great Cathedrals of Europe. Tactically, this would have made no military sense at all, as there would be few better ways to destroy a people's morale than to wipe out their cherished national shrines. In a *real* war these would have been blasted first—even before attacking military targets!

And what of the body counts? Leafing rapidly through the pages Adam quickly found that the *Encyclopaedia Britannica* lists 135 specific subtopics under the heading "World War II," everything from "Antarctic Operations" to "Motion Picture Industry Policy Change," but offers not a single heading for "Casualties" or "Mortality Rate." Oh Flanders Field, what lies then beneath your silent sod?

Adam stood up and wandered restlessly around the room, his forehead webbed. The face of warfare had changed in history. From rocks and clubs, arrows, spears and cannonry to the truly remarkable means for annihilating the entire species in a matter of seconds. And yet, even though we have long had these extremely advanced military capabilities they were not resorted to in the Korean and Viet Nam conflicts. Why? Because computer-controlled nuclear warfare does not offer the charming *desiderata* so lusted for by the latest crop of our adolescent Rambos. There was no derring-do, no chance for heroism in pushbutton warfare. Could he later boast to his children that he'd pressed the button that atomized three billion human lives into eternity? No. So it was still rifles, mortars, jeeps, terrorists and helicopters—warfare with a flair. Which would mean, then, that these antique weapons are a little more than *macho* playthings for the wet-nosed, hard-on, pimple-popping would-be warriors of the world?

Meanwhile, back on the homefront, this fantastically scripted drama had been systematically reinforced by a steady battery of news stories about the conflagrations in the Pacific and European Theaters— *Theaters! Damn!* But his friend Hank Davis, then a U.S. Navy Commander, had given Adam one good man's firsthand account of what really happened to *Mister Roberts* and his friends.

"Tell you about the war? Sure, I'll tell you about the war—there wasn't any goddam war! Five years we ploughed our cruiser up and down the Pacific looking for action. Sure, we all heard about the great sea battles going on. We were ordered into a lot of them, but they were never there when we arrived!"

The folks back home never knew what he had learned. They read the newspaper accounts, saw the newsreels, and swallowed the whole hog without so much as a belch. The food and gas rationing, which worked no real hardship on anyone, had made it all seem more real to the homefolk. Who could doubt one bit of it?

Military conscription—the infamous Draft—had also made its contribution to this spurious sense of reality, even though its most important function had nothing to do with recruiting soldiers. It was created to help the freshly muscled, pimply-faced, underaged high school heroes get away from home. Smiling reluctantly, Adam imagined a bizarre domestic dialogue of the Forties:

"Dad, I'm eighteen now—can I join the war and go kill Japs?"

"Hell no, boy—it would break your mother's heart. You get on back to school now!"

Ah yes, the Great War had set us free from the awful vexations of hearth, home and scholarship. It had enabled a massive Rite of Passage on a planetary scale—thank the gods. It was so arranged that we were "forced" to go—given "no choice." All except for a few conscientious objectors, that is, who were offered the equivalent psychological emancipation by way of the Medical Corps or some other light duty.

Adam pressed his temples and calmly wondered if he might be going mad. It could happen, even to famous psychiatrists, and here he was conjuring up the most titanic delusion the world had ever known. But there it was, the very real possibility that the Great Wars—a new one every generation—had all been skillfully designed to last only long enough to complete the task for which they were originally intended—long enough for our late adolescents to get a bellyfull of what they *thought* they wanted.

Wars are scripted and produced for youth? And for those adults who harbor a residual instinctual need for high adventure, destructive aggression, vengeance and hate-fulfillment? And for the excitement and fanfare—the throbbing beat of martial music—and for the other fringe benefits of a wartime *fiesta*? Adam well remembered the onset of World War II. It had not been greeted with tears of anguish and a gnashing of teeth, but with an enormous burst of excitement and a national upsurge of energy and patriotic fervor. It was party-time for G.I. Joe and Rosie the Riveter, grinding groins at the local U.S.O. to the stirring strains of "Don't Sit Under the Apple Tree" and "Praise the Lord and Pass the Ammunition."

Heady with his burgeoning madness, his mind dazzled and lightly afloat, he leaned against the wall and blinked his eyes, trying to sweep away the malignant delusion. He found he had no explanation for the curdling tragedies at Hiroshima and Nagasaki or the attempted genocide in Nazi Germany—but neither did he altogether believe any of them. As heart-wrenching object lessons made to seem real they had been very strong medicine, instructing us at bowel level on what we are capable of. And yet, all he knew of it personally was the chilling picture on the front cover of *Life* magazine, showing the stark outline of a human figure—the victim himself presumably atomized by the nuclear blast—on a Hiroshima walkway.

For more information on that he would have to consider a consultation with Jasper Maskelyne, the *War Magician*, who during WW II had managed to hide the Suez Canal, relocate the Alexandrian harbor, launch a counterfeit fleet of submarines and a phantom battleship, to send Rommel's famed Afrika Corps "into confused retreat," and to create entire mock armies. Moviedom's special effects had come a long way since the original *King Kong*, regularly and believably depicting everything from the assassination of national leaders to phony space launchings to the explosive finale of the late, great planet Earth.

He exhaled deeply, sank slowly to the floor and stretched. He was exhausted, but sleep eluded him. In a twilight state of mind he saw the emaciated cadavers at Auschwitz, the corps of amputees in wheelchairs, the quadriplegic fruits of the war that really was. But something was missing, somewhere. During WW II one of the more scandalous media hypes had been that draftees of low I.Q. were being discriminated against, sent to the frontlines, while the brighter kids were settled into safe and cozy rearline desk jobs. True, likely enough, but where had been the difference?

As we measure I.Q.'s, he reflected thoughtfully, lower intellectual attainment is generally associated with aggressivity—joyful aggressivity. He then recalled the platoon just returned from the horror of Iwo Jima, back from battle to the good life of radar training school. They were not pale, long-faced, devastated, but still a-burst with hell-raising high spirits. One of their favorite amusements had been dousing each other with lighter fluid then tossing lit matches after—all howling with laughter as they rolled on the floor to put out the flames. *There* was the difference. It had been discrimination, all right, but rational discrimination. They—we—were all doing what we wanted to be doing, both the lowborn and the high. It was all voluntary—self chosen. International *therapeutic enmities* had been deliberately fashioned to gratify the instinctual bloodthirst of the Earth's young Neanderthals—the latter days sons of glorious Sumeria? Or, Adam wondered painfully, are we still an imperfectly mingled hybrid strain?

He struggled to force his thoughts in other directions but could not. He had been there, all right, and had forgotten none of it, and his own remembrances were far and away the most reliable source of information available to him. Think, think!

Consider it, Adam, my friend, how heroically you risked your life for your country in WW II (ha!) at an age when you urgently needed to do exactly that. But T.H.E.Y. persistently declined your many requests to be permitted to charge up those South Pacific beachheads in the face of cannon, musket and bayonet. And you were secretly glad of that, even then, though you didn't quite realize it. Howard Hughes. Richard Nixon.

Winston Churchill. Mao Tse Tung. Stalin. Great thespians all?

And just think how hard it is to keep peace in one family or one neighborhood—so just how do you preserve a semblance of peace and order and a decent way of life among nearly five billion of us potential killers, thieves, rapists and shrieking fish wives? Well, you give us plenty of vicarious outlets for our destructive drives, and a chance to use our particular little gifts and needs in the ways to which they are best adapted—and then reward us for doing it right. Confess it, Adam—you still need to see a little vicarious bloodletting on the screen to calm the murderous beast within you, just as gladiators need gladiators and lovers need lovers. The net pleasure-pain balance in our lives probably comes out about the same for each of us, whether we're born rich or poor, scholar or mechanic, male or female, black or white.

Funny-phony mayhem and mass murder. What I am doing now, he laughed to himself, is composing a detestable ode to hideous warfare—not warfare as we've heard about it but as it has really been. The need for it starts with *us*. We are all instinctive, natural-born bigots. Beautiful words about tolerance and brotherly love mean nothing to us when a black family moves into our neighborhood or Sis starts dating a Chicano dude. We giggle at foreign dialect jokes, laugh at gags about homosexuals, at pantomimes of women squeezing out of their girdles—at anything the least bit foreign to our own ways.

We are all aliens to each other, xenophobic to the utmost, and the great "wars" have done more than any other social force to reduce these feelings of strangeness and unfamiliarity and to let us get to know each other. The American Revolution, virtually bloodless, melded a thousand different tongues and colors and made neighbors of angry strangers. The African slave trade brought thousands of dirt-poor peasants to a new land where, like the rest of our low-born rough-n-tumble ancestors, they had a far better chance at a better life than they would ever have had back home.

World War I introduced living Americans to living Europeans—all expenses paid—courtesy of the U.S. Army Travel Service. WW II added Russia and the Orient to our experience, and us to theirs, at last bringing an end to the Gilbert and Sullivan picture of the *Yellow Menace* that once dominated the Western mind. It is interculturation by exquisitely refined plan and conducted with computer accuracy. It has carried food and medical supplies to where they are most needed. It has razed slums, dispersed a hundred troops in a hundred different directions, then sent word to all that the rest were "killed in action."

War has spurred science and technology. It has enlivened our senses and awakened our minds. "War" has made it possible for callow and aimless young men to appear fiercely independent and brave, even as they are being almost totally provided for and protected—and trained!

"War" has made prosperity, fostered education and enabled democracy (of sorts). It has brought humankind from the brutal and wretched dog-eat-dog miasma of the jungle to a world of organization, intelligence, long life, a chance to make it and a chance to love. It has converted an animal brain to a human mind.

And the most beautiful, incredibly glorious thing about it all is that "war" is a divine fiction; scripted, produced, directed and cast to give us all what we have most wanted while protecting us from our own terrible ignorance of just what it is we *do* really want.

I should know, he thought once more, remembering. I tried, sort of, to get myself killed in WW II, but that big computer in the sky would not let me do it to myself. Instead, it gave me a chance to learn, think, respect myself and other strangers, to grow up a little, and to safely satisfy my violent and rebellious needs as an unwitting spectator at the greatest, most beautiful show on earth. T.H.E.Y staged it all for me—for us?

17

Erasure of Our Protohistory

With excruciating effort, Adam forced his mind from the tantalizing warfare delusion and turned to hard physical evidence as an antidote. Another vast mystery—the commencement of our species on this orphaned planet—once again jumped to the forefront of his thinking.

He grimaced thoughtfully; origins, origins—not even the experts are agreed—which is, of course, the usual state of things. By the best available estimates, the earth itself is somewhere between three and four billion years old, with that resounding echo of the Big Bang creation of the solar system going back to about ten billion. Man, himself, has probably been around two million years, maybe closer to three, or even more. In Nevada, the clear print of a shoe-clad human foot was discovered and found to be 15 milllion years old. (And one like it was discovered in the Gobi desert, also millions of years old.) Another humanoid skeleton fossil, found by Hurzeler and de Terra in Tuscany in 1958, was dated to ten million years ago. Yes, in the conventional evolutionary time-scale, our species sure developed in one helluva burst of speed. Like "out of the blue"—perhaps literally.

Awed by the very thought of it, he reflected for a moment on the famous cave paintings of Europe, where sketches and fragments strongly suggested the active existence of art schools there some 15,000 years ago. Even more staggering was the fact that "pre-historic" sculptors left rock renditions of Tyranosaurus and Stegosaurus in Arizona and Washington. And giant, monumental sculptures of people of all races, at least 10,000 years old, have been discovered in Peru, along with figures of animals presumed by modern paleontologists to have been extinct long before man's appearance on earth. Stra-a-a-ange things are happening.

Even the amiable and learned *Seth* speaks fluently and specifically of human (or humanoid) cultures antedating those we have learned of, and by many, many millenia—our lost protohistory. The most recent archaeological findings puts the origin of our species at somewhere between 1.5 and 3 million years ago, and yet we so readily accept that our crude stone-age culture did not develop until 10-15.000 years ago. What, indeed, were all those people doing for those hundreds of thousands of years?

Let's assume for a moment, he pondered, that they were doing the same things we do—perhaps even better than we do it. But how can we possibly let that one get past our overinflated, self-centered egos? And yet there is evidence. An unmistakable computer part excavated from ancient Cretan ruins. Electroplated materials recently found near Baghdad date back to 2,000 B.C., and those accounts of twenty-five ton slabs of granite being lifted and moved by sound waves squares with Seth's account of Lumanian engineering skills. Incredible!

And there seems to be no doubt now that the prophet Ezekiel was, in literal fact, visited by "men" (Our Father who art in Heaven?) from elsewhere in the universe on four separate occasions over a twenty-year period, as recently demonstrated by an engineer and scholar of the first-order.[1] Brilliant bit of deduction, inspired by von Daniken's *Chariots of the Gods*. (A whole rash of those creatures-from-outer-space books being put out, he noted. Hell, maybe they just sell well. But, then again, why is that kind of far-out thing selling so well at this particular time and place in history? Are we, the People, gradually inching our way toward some newer and more promising point of reference?)

It's hard to take, of course—that we're just another harvest in the rotating crop of biohistory. But only vanity, vanity—all is vanity!—could blind us to the obvious possibility that we are *not the first*, not the *best* and not the *only* creatures in the universe.

Let's face it. In 1961 the Green Bank scientists estimated conservatively that there could be anywhere from ten to fifty million planets inhabitable by man. Inhabitable as they are, that is, without special terraforming or other artificial life-support systems. And, in 1964 Stephen Dole of the Rand Corporation put the upper limit at 600 million such planets.[2]

As for knowledge of the universe, of science and technology, and of man, we of today truly do stand in the shadow of the "ancients." The Egyptian priests of "antiquity" had been at careful record-keeping, especially on their highly refined astronomical observations, for somewhere between 10 and 50 thousand years—and one authority (Simplicus, 6th century A.D.) even puts that figure at over 600 thousand years! Jesus! And speaking of Him, the Vatican Codex puts the origin of the Mayan calendar at over 18,000 years B.C., and Plato quotes the Egyptian priests as dating the sinking of Atlantis at just short of 10,000 B.C. (could Roc be wrong, he wondered?)—which closely accords with Zoroastrian texts that declare "the beginning of time" at about this same date.

No, he thought sadly, knowledge has not accrued to us in a steady, linear fashion. It has risen and fallen, waxed and waned, progressed and regressed. Many Renaissance scholars truly believed the earth to be the flat center of the universe, but 4,500 years ago the Chinese scholar Chi-Po told his emperor that the earth was afloat in space, and the philosopher astronomers of Periclean Greece understood not only that, but even conceived of an infinite and centerless universe—in which they anticipated Einstein and his special theory.

The same for technology. Millennia ago Heron of Alexandria built a steam engine combining both turbine and jet principles—and an odometer. Excavations in Pakistan reveal the existence of planned cities, thousands of years old, complete with streets and sophisticated water supply and sewage systems. Then there are those 8,500-year-old fragments of tapestry discovered in Turkey—the equal of today's in workmanship; like those skillfully woven sandals found in a cave in Eastern Nevada, over 9,000 years old and also comparable in quality to modern products. The Suez Canal was *first* constructed some 2,500 years ago, and an artificially straightened elephant tusk and a handcrafted bone needle have been dated to 30,000 years ago.

Adam grunted discontentedly. Elephant tusk and bone needles and cave paintings all perpetuate that picture we have of the slant-browed, ignorant apeman with a big club in his hairy paw. Cro-Magnon was a tall, handsome and highly intelligent chap who's been around for some 30-50 thousand years—at least—and has no clear evolutionary predecessor. (Neanderthal man was not his ancestor—they were partial contemporaries.) No, Darwinian evolution could not explain his appearance. He came on-stage much too rapidly, and after a 12-million-year hiatus void of any forward movement in the *Homo* fossil record. The extraterrestrial import theory again. It just could be, couldn't it?—that others came before us, mixed their genes with those of our lowly and apish earthbound ancestors, taught us how to fend for ourselves, set the whole process in motion and then left this superior new hybrid breed of creature to run his own show—then abdicated the scene and left it to run out its own predetermined and foreseeable course. Sired by the galactic Gods—the starmen? Were we, in fact, created in their image, not mystically but quite literally?

That's not too far out, he decided. After all, there are clear and unmistakable references to atomic detonations in ancient Hindu Sanskrit texts. And old Brahmin science texts split time measurements clear down to *kashta* units, one three-hundred-millionth of a second, or 3×10^{-8} —which just happens to closely approximate the life span of certain sub-atomic particles. What need had they to slice time so fine if they were not, in fact, deeply involved in and knowledgeable of nuclear physics? Even the European cave creatures left complex astronomical notations, recorded in linear symbols, on the walls of their dwellings—and dating back to some 30,000 years ago.

This same strange progression and regression of knowledge appears also in astronomy. The two small moons of Mars were supposedly not discovered until 1877, yet they are clearly referred to in the *Iliad*, and by Kepler (early 17th century), by Voltaire and Jonathan Swift. Then there was the mysterious moon of Venus, discovered by several reliable and independent observers in the late 17th century. It disappeared for a whole century then reappeared in 1886, then disappeared again. Not unlike Lescarbault's evanescent, discoid planet *Vulcan*, which he sighted in 1859 soaring across the face of our Sun. Just what was that one all about, he marvelled—some sort of transgalactic space platform or city? And what of Marduk?

Is there intelligent life elsewhere in the universe? Adam laughed aloud, a little bitterly. Hells bells, what kind of a stupid-ass question is that? It's no question at all! The truly burning, searingly impossible question is, rather: Is There Intelligent Life on Earth? A bumper sticker query, maybe, but valid even so.

Yes, there is intelligence somewhere on earth, apparently, and we are in some kind of tenuous contact with it. Whoever they may be,

T.H.E.Y. seem to drop down historical and other information when the time is right: when they're ready for us to have it or when we're ready to receive it—or both? *The Peoples' Almanac*, debunking the American dream, converting our presidents to mere human beings, clueing us in that television and the internal combustion engine have been around for one hell of a lot longer than we realized. The sudden influx of oriental religions, and the *Seth* books—opening the American mind to reincarnation as opposed to the popular oblivion-theory of death. Isaac Asimov teaching science to the masses. Daniken and his *Chariots of the Gods?* Tomas's fascinating *We Are Not the First*. All of them right on schedule, apparently, and all of them saying about the same thing. Others came before us, erased the evidence of their presence and vanished—like the fugitive Indian brushing away his foot tracks as he makes good his escape. Not a trace. Well, a *little* trace, but only an expert tracker can find and follow them. Is that what the Insiders are doing? Leaving just enough evidence for the curious and capable to track them down by? A screening process? "Many are called but few are chosen?"—or is it that very few choose to follow the traces beyond their own front yards?

So many things we think of as new are not that new. Even little things, like contact lenses—Montgomery Ward had them in 1889. And Henry Ford did not invent the automobile as they told us he did when we were kids—there were Fiats running around in Europe before the turn of the century. CB radios have been around for years unnoticed, then for no announced reasons the FCC relaxes the regulations governing their use, and simultaneously the Insiders' big electronics factories and retail outlet companies flood the country with them. More technical training in the alluring guise of fun and games— Polytech U. in recreational clothing. Why? Who knows. Preparing communications technicians for extraterrestrial travel, I suppose, just as pleasure boats and automobiles and airplanes train piloting technicians for the same purpose.

Corollary: Most of the work people do is one inessential routine or another. Could be that it's been arranged primarily, by T.H.E.M., as occupational therapy for the mass of mankind—or possibly as an elementary prerequisite to that Great Graduate School in the Sky.

Something like that. It must be, because those vehicles are intrinsically pointless—far costlier and less efficient than mass transit systems—which means that their presence in The Program is serving some other, quite hidden purpose. Yes, he concluded, our technology—

or certain information about it—is being manipulated from on high, somehow, and on a meticulously programmed basis. And now we hear that Texas Instruments has a little telephone attachment that lets you make direct calls to anyone you like—without going through Bell or any other telephone system.

Just what the hell is going on, anyway? All of these lavishly advertised products, the crockpots and the microwave ovens and the cosmetics, are in themselves essentially useless. So what is the real purpose of all this senseless and horribly extravagant advertising? Remember your basic Freud, Adam: in all symbolic expression there is latent or hidden, as well as manifest—or obvious—content. A TV commercial for a microwave oven seduces the consumer into not only buying one, but of then learning something about its operation—and that a Hertz is something *other* than just the #1 car rental company.

There are a few clues, though, here and there. A sitcom episode, without prior notice, is postponed to make way for a fifteen minute lecture on how to program your Space-Age digital kitchen range—so the American housewife can control how crisp the family bacon is? Hardly. Housewives of America, he declared grandly, you are being tacitly trained as flight technicians for intergalactic space travel! The bacon is a bonus.

That's a fairly palatable thesis—if true. You give a kid a gun, a car or a typewriter after he's learned to use them—not before—so he won't kill himself or someone else or wreck a costly piece of equipment. That could be the answer: they're letting the new technology down to us as we're able to learn its uses and then to use it. Face it, my friend—if Goldy's a retard, then so are you! That kind of judgment is all very relative and arbitrary. Good God, you can barely handle the four basic arithmetical functions on your trusty little compact calculator. So what do you want with more? Unless, of course, you can retain people like Gilth and Bairny to handle the hardware for you—whereat you become an administrator. Oh, woe!

Back to origins, he admonished himself. If there were—are—highly intelligent Others who set our Program in motion—how did they do it, and how did T.H.E.Y. manage to get themselves behind the scenes so completely? The deliberate and systematic erasure of "pre-history" was obviously not an easy task. From today's detached perspective it's easy to see that it was largely accomplished through the destruction, by arson, of the fabulous "ancient" libraries of Pisistratus in Athens, the Temple of Ptah in Memphis, of Pergamus in Asia Minor, of Carthage and Alexandria (the best-publicized of these calculated torch jobs), and the carefully premeditated and perpetrated mass book-burnings by Tsin Shi Hwang in China and by Isaurus of Constantinople—both of them *Illuminati primi* no doubt.

Tactically, he ruminated, the destruction of the books was a sort of necessary evil—it had to be done to make T.H.E.I.R. program operable, though presumably the books were all microfilmed and safely stashed away before the originals were destroyed in the flames set by the Masters of Enlightenment. Millions of volumes of information connecting us with our mysterious predecessors, all wiped out, thus successfully sealing them off from us—forever? It wasn't just a missing link—it was a deliberately broken link.

Today, of course, T.H.E.Y. hide behind organizational complexity, and the organization of that huge corporate jungle is as impenetrably dense as that of the banking system.

Pondering that one, he rifled through a stack of books and pamphlets until he found a thin catalog of "Selected U.S. Government Publications," and on page 11 found what he was looking for, Item 125L: "Disclosure of Corporate Ownership. A 1974 publication that reports the responses of several hundred of this nation's largest corporations to a Congressional request for the identities of their 30 principal stockholders." Wagging his head in amused disbelief, he laughed aloud and harangued the wall: "Ladies and gentlemen of the Congress, you'll never, *never* make it to the top of T.H.E.I.R. pyramid by pissing around its base like that . . . can't get to Heaven in a rockin' chair, *Oh!* you can't get to Heaven in a Ford V-8!"

Smiling smugly among themselves, T.H.E.Y. lurk above our own *Financial Ceiling Zero*, the level at which the world monetary system becomes too complex for the mortal mind to grasp.

Crazy, maybe, but happily I'm not alone. Charles Fort said it plainly enough. "Maybe we are property—property of a cosmic supercivilization breeding gods out of monkeys." Like George Schaller's perplexed gorillas, Adam scratched the top of his head wonderingly and murmured again, to himself, "Yes, we are being bred—cultivated—like hothouse orchids."

A most repugnant notion, of course, and our incorrigible egotism bids us cast it out at once! Interesting though, he mused, how readily we accept that we breed and train dogs and horses and fighting cocks, yet we bristle and recoil at the mere thought that we ourselves are being bred and trained; but we are, no? And the good old U.S.A. is one of the largest human husbandry farms on the face of the earth—the Spaceship Earth: white, black, yellow, brown, and red—the Illuminati program—a palette of carefully recombined alleles to produce new breeds to perform new tasks for T.H.E.M. How might that work? The black blood makes us stronger and more peaceful; brown, prouder and more sensitive; red, wiser and kinder; yellow—smarter. Something like that, I suppose, though I'm sure the Ultimate Computer has it doped out in much finer detail than that.

What the hell, he muttered, letting his imagination run amok—why not? The generations of our *known* historical era *are* just another crop, only one out of hundreds—maybe thousands—that have been planted, fertilized, tilled and harvested before us. The chilling question is, who are those celestial superfarmers above and beyond the local Illuminati, and where does their program point? T.H.E.I.R. Phase I objective seems clear enough—someone up there is trying to wake us up from the primordial sleep, to seduce us from apathy and to fire us with a vibrant lust for life. What happens next, though, is just too far for us
                                   clear
                  a   day,   can   e-e-e
mere mortals to envision. On   you   see for   ve - e - er...
"My ass!" he bellowed inwardly—"I can't even see beyond the tip of my nose. It's just too dark down here, you brilliantly Illuminated bastards! How about turning up the lights a little?"

Beginning to feel like a dim-witted Neanderthal man, he nervously reminded himself that he was, in fact, an honest-to-God *Homo sapiens*—a direct descendant of the superior Cro-Magnon strain. No, not a hairy brute with a club in his hand, but a meditative, calculating creature working at his abacus and sextant, planning and plotting—forming, somehow, the destiny of his own progeny. Ten thousand years old at least, the abacus, the original binary digital computer, the alpha and the omega of the banking industry (and as for the hairy brute, the Piltdown fraud was a clear enough clue as to how that sort of thing can be arranged;[3] early man—precocious genius or imbecilic beast?—you pays your money and takes your choice, no? For all we understand of it, all relics and artifacts—like the Piltdown man and the Dead Sea Scrolls—could easily have been salted into the riverbeds and mountainsides. Old *Seth* himself has pronounced the Dead Sea Scrolls a fraud, and, as a former Pope, he should know!)[4]

They kept records, surely, on the growing population of the species. One could almost hear Jethro explaining to his good son-in-law, Moses, that he would have to organize the legions of mankind—by the thousands and the tens of thousands. Keep a census on them all, a running inventory, and teach them morality. (But how! Adam wailed inwardly—how do you teach the unteachable?) Keep control of the money, of course, because it is through money that the nations and their governments shall be regulated. And every bit as important as the money is the control of all public information sources, from the Holy Book of the Hindus to the Bible and later books, and the newspaper, radio, the BBC, NBC, ABC and CBS—and the cinema. All of them. All of it run by incognito angels of the invisible powers behind all the thrones of the world, in an administrative hierarchy that spiraled up, up, up—to where! Farther, to be sure, than the human eye could possibly see.

It was organized, and still is. Consider this, he demanded harshly of himself: In 1951 Pope Pius XII proclaimed the Archangel Gabriel as patron of all electronic communication industries, thus perpetuating his historical function as a messenger of God. If one were to take a strictly fundamentalist view of The System then, Adam mused, he would have to interpret "Captain Kangaroo," "Sesame Street," "Mary Hartman," the evening news and the late, late movie and the commercials, too—each and every one of them—as messages from God, courtesy of the Archangel Gabriel.

A frivolous notion, perhaps, but not inane. Those programs are educational and entertaining little morality tales—and "Mary Hartman" is surely group therapy for the masses. That tube sure teaches a lot of law and medicine. And science. Ethics. Manners and morals. *The Bill Cosby Show* and other sitcoms are indeed like real life, as is *Mary Hartman*. That, in fact, is the problem. Nessa Hyams directs the show. Anagrams to Essan Shaym. Is that what Mary and her friends are—the bumbling, ignorant, emotionally screwed-up shame of the Essenes? The Illuminati? In any case, it is pedagogically sound principle.

Yes, teaching in the guise of entertainment *is* the best kind of all—when you don't even know you're being taught. My good colleague, psychiatrist Bruno Bettelheim, found that out in his famous Orthogenic School. There, kids who couldn't read or write, but who turned on to ideas of "kill" or "burn," could soon learn to spell those words because they were interested. And did the learning of those dangerous words move them close to the deed? No! It moved them away from it, by interposing thinking—delay—long enough to spell the word and discharge some rage in the mental image it represented.

It's like counting to ten when you're angry. Up from the jungle?

And yet it all seems so opportunistically chaotic, supply-and-demand, programs coming and going haphazardly—or does it just seem that way? It could all be part of a master program intricately constructed to work highly specific effects on the mass mind(s). With all those manifestly pointless commercials and those endless and mysterious subliminal flickers thrown in here and there. All those dead arms and legs draping across the tube in quick flashes, the skull and crossbones, and those tiny little flicks of people screwing and eating each other—why? And that gruesome, faceless Dristan commercial—have T.H.E.Y. begun inuring us to the sight of faceless extraterrestrial comrades in preparation for our first encounter with them? Is that it? Well, maybe—just maybe—it isn't all as random as it seems. A monumental, incessant brainwashing of the mass mind. A meticulously methodical conditioning not merely of individuals, but of entire populations? Incredible, yes, and ingenious.

It was now dark outside, and quiet. The hour was late and his mind was racing. Take Genesis as a metaphor. See the doughty Nimrod seeking to build a tower to the private dominion of the Almighty—what brazen presumption! Now see him struck down to earth, and a great confusion of languages set upon him and his fellow-conspirators, that they might never again enter into a collusion against the invisible masters—or Master? Divide and conquer. Nation against nation and race against race.

If I were king! How easy it would be, he thought, to make that program work, with five thousand or five million or five billion people. No difference—the principles of management remain the same. Why, you could do anything you wanted!

From that lofty retreat where dwelleth the local G.O.D.S., he thought, how simple it would be to lure whole masses of people from one place to another to where their particular services are needed—and their opportunities are greater. Free land is offered in Oklahoma. Gold is discovered in California (a few thousand dollars worth, he thought drily—that great gold strike happened only in the newspapers), and now the enormous oil wealth of the U.A.R. is paying handsomely for another big drain from here to there. Human avarice is one of our more reliable instinctual traits; money moves us. Rich oil deposits are uncovered. Our mortal Everyman finds these little temptations quite irresistible, though no one forces him to pursue them. He may still opt for the brief, idyllic, ignorant and dream-like existence of the happy savage—and indeed some still do. But Everyman will take the bait quite voluntarily and in so doing he will work, and in working he will think, and in thinking he will live. At times strenuously, to be sure, but overall he will live longer, and better, than had he chosen the native state of motionless stagnation.

The Master Headshrinker in the sky, on Old Olympus's Towering Top—or even higher, seated at the supreme computer console—at the nerve center of the world. How would I actually go about it he asked himself. How? In practical, down-to-earth and very nitty-gritty terms? How?

He stood up with a lunge and began pacing the room, carefully, doggedly hatching out his hypothetical plan for running a proper kind of world-wide civilization.

1. Blumrich, J. (Chief of NASA's Systems Layout Branch) *The Spaceships of Ezekiel* (New York: Bantam Books, 1974).

2. "The Possibility of Intelligent Life Elsewhere in the Universe." Report prepared for the Committee on Science and Technology, U.S. House of Representatives, Ninety-Fourth Congress, U.S. Government Printing Office, Washington, D.C., 1975.

3. Wilson, David, *The New Archaeology* (New York: Alfred A. Knopf), pp. 22, 235, 255, et seq.

4. Roberts, Jane, *Seth Speaks* (Englewood Cliffs, N.J.: Prentice-Hall, 1972).

18

If I Were G.O.D.

Why shouldn't I, Adam asked himself? After all, Steffens had once played G.O.D., too. And as such, looking down on this little ball of clay, he had decided he must do something to help us all keep up with the changes He was making. And *that* He would do by creating a "political thunderstorm," one big enough to be noticed by all but not too big to be understood. He would fire down a thunderbolt that would destroy old ideas and principles and create a new light—like the romantic figure of Mussolini—that would illuminate all the nations of the world. (Mussolini? I thought he was a villain.)

Enough but not too little, Adam pondered—an important principle in the rearing of a species. Provide enough stimulus-input to stir us from our animal dormancy, from our powerful native inclination to squander our lives at playing in the sun, eating from trees, balling and boozing. Enough to excite us to purposeful action, there to realize the pleasure of a kind of thinking we seldom get to on our own unless we're prodded to it. But not so much stimulation as to overwhelm and confuse us, which could readily render us catatonically frozen through our inability to process it all meaningfully. Either of these extremes could easily be arranged through the media (from no news at all, to terrifying tales of man-eating monsters invading the earth from outer space). But is it? Apparently not—it all seems to be carefully balanced—just enough to keep us on our toes and moving, thinking, problem-solving, choosing, acting. Yes, T.H.E.Y. have managed somehow to achieve a regulated balance between the killing monotony of a stimulus-input underload on the one hand, and a mind-shattering overload on the other. Again, the carrot and the donkey—just enough to keep us on our toes, *moving* it, *thinking*, puzzle solving—waking us up from the big sleep of nonexistence. Or are they trying to torment us into the funny farm?

Such madness, he chided himself. The very idea that such exquisitely refined manipulation of social institutions could actually be conducted from some lofty economic aerie does sorely tax credulity to the utmost. And, yet, if you put yourself in that position, you can see that it really might not be all that difficult to do; it's all in the mind of the beholder—the beholder of the media. Just theorizing, of course, but if I had a few trillion dollars stashed away—or even if everyone in the world *believed* I had that much at my command—and I wanted to increase my capital and political control in the adjoining "nations" of Oz and Utopia, it would be a lead pipe cinch to run my little number on both of them. I would simply buy up the television networks, newspapers, magazines, and publishing houses in both countries and start playing my little games with the people's minds.

With this kind of backing I really could do with them anything I might choose. The elected presidents of these two poor but peaceful little nations are actually on my payroll, so naturally they do what I tell them to. If the people begin to complain too much about the policies I have given them to enforce, I use the media to explain why they are necessary. If this doesn't work I simply buy myself a reform leader, set up my obsolete incumbent for some scandalous activity that forces him out of office, one way or another, and replace him with my new presidential mouthpiece. He has the support of the Congress because most of them are also in my pocket—they don't cost that much and they are so corruptible! If one of them, or any other snoopy intellectual type, pokes in too deep and starts to put the picture together, I first give him a grant to continue his studies, and if that should fail, there are still plenty of other things I can do to keep him in line: I can put the heat on him for cheating on his income tax, frame him for giving government secrets to the enemy, or for some kind of bizarre sexual misconduct which the people have already been conditioned to believe—through a deviously inculcated body-guilt trip—is simply dreadful. Or I might start sending my private police around to drop in on him now and then—or have him done in, if necessary. The possibilities are numberless.

If I need to build my army, I flood the television and newspapers with stories of border skirmishes between Oz and Utopia, and if there are no real skirmishes going on there, I can hire the people to play the parts and a few good script writers to put the scenario together—although there are always enough hot-heads around to do it on their own. If inciting them to patriotism doesn't work, I cut down on the flow of money, which is being regulated by my National Currency Control Board (which they think is theirs), raise the pay and the fringe benefits for soldiers, and offer them free training for doing the kind of labor I will soon be needing as my plan progresses. This will be chiefly technical in nature and will include very little in the way of philosophy, history, economics and political science. Those departments are being handled at my universities, where my well-compensated "intellectuals" are busily conveying my policies to the upper-class students and writing speeches and position papers for my political puppets in high office.

I can do the same thing at the more local offices of my policing arm, again by reducing the amount of money circulating while jacking up retail prices, thus creating inflation-depression, "increasing" the crime rate (rape, drug abuse, violence in the streets—whatever is most popular) by playing it up big in the media, the way old Lincoln Steffens and his friends once created that ersatz "crime wave" in New York, while at the same time glorifying the role of a police officer through the same channels, and finally by lowering entrance requirements for these jobs, raising the pay, and supplying resplendent uniforms and any other ego-satisfying accouterments that might appeal to my personnel at this level of operations.

Legislation, and the enforcement of laws by police and judges can be controlled in much the same way. I find that it is seldom necessary to buy off these lesser functionaries directly; they can be had with little gifts of power, public esteem, and enough economic pressure to keep them busy on their off hours figuring out how to get enough money coming in to maintain their cherished status. A great inducement, money—great!

To simplify my operations, and to keep them secret, I also flood the media with a variety of attractive distractions, like well-timed and spectacular murders, kidnappings, riots, open conflicts between small but earnest special interest groups and plenty of entertainment—but all of them little morality tales in disguise. If the people won't study law and medicine and philosophy, I'll sugar-coat it for them in "L.A. Law", "St. Elsewhere" and "Gunsmoke."

I am also careful to maintain the appearance of an active and authentic opposition to the policies I am enforcing. Through the media I easily make the world look like a terrifying, dog-eat-dog jungle of ruthless competition. This will take care of the less educated classes, but the eggheads—the "free-thinking" TV-snobs, they're as easy or easier than the peasants. Their undoing I can easily accomplish by directing my top-drawer "intellectuals," now much respected by the people, to write articles and books which, though appearing to be very critical of my policies, are actually quite harmless because they are very long and tortuously worded, much too dull for the average scholar and also much too expensive in the form in which I have arranged to have them published. The average mind, I have learned from long experience, is easily controlled by simple slogans and fear tactics to which the newspapers and television channels are especially well adapted, but the brighter ones must be flattered into line with a show of respectful indulgence.

By these measures, I have now convinced the previously peaceful voters of Utopia and Oz that their two nations have sharply conflicting political ideologies, and that, for their own good and for the good of the world at large, one must defeat the other in warfare; and I then instruct my governmental officials and military leaders to commence the conflagration. The materials they use to fight this war are, of course, supplied to both sides by my factories and at the usual outrageous prices. The war itself costs me nothing because I have arranged to have it paid for through taxes levied against the citizens of both countries. The money needed by them to finance the war is also provided by me at a wholesome rate of interest. Then, in the course of the bloodletting, anything of value in the way of saleable commodities is passed on up to me by my agents. Peace is, at my convenience, reestablished by a reverse laundering of the public mind along with another, carefully engineered complex of distractions, economic pressures and just enough *petite* rewards to keep the people docile and in a hard-working, money-earning frame of mind.

After this, I simply keep repeating the operation clear around the world, timing all activities with the sure foreknowledge that the historical memory of the general populace is very short. Moreover, any accurate memories they might retain of past events are easily modified by adjusting the tone and the content of the books they are required to read in the schools they are compelled to attend. Through all of the media available to me, I keep reminding them of what a valiant job they have done in the past, and how well off they are in every way for having done it.

It is true that my system is not absolutely foolproof. There are little flaws here and there. My name and some of the upper level fronts for my operation are bandied about in hushed rumors from time to time, but I am so far removed from the earthly arena in which my players carry out their assigned roles, and so well protected from them by my carefully engineered and extremely complex organizational structure, that no serious opposition ever develops from the lower or middle (governmental) level of my operation.

My only serious problems are created by other groups who are as quick-witted, determined and well financed as I am. We are after the same thing, but even though we are in deadly competition with each other we are vigorously agreed that the people beneath us will never learn of it. Our long-range objectives are to own most or all of whatever property is available, and to exercise most or all of the power to control and regulate that which we can possibly get our hands on—and we are no longer thinking of this one little planet alone, but our plans for future extension of our progressive activities will be greatly assisted if our ordinary, earthbound minions are unified into a single-hardworking labor force that will continue to pass up the money we need to prosecute our humanitarian (?) goals.

Now, if you should ask me in a privileged conversation why I am doing this, the answer would be easy to give and reasonably truthful. I am doing it for the same reasons you are doing what you do: mostly because I was born to it and taught how the system works, and because I am a good person who sincerely believes in the rightness of doing the job that I have inherited from the people who are nearest and dearest to me. These are really the same reasons that you became a plumber, because you were born the son of a plumber and learned much about his trade while growing up within his sphere of influence, and because he recommended it to you as a good way of earning a living by helping other people solve plumbing problems that they are unable to solve themselves. And this is a good thing for a good person to do, is it not!

I do understand very well that you might resent the many deceptions I practice on you, that I control your life and move you and your people around like pieces on a chessboard. But this is necessary to the success of my operation, which in turn is necessary to your success and to that of all humankind. If I told you what I was doing, and how, it would be like telling my opponent on the other side of the chessboard what my next six moves are going to be, and obviously it would also put you in a position to prevent either of us from moving you around at all. If that happened, then my opponent across the board would probably win the game and he—and his purposes—are not quite as good as mine.

To be sure, we also understand and sympathize with your complaints that too much work is required of you, too little pleasure is returned. To this, with apologies, I would have to speak in technical terms—regrettably over your heads—about yourselves. I am not patronizing you! And to prove it, I'll say the words and leave them for you to decipher—if you will!

Repression engenders sublimation and creativity—sexually energized thoughts and actions but without loss of direct sexual pleasure in the total life span. There is, rather, an increase in it, because it has been stored, like interest-drawing money in the bank. And it has also been made spicier by clothing, complexity, fantasy, postponement, tantalization and exciting games. In short, my system does not penalize you—it pays you. Under it you do not lose life—you gain it.

And next you might complain that our operation might of necessity leave you maimed or dead. This is quite true—but only if you choose it! And, we also have our casualties. Our mid-level operatives who manage national governments are often subjected to extreme emotional stresses, and for the good of the system are commonly required to say and do things that gravely violate their own principles, because they do not really understand the necessity for this. Also, it is occasionally necessary to depose them and subject them to public disgrace, which is also as bad as execution for the person who is so vain and ambitious as to seek out—and sell out—for the moment of public glory that this position brings to him. But they will have *Secret Honor!*

At this level and even higher up we are also exposed to the dangers of political kidnapping, assassination, contrived public scandal—or worst of all, by some unanticipated and successful move by an opposition group.

True, it is a most disagreeable feeling to grow up believing that you are a free, self-determining and unique human being, only to realize later that you are actually but one of billions whose lives and destinies are being secretly arranged for you by powerful and all but invisible demagogues who *do* consider themselves superior to you and, therefore, quite properly your lawful masters. Although it may sound heartless to you, please consider the possibility that there may be some truth to their claims of superiority, and that the best thing you can do about it is just forget that this wild flight of fantasy ever entered your mind in the first place. Then you will be, in a sense, free to go about your life, working at fairly congenial tasks, and enjoying the loving company of your family and friends while working for that certain degree of status that will win for you their appreciation, admiration and approval.

Those, essentially, are the same things we are after in our own inner circle. When you consider the options it really isn't too bad a system. Without it, you would all be bald and ignorant apes grubbing about for food in the forests and over the plains, fighting constant battles with other marauding tribes, with no decent medicine to treat you when you fall ill or are injured. Of course, you might be injured or killed in one of our wars but under our system you stand a much better chance of living to a ripe old age than your ancestors ever had in their jungle habitat, *and*—you can do it more comfortably. You also have doctors to relieve you of pains when you are sick, teachers to provide you with information about the earth and the universe, about people, and how they work and organize themselves.

If you are a woman, it is no longer necessary to bear and rear many children and thus deprive yourself of an opportunity to live your own life. There are really a great number of advantages to the system, and if we could trust you to recognize this and to cooperate with it, within reasonable limits, then we might feel free to reveal more of ourselves and our operations to you. Of course, this would mean that we would have to loosen our control on you just a little, require somewhat less work of you and offer you a few more pleasures—and, perhaps to involve you in fewer wars.

At this very moment, in fact, we are seriously considering the possibility of acknowledging the fiction of "nations" and paying you somewhat more directly, as honest mercenaries, to accomplish certain economic tasks that really need to be done. We are also deliberating the possibility of according you those basic conditions you need to live out a life with reasonable comfort and dignity: the right to shoot off your mouth, practice your favorite superstitions, spread your thoughts around freely, defend your own life and the lives of the people who mean the most to you. To have your own little piece of territory and to be safe and secure within it, and to be treated fairly when you find yourself in conflict either with us or with your neighbor.

The other laws, however, are really of little or no concern to you, as they have to do with the management of money and power. Remember, there is nothing new in any of this. It has been going on ever since our species left its primitive roaming and food-foraging way of life and settled down to farming and building cities. With this the creation of "money" was both necessary and inevitable, and what you like to call the "corruption" of it is just as necessary and inevitable. Remember, it was one of your greatest teachers who told you: "Render unto Caesar that which is Caesar's . . . " and so on.

Adam frowned. The media plug that same theme constantly. The work ethic. Produce and create—as in work your ass off for peanuts! But we do live longer, and better, and everything added and subtracted we also have more fun and a profuser variety of experience.

Then, also on schedule, comes "Roots," the saga of an American family. During his manhood training, Kunta Kinte had been warned against exercising the stubborn but inevitably fatal courage of the wart hog. But he did it anyway, after his enslavement, and bravely endured the wart hog's fate. But his grandson, George, saw it clearer, resolving to look straight ahead—not back over his shoulder—and make it big where he happened to find himself. After all, he was the best cockfighter in the whole territory, and proud of it. It was also the way to money, and money buys freedom.

Money: the best rewarding CS of them all! And from it all came Alex Haley, a beige-colored American artist—an upperclass intellectual. Kunta Kinte and Chicken George and Tom and the rest of them all paved the way for him. It's a story about a process of refinement. Like the Lorne Greene (who played Kunta's bad white Massa) Alpo commercial right after the end of the last episode—ah, strange coincidence!—about sheep dogs! Their behavior is instinctual, he said— you can't breed it out of them! But you can, by mixing their alleles with other breeds—and you can also program it out of them. CS! CS! CS!

Getting there, he thought, but I haven't made it yet. The Rosetta Stone is still missing; something obvious—it's right under my nose but I'm missing it. I'm too far into a groove—better break up the log jam and see how they rearrange themselves as the river of thought moves them on. A few minutes of calculated, self-imposed insanity might do it. Maybe I should let myself go nuts on numerology for awhile, a la

Simon Moon! T.H.E.I.R. two big numbers are 5 and 23, and 2 + 3 = 5. The sum of the digits of 1976 = 23. During the Horta episode of "Star Trek," Kirk directed Dr. McCoy to join him on the *twenty-third* level. In the Fortran computer language the asterisk is a multiplication sign, so "M*A*S*H," which anagrams to "sham," yields a numerical product of 1976, our fabulous bicentennial year that's being so hilariously satirized and celebrated all over the media.

And then there's *The Education of H*Y*M*A*N K*A*P*L*A*N*, which multiplies out to 1,076, 275,200, probably a world population figure somewhere toward the end of the nineteenth century—should have been called *The Education of the Entire Human Species*. The jokers! Here's another asterisk clue title, that obscure movie, "S*P*Y*S," deliberately misspelled, with a product of 144,400. Curious figure. Possibly the 144,000 members of the twelve tribes of Israel plus a mysterious 400. Four hundred? *The* Four Hundred. High society. The upper crust. The Insiders? How very clever of them!

19

"23 Skidoo" and All That

And precisely what is the meaning of the ubiquitous number "23," ever associated with the *Illuminati*? It is without question the most often recurring number on prime time television, from floor levels to apartment numbers to the pasta-form "23" in the dead center of a Chef Boyardee alphabet soup commercial currently on national television. Mystery writer Elmore Leonard finally made it in his field after 23 novels. Richard Bach's *Seagull* was rejected by twenty-three publishers and then went on to sell twenty-three million copies. There are twenty-three nationally televised "Weight Watchers" menus, and twenty-three gratuitous heat wave deaths in *The Secret Files of J. Edgar Hoover*.

And there's always "23 skidoo," of course. What else? Out of 150 biblical Psalms, only one has ever had much publicity—the twenty-third: "The Lord is my shepherd, I shall not want . . . " He leads me, protects me . . . intriguing.[1] The pyramid, notorious Illuminati symbol, has five surfaces, if you include the base. The five-sided pentagram is their other biggie. Pentateuch. Pentagon. The five-circle symbol of the Olympiad. Does it mean that our whole planet is being run by only twenty-three of them? Or is ours their twenty-third captive planetary colony? Oh, garbage—garbage! What are you doing, Adam! You're going nowhere with this nonsense. Get back to logic.

1. Shea, Robert and Wilson, Robert Anton. *Illuminatus! The Eye in the Pyramid*, New York: Dell Publishing, 1975.

20

Profit In Poverty

Goldy, dozing lightly, and naked amid a pile of satin pillows on her chaise, roused partly awake when he entered the room, stretched and moaned luxuriously. "Hi, Adam. How ya makin' out?"

He flopped down beside her, idly stroking her arm with his finger tips. "Okay. But I have to ask you something. You were talking about me and my classy uptown friends earlier. If I had a big party with them, well—would you like to join us?"

She shook her head lazily. "Nope—'course not."

"Why?"

"I wouldn't have no fun listenin' to all their big words an' feelin' like a dummy all the time."

"You wouldn't feel—left out?"

"Nope, no more'n you would, if I didn't invite you over ta drink beer and play pinochle with me and some of my lady friends." She rolled over and embraced him, adding, "But that don't mean I don't love ya, Adam—just different strokes fer different folks, see?"

"I see, yes."

Moving against him she asked, her face lifted innocently to his: "Ya wanna screw around some, Adam? A blow-job or anything?"

He patted her appreciatively. "Don't tempt me, Goldy. But I don't want to interrupt my train of thought, such as it is."

"Then," she asked, her tone of voice unchanged, "how about some scrambled eggs and bacon?"

"That I can use," he thanked her.

While she put their breakfast together, he ran it out to her, in simplified form, his little allegory on how the world might be run if he were king. She heard him out patiently, smiling and nodding now and then, seeming to understand. Then she put their plates on the table and sat down beside him, her voice apologetic, almost beseeching:

"Guess maybe I don't know what you're sayin', Adam, but it sounds like well, so gloomy and down-in-the-mouth."

"How do you mean?"

"Well," she shrugged, frustrated by her own verbal inadequacy, "it's like my daddy used to say: if ya can't say nothin' good about nobody, then don't say nothin' at all."

Making a conscious effort to conceal his irritation, he replied, "Something good? About T.H.E.M.?"

She shrugged helplessly, acutely aware that if it came to an argument she would be instantly and overwhelmingly outclassed. "All I mean is, well, you 'n' me, we ain't got it so bad, ya know? We're both doin' okay, now ain't we?"

"Sure, Goldy—sure. You are and I am, but what about the other poor, suffering wretches in the world?" But then he abrupted himself with the reminder that Goldy was there to be listened to—not argued with. She did have a remarkably unique knack for asking him the questions he never seemed to ask himself.

She took his hesitation as an opportunity to polish off her point: "I mean—these people you're talkin' about. Maybe they ain't such bad guys after all. Maybe," she said wistfully, bracing herself against his possible counterattack. " . . . maybe they're even tryin' ta help us?"

Preposterous! But it was only an inward bellow of scorn. Outwardly he remained calm, and, once again back in his cell, he admonished himself to honor his own rule-of-the-house, which was to remember that Goldy could be more right than he. But trying to help us?—that was a bit thick! Why? And how? By robbing us blind? Pitting us against each other in mortal combat on the great battlefields of the world? Obviously not, Adam, but you're not giving Goldy her due—you're simply restating your own argument. But, *poor* Goldy and her wishful, child-like mind—she even hit me with that mawkish old chestnut about how nice it would be if somebody gave a war and no one went. Pathetic!

Trying to help us. Hmmmm. It's possible, I suppose, that the invisible managers are trying to goad us into a worldwide, pacifistic sit-down strike to prove that we have learned something about not fighting among ourselves. Or, to show us that we have the power to get for ourselves whatever we want, if only we would use that power. If . . . if we would actually put our outspoken desire for peace and freedom above our ancient, inborn lust for money, power, personal prevalence. They could be testing us, until we demonstrate—not merely in hollow words and happy slogans—but in our living behavior, that we have at last learned these lessons—learned them not only in our heads but deep inside our hearts and bowels.

Thirty thousand years—or longer. Yes—admit it. It is conceivable that they themselves learned these lessons long, long ago, but then realizing that we humans are far more animals of habit and passion than of thought and reason—whose primitive intellectualizations might never be enough to regulate our behaviors nonhypocritically—that we have indeed an astonishing genius for talking good while doing bad, and that . . . Yes . . . that we must therefore be operantly conditioned, like the pigeons in Dr. Skinner's laboratory, to *learn* what we must do in order to achieve the things we claim to desire. Peace. Integrity. Autonomy. Fraternal and sororal love without envy or jealousy.

Conditioned—yuck! Pacing restlessly from one end of the small room to the other, Adam bridled at the thought. Trying to help us! Dammit anyway, Goldy, you poor, gorgeous, innocent trusting retard—what did you have to come up with that one for, anyway? And that other silly little question she dropped on me about their leniency: "Gee whiz, Adam, if they're as all-fired strong as you say they are, how come they didn't take us over or blow us all away a long, long time ago?" Damn! Paradox of paradoxes. It was true—they could obviously destroy us—every last one of us—any old time they wanted to, but, instead they are merely playing chess with us. Or, Chinese checkers, or Russian roulette—depending on just exactly *who* they are.

But the poverty, and the wars—the wars! My own father and his friends—caught in the hideous throes of WW I—what horror! Only thing is, they didn't seem to think so. Mademoiselle from Armentiere, *parlez vous.* How you gonna keep him down on the farm—after he's seen Paree? We beat the Kaiser and the Hun. When Johnny comes marching home again, Hurrah! Hurrah! He joins the VFW and reaps veteran's benefits. And the same with you and your friends, Adam. You were bored with college and couldn't wait to get into the next and newest War to End All Wars. Punky, bragging, breast-beating, smart-ass kid looking for a chance to be spiffed-up hero and world adventurer.

It was really hell, now wasn't it? Well, no, not exactly—not for me. The pissers wouldn't even let me get into the fighting. Just one damn radar engineering school after another, then a short stint on the Marine Corps newspaper down there at good old Cherry Point, North Carolina. My God, I tried three different times to get into ninety-day-wonder school so I could go charging up those southern Pacific beachheads and cover myself with glory. Or with my own blood and bowels, more likely.

All right, he grudgingly admitted, it was a good thing. Gave me time to get my head together—get on my own. A chance to get away from home and be totally cared for while appearing heroically independent. And when I got back from it I was burning to get on with my medical training, with all that electronic engineering training they inflicted on me in the Corps giving me a head start in math and physics, dammit! And then there was the GI Bill to pay me all the way through—clear through internship!

Fine! For you, my friend, and the other lucky ones who made it back from the battlefields of Detroit, Chicago and Corpus Christi. But what of those countless thousands who didn't come back? The dead and the maimed? And what of Korea, just a few years later—and then that ghastly debacle in Vietnam? By then, of course, the patriotic fervor of the young was far less than it had been, and a new breed of American youth decided to reject their Uncle's greetings and just not go to war. And they didn't, many of them. Instead they burned their draft cards, resisted and fled to foreign countries, and looking back we see that they were punished far less for their mini-treason than were the ones who were wounded or killed in battle? Survival of the fittest? or you get what you ask for?—as in "seek and ye shall find."

Yes, he went on, most of our pain is self-chosen. We may move toward something or away from it—make ourselves captive or free. After all, legal provisions do exist for us to defend our civil rights but we must learn how to use them—and then do it, or otherwise it looks as if we are saying—or rather demonstrating by our inactivity—that we do not really want them. And the same principle applies to consumerism. After all, there is not one single thing out there that we have to buy if we really don't want to, which makes it very pointless to complain about prices.

It also makes it futile to bitch against the huge income tax and social security ripoffs, because it's easy enough to defeat those by simply having no income, which one could do with a couple of acres of land and a simpler way of life, aided and abetted by existing public welfare funds. And all of this, I suppose, could be interpreted as an effort on T.H.E.I.R. part to teach us how to live for ourselves, by ourselves, without money, while at the same time giving us the option to go the money route if we choose to.

Can I deny it? Inflation or not, we now have actually more goods and more choices, more different ways to go, than we have ever had in history. It's almost as if those invisible masters or teachers, whichever they are, are forcing us to solve problems, to think, and to make active decisions to determine the course of our own lives. Could it be true?

He interrupted that line of thinking and commenced admonishing himself for this acute and uncharacteristic bout of optimism. What about the evils of poverty? "The poor, they are always with us . . . " True, true. And yet, the presumptions we make about the poor can be as bizarre and wide of the mark as those we make about the wealthy. That's one important difference, Adam, between you and your toney intellectual liberal friends. They generate their pity and their indignation for the poor from afar, from the remote comfort of their lavish pads, whereas you work with these good people daily and pity them not at all—no more than they envy you your paltry prosperity and petite prestige. Now why is that? Because, essentially, even though you lik: them and they like you, the two of you really don't want to swap places with one another. You were born in different places, grew in different ways, and are going in different directions all in your own unique ways. How would you, Adam—or anyone else—look and feel in the clothing of someone half his size or twice his size? It's all a question of fit.

There is surely no person more miserable than the one who finds himself in a job for which he is not qualified. Adam well knew that there are a dozen or more occupations well-designed to make his life miserable, were he foolish enough to occupy them: insurance actuary, auto mechanic, supermarket cashier, computer programmer, and so on. But one job he could certainly handle with comfortable aplomb is the Presidency of the United States of America. In that job there is really not much to do but mouth a string of meaningless platitudes during State of the Nation addresses and at "crisis time," while keeping your own political party in line with casual promises and blatant intimidation. What could be easier? Having a professional actor as President is perfect—it's about all the job really calls for.

National leaders function pretty much as office managers, he decided. They are not responsible for starting major wars, moving national boundaries, or selling off international canals. Moreover, one cannot start a war without enormous sums of money, and bankrupt nations can procure such sums only by borrowing. And from whom do they borrow that money? And if they succeed in it, who will call the shots? The bankroller, of course.

Goldy aroused drowsy but smiling from a light sleep as Adam eased himself down gently at her side. "Oh, Hi, Adam. You ready for a little break?"

"Not exactly, Goldy," he said softly. "My thinking is flowing well but I have a problem. I'm into some fairly heavy material on the psychology of economics—wealth and poverty—dull stuff, y'know? Which means I'm running a serious risk of boring my readers. It's time to run in a little more sex to perk them up again—catch their attention. It's an old Illuminati trick I learned in the Marine Corps."

"Is there anythin' I can do t'help?" she sighed cozily, curling up to him with a wiggle.

He slid his hand slowly over one of her breasts and trailed it down over her firm, flat belly. "Let me ask you some questions about what it's like to grow up poor. Now, tell me. What was it like—being so dirt poor all of those years growing up on the farm?"

"Fine. At the time, I mean. Y'see, I didn't really know we was poor. I jus' thought everyone went t'bed hungry at night—an' slep' cold and everythin'."

"Were you happy then, would you say?"

"Oh, sure. We had lotsa fun. Well, guess I wasn't en-tarly happy, else I would a stayed there m'whole life. When I got older, I seen that people with more money got t'eat reg'lar, and they had nice clothes and cars an' things, so that's when I decide to move up here to the city and make me some money."

"So, John Wayne is right after all—everything does turn out for the best."

"Oh, sure, Adam—I known that for a long time."

He then pressed her with one last question: "Goldy, back when you were real poor and struggling to get established here in the city, how'd you have felt if someone had just handed you ten thousand dollars, free, with no strings attached?"

She smiled at the thought. "Tickled pink, that's how."

"Would it have helped you, do you think?"

"Oh—that. I dunno, Adam. My daddy used ta say, a fool and his money are soon parted. That's me, all right. I was shootin' smack at the time, an' drinkin' too much . . . if I'd a had that kinda money I'd a blown it in a week or two 'n' prob'ly killed myself doin' it. No, it was better fer me t'make it on my own—it seemed rough at the time, but it was—y'know—kind of a adventure."

"Thanks, Goldy—you've been a big help."

She immediately slipped off into a contented sleep as he returned thoughtfully to his cloister.

All right, we bleeding heart liberals don't really know a damn thing about poverty, but Goldy—who was there—she understands. So did good old Lincoln Steffens and his rich friends—they came to understand it in time—even though they themselves weren't poor. Like Joseph Fels, Linc's millionaire friend from Philadelphia, who once came to him with a real psychophilosophical poser: Is it possible to give free money to individuals or worthy causes without injuring said persons or causes? Unable to come up with a satisfactory answer they had joined forces with a few worldly-wise friends and tested the question empirically, in the field, and finally concluded that one of the best ways to stop a creative person cold—or to abort a worthy cause—was to lay a lot of free money on them.

It had been the same with department store magnate Edward A. Filene of Boston, who tried every way he could think of to persuade his employees to take his store away from him and run it themselves, for their own greater profit. He failed in this, finding them interested only in a few more pennies on their paychecks and another extra half holiday every now and then. They just didn't want to be tycoons or—to put it another way—they were actually quite satisfied with their sweatshop slavery—their *relative* poverty.

So that could be the moral of that story; we all plateau at whatever level of activity is most suited to our desires and capabilities—or, because we're innately lazy and inertive—perhaps a level or two below that. A reversal on the Peter Principle. We go where we want to go, do what we want to do, and there's no use trying to deny it; there sure is plenty to do out there—choices and chances all over the place.

Like the poor people I work with out in the desert boonies. They complain a lot about having too little money, just as I do—as most everyone does—but offered a chance to make an easy extra buck or two—what happens, time and time again? A sheepish smile and a bashful confession: "Aw, that's okay—I guess I'm doin' okay as I am." All they really want from me is a little respectful friendliness, a renewal on their prescriptions, and a letter to support their application for a Social Security supplement or disability income or unemployment compensation or veterans' benefits.

It had taken him almost three years, in fact, to finally learn that poverty, in itself, was not a cause of mental illness, and that out-of-hand gifts of money were not a cure for either poverty or mental illness. The realization had helped relieve his depression. That, and recognizing at last that most of the people in these poor little communities were actually quite happy, quite content with their lives. The few who weren't moved on, and up, to other things, or down—and a few even went out.

The poor, they are always with us. The rich, also. And the several strata of the middle class—but all of them in flux. The comprehensive pattern from one generation to the next, he had to admit, was unmistakably from relative poverty to relative affluence. Was Kunta Kinte really unhappy on that southern plantation, or was he, too, doing what he wanted to do? And the same question for Chicken George and his son, Tom, Alex Haley and Adam Trasy Solon? With too much money and ease we grow proud, insufferably arrogant, complacent, and we have a mighty tendency to go native—to seed. As noted neighborhood organizer Sol Alinsky once remarked, "Poor people are fine, until they get a little money in their pockets—then they turn into real shits like everyone else."

Just like the happy savages: eat, drink and screw. Hardships spur us, and war—and most of those we make for ourselves anyway.

Hungry mice run faster. What was it a famous friend of his had once said? "The more kids I have the deeper in debt I go, and the harder I have to work—which is the best thing possible for me." Yes, most of us do indeed owe our soul to the company store and spend our lives working to pay it all off. Idle hands make mischief—that's what Goldy's daddy would say. Make work for the devil. John Henry was a steel-drivin' man. Sixteen tons and what have I got?

Pleasure in poverty and misery in wealth: paradox, oh paradox! And just where is all this taking you, Adam, in your heroic quest for the unscrupulous Illuminati? Who are T.H.E.Y., anyway, those phantom demi-gods who own the company store of the world, and to whom we owe our money and our souls? Who, and where, and how—and, *why*? Where are the clues to the puzzle, and what is the puzzle itself?

Frig it, he sighed, then chanted quietly to himself: "Adam, this is stupid stuff—you swill your liquor fast enough. . . . "

And, who, precisely, is John Galt?

"Those are very ominous clouds on the horizon, Jasmyn. Let's get back."

"We should anyway," she agreed, turning their sloop into a beam reach and heading for shore.

"By the way, your favorite Earthie did quite well on the Playing God maneuver. He's also doing surprisingly well on the Money and the Media, I must say."

"He'll make it," she observed calmly.

Sandol laughed. "Not a chance. He'll never shake the paranoia—they never do."

Her confidence was intact. "He will. He's loose as the proverbial goose. Anyway, I still reserve my entitlement to one clue—when the time is right."

Sandol shook his head. "He hasn't a prayer. You can go ahead and give him the whole story if you like—he'd never buy it."

"He's much brighter than you think. We shall see."

"Where do we dine tonight?" Sandol asked, changing abruptly from his least favorite subject. "Palm Springs, Paris or Hong Kong?"

"I'll have dinner in San Francisco—you back home. I need a holiday from you, Sandol. Your jealousy is polluting my space."

Sandol was jarred. After a long, tense pause he answered her. "I thought I was improving."

"Not notably. You go home this evening and come back next week—Earth Time. It will do us both good."

"You're planning to visit him again?"

"See what I mean? My plans in that regard are not your concern. You really must try harder."

21

Tyranny of Instincts

And all along, Adam suddenly realized, he had been waiting for *it*; it—the sound of a brain-splitting shot, or a high-powered plastic explosive lofted through his window. T.H.E.Y. knew where he was— he had no doubt of that. And now there he was, deliberately endangering Goldy—poor Goldy and her not-so-innocent customers. He was certain T.H.E.Y. would get him sooner or later, and wouldn't that be exactly their style—to wait until he was right on the brink of his great discovery and then douse his lights? But so far there was no gunshot, no bomb bursting in air. It was something else.

His arrant ruminations were suddenly interrupted by the ugly sounds of a dog-fight on the sidewalk outside his window. Parting the shade, he saw a big German Shepherd and a Black Labrador—also huge—pawing the air, circling and tearing at each others' throats with slashing white fangs. Then one of the peace-loving onlookers, a young man in a business suit, foolishly stepped forward and tried to draw them apart, but with predictable results. Shouting with pain and fear, he leaped back, his hand gushing blood.

"You poor simpleton," Adam murmured to himself. "Your interference was sadly misguided. Those creatures were born to fight—and they're paired off perfectly—just like a good marriage, or Fred and Ginger waltzing. Stop them from doing what comes naturally and you'll just have a couple of miserably depressed and frustrated psychiatric canine basket cases on your hands. They'd rather die fighting than be deprived of the right to fulfill their biological destiny. Like those game little quarter horses, who become pathetically neurotic if they're not given the chance, now and then, to dart around an open prairie cutting cattle from the herd. The same for fighting cocks, sheep dogs—for all of us. It's a need—a desperately powerful need—being met in the open by two mutually consenting and evenly matched, driven and lusting gladiators.

The impromptu little spectacle was opportunely relevant, he would realize later, as was the turning on of the signal light over his door a short time after the dog-fight ended. Goldy's first customer of the day was a robust, good-looking gentleman in his early forties. He looked familiar—with a face that appeared in the newspaper from time to time. A councilman, perhaps, or a state representative. No matter. He was serving well and being even better served. In silent admiration, Adam watched Goldy perform her ancient art. Yes, an artist at her trade; made for it, devoted to it, loving it—and a master at it. A poor, uneducated girl from a red-clay dirt farm in central Georgia. Her father a sharecropper, she had gone to bed hungry most of the nights of her childhood. But now, just a few years later, she was a prosperous working girl.

As her financial adviser, Adam knew that she had more than enough in the bank to start a beauty salon, a classy and profitable restaurant— in fact there were many ways she could go now to spare herself the degradation of whoredom. But she didn't want to be spared, because she didn't feel at all degraded and she was getting wealthier every day doing a job of work she loved to do. And you, Adam, if you can be honest with yourself for a minute, isn't it just about the same with you—for all of us—in spite of all our carping and moaning and bitching about how bad everything is?

Yes, just as Big Money was—somehow—the essential instrument in the regulation of large populations, so was self-instruction the key to learning by the individual. There simply was no way to "teach" those snarling brutes beyond his window to behave like sweet little lap dogs. If they lived long enough, and suffered enough painful battlescars in mortal combat, they might in time decide upon a more peaceful lifestyle. But they would surely have to reach that conclusion on their

own, in their own way and in their own good time. No one could teach
it to them, except possibly by some cruel conditioning "behavior
modification" technique that could be as bad or worse than the battle
wounds themselves. And even if successful in training them to modify
their behavior, the intrapsychic damage worked by such a technique,
however invisible, would surely be far worse for them than mere
physical pain—or even death.

We human students are essentially the same, he well realized, again
pacing the floor and now quite oblivious to Goldy's lusty lurchings and
guttural outcries. We can learn, but we cannot be taught. We need
heroes and villains; skyscrapers, temples and pageantry. We need
excitement and entertainment—we need to be told stories. Jesus knew
that, which is why he couched his moral principles in parables—so that
they would be attended to, understood and remembered. Abstractions
mean very little to most of us; only real experience, or something very
close to it—like gripping drama—can really grab us where we live.

With an amused little smile he recalled one of his last "teaching"
sessions with Telman Durst, before the latter completed his training,
"grew up," and became a full-fledged psychiatrist by official decree of
the American Board of Psychiatry and Neurology. To be sure, Telman
had been a reasonably bright and knowledgeable resident, though
greatly given to chronic pontification. Not only did he pontificate,
Adam thought, but he did it so nasally, and still does. Perhaps some
Benadryl would help, or a nasal inhaler.

"You see, Dr. Solon," young Dr. Durst had droned on, "Harlow's
work with the rhesus at Wisconsin demonstrates convincingly that the
primate mother who has herself been deprived of an adequate
mothering experience is unable to present normally to a male, for
copulation, when she comes of age. But, if she is locked in a rape rack
and forced into pregnancy and motherhood, she subsequently proves
to be a cruel and grossly inadequate mother herself."

Adam had nodded indulgently. "Very interesting. But do satisfy my
curiosity, will you? Where did you get that information—what was
your source?"

Telman had been surprised, caught off-guard. "Oh, I can't say
exactly—some ethology journal I imagine. I could locate the reference
for you if you like?"

"Oh, no, not necessary—thank you all the same."

Adam was flabbergasted, even though it had happened a thousand
times before in his twenty years of teaching. He himself had given that

information to Telman during a supervisory session just three days before, and it had taken his student no longer than that to totally repress all awareness of where he had learned it, and from whom.

Yes, it is vitally necessary that we somehow manage to convince ourselves that no one has ever taught us a single thing—we did it all by ourselves. At that time, he now recalled, he had looked at his reflection in the glass door opposite his desk and shaken his head. "Give it up, you stupid fool! If you were a professor of surgery you could teach the trade okay—where and when to cut, and how to tie knots and reperitonealize and bend broken bones back into shape, but you might as well try to push a wagon uphill by its rope as to tell a Dr. Telman Durst the difference between mental health and mental illness, or to help him discriminate between better and worse behavior. It's hopeless—even when they come to you begging for a viewpoint, it's hopeless."

And yet, he admitted, pure self-education is a very chancey thing. Even those super bright kids back in Ann Arbor, the sons and daughters of professors, had once admitted to him that they could not trust themselves to a completely open schooling arrangement—with labs and books and teachers available to them but assignments not given and attendance not required. They still needed a supportive structure to urge them on—assignments and periodic examinations to goose them along. And they were just about the brightest, most self-actuating kids in the world.

Yes, it's true. We *sapiens* are intrinsically lazy animals, greatly subject to vegetative inertia. We need motivation without coercion—inspiration without tyranny—something like programmed self-instruction with suitable rewards for progressing, and no punishments for dropping out at our own optimum level that each of us chooses for himself. Yes, something like that.

We humans—our convictions and beliefs are as dear to us as our very selves—they are our very selves, and, once formed, they set like concrete. A good teacher soon learns that it is impossible to impart beliefs to students. No, he could only offer them a *choice* of beliefs and then disappear from the scene, leaving them to determine their own— their very own—directions. A few years earlier, he had enjoyed the honor and pleasure of working on that one during the first of his five colectureships with a most exciting and statured lady. Yes, he recalled he had just finished his lecture at a major symposium in New York, on the pitfalls of the psychosomatic concept in general medical practice, and as he was gathering up his notes from the podium, he saw a familiar figure barreling down the aisle toward him. Rotund, hair crimped, flashing intelligence and energy—Margaret Mead herself.

"Dr. Solon—you must be careful what you say to these doctors. Some of them have never even heard of the psyche!"

"I know that, Dr. Mead, but they do have a long medical tradition behind them. They can know it's there and deal with it without knowing its name."

"But, it is *very* important to tell it to people *both* ways. In the early forties I told young mothers it was a good thing for them to nurse their babies. A few years later I found I had to tell them it was fine *not* to nurse their babies. When you become a public authority it is imperative that you offer people a choice, or many of them will become very upset."

Adam nodded. She was right, of course. (And he was glad of that—he knew better than to argue with her as there was simply no way to win.) People must be given the opportunity to believe whatever they need to believe—until such a day as dispassionate reason should prevail *in the Weishaupt way.*

He stopped in his tracks and shook his head, wondering where that odd phrase had come from—far out in left field? That was Goldy's idea, not his . . . and his mind trailed off to a blank.

22

America-A Planned Area Development

Dropping crosslegged to the floor once more, he began to pore rapidly through a small stack of American history texts, skipping by subject index from one to another, checking occasional bits of information against the *Britannica*—and most especially against the Lincoln Steffens interpretation of people and events. The great journalist had been there, after all—right in the middle of American history—equidistant between the Founding Fathers and Adam Trasy Solon—for a half-century of inquiry, observation, interrogation and investigation. And of *thinking*—my God, what a relentless questioner of events, and uncanny analyst of people! A student of history and front-row participant in it.

Strange, he thought—our sense of time. Steffens was as close to Washington and Madison as we today are to Woodrow Wilson and Franklin D. Roosevelt. And yet in our books, and in those "Bicentennial Minutes" on the tube (sponsored by the big corporations, of course) it's all made to seem so ancient—but it wasn't really that long ago. Only yesterday. And look what's happened in those few short years— millions of acres of wilderness transformed into a wealthy nation of cities and industry and universities and . . . and . . . we think we did it all by ourselves. Motley bands of ruffians, convicts, obnoxious religious zealots, soldiers of fortune, slaves, bondsmaidens and whores—almost as if handpicked to be perfect for the job that was here to be done. And with money leading the way, trailing tantalizingly ahead of us like the carrot on the stick dangling always just out of reach in front of the hungry donkey's flaring nostrils, bringing him on, inspiring him to move it! Move it! Move it!

An eerie and at that point quite unacceptable—even bizarre—notion crept insistently into his mind. The American adventure a *real estate development*? Not packs of chattering, semi-intelligent apes rampaging across a wilderness land at all, but moving very purposefully and according to plan—not their own—but another that had been elaborately drawn up and secretly laid out for them to fulfill—though unbeknownst to them? Repugnant thought! He laughed at himself, suddenly crying out to the blank wall—"We did it all ourselves, my ancestors and I! We had no help from you!"

Duped, euchered—even subtly coerced into doing a supremely dirty job of work for those invisible, string-pulling puppeteers so far above and behind the proscenium of the world stage? Old William said it, now didn't he? All the world's a stage, and we're all actors on it. A figure of speech, or so it is taught—a fanciful metaphor. But if literally true (Mr. Shakespeare did, after all, have quite a broad grasp of people and things, much as Mr. Steffens had, in his rather different way), just what would it mean? If not a rigged game of sorts—a staged drama?

Adam found himself fretfully stuck on "coerced." Pure anathema to the liberty-loving, resolutely self-determining American stalwart. He resisted the implication of it, and, leafing quickly through the familiar terrain of the Steffens autobiography, found vindication for himself. A choice had indeed been given us—as a people—according to the Steffens view of it. The influential and much-loved Thomas Jefferson had staunchly espoused a true democracy, a nation of small and independent freeholds, predominantly agricultural and free of the much advertised horrors of the European Industrial Revolution. And in the other corner, weighing in with about the same muscle and clout, was the aristocratic Alexander Hamilton (with Father George, by the way, close at his side) coming on strong for oligarchic government with heavy federalization of powers and, in essence, rule by the well-monied and educated "upper class." That had been our choice, and we made it, ultimately, for Hamilton; industrialization, money—and government by the few.

That silly legend about Washington having been replaced by an imposter, Adam Weishaupt, founder of the Bavarian chapter of the infamous *Illuminati*—yes, silly. But a clue? A clue to a set-up of some sort—that hidden blue-print that keeps coming to mind? Oh, damn, damn, he moaned, and fell from there to ruminating loosely on what he was rapidly coming to think of as the mythology of the great American Revolution, and of American and other history in general. Not such an heretical notion at that, he consoled himself, as Mr. Steffens himself, in the course of his historical researches in the best universities of Europe, had quickly concluded that History was "crying out to be rewritten." To be sure, our own published history is a downright comical dramatization of what a little tampering in the beginning can do to modulate the convictions and the national self-image of the generations following.

In 1775 the people of Virginia were trying to negotiate a peaceful settlement with England when young Patrick Henry (an undercover agent of the Enlightened Ones?) leaped to his feet and cried out his famous speech about preferring death to enslavement, when in fact the only slaves around were the black people out in the fields, and even they were better off than they had been, starving to death and stagnating in their native Africa.

And then, less than a month later, at the celebrated battle of Lexington-Concord, out of the 77 volunteer Minute Men (Yes, they were all there of their own free choice) who faced the British force of some 700 troops, eight were killed and ten wounded—with the British suffering about twice that number of casualties. Final score, all told for both sides: fewer than twenty dead and twenty wounded—valiant men all—like the powerful and courageous canine gladiators who had so recently settled their differences, in their own instinctual and God-given way just outside his window. Like Kunta Kinte, the brave Mandingo warrior. The thought passed through his mind that more men had died in the American boxing ring than met their glory in that fabulously publicized opening battle of the great American Revolution. Hell, he grumbled, the only reason *that* shot was heard 'round the world was because of the tremendous amplification it got from the press and the elementary history texts.

Then take the famous battle of Ticonderoga, he hastened on. It turned out to be little more than a personal contest between an ambitious young Benedict Arnold (foul traitor, he!) and the outlaw roughneck, Ethan Allen, neither of whom were acting on the authority of the Continental Congress. This is war?

And then there was the colorful old General "Mad Anthony" Wayne, so named because of the orders he gave his troops prior to the Battle of Stony Point: unloaded muskets, with bayonets fixed, were to be shouldered, but no shots fired—under pain of death at the hands of the nearest officer—and the fort was to be taken by a shouting bluff only. Good Lord, Adam agreed disdainfully, small wonder they called him "Mad"—what a bloody dull way to fight a war—I can see better stuff than that on television, or in the local movie house, any time I want to. Splendid catharsis for us instinctual killers! Yes, another searing moral question of our time. Too much violence on the tube? Too much sex in the movies? Don't worry about it—maybe the dose is exactly right—ever think of that? could be that T.H.E.Y. know our emotional nutritional needs very well indeed—better than we do?— and T.H.E.Y. blend the stimuli they feed us as a good chemist titrates his reagents, or a good horticulturist his plants—perhaps there is no overdose, nor underdose, or anything. There it is again, he thought: are we being cultivated?

That great Revolutionary naval hero, the redoubtable John Paul Jones, was much better suited to the role than was old "Mad Anthony." Earlier in his career he had served as first officer aboard a slave ship, and was once charged with murder for having had a crewman whipped to death for laziness, and after that he fled to a commission in the new Continental navy to avoid yet another murder charge. When the Revolutionary War was over he signed on as an admiral in the Russian navy, where his skillful victories over the Turks went largely unrecognized by the rest of the world, poor chap!

Are these things really wars, he suddenly wondered, or oversized dormitory panty-raids blown up by the media into something they really never were? Extra! Read all about it. Joe Doaks gets a speck in his eye! Remember the Maine! Remember the Alamo! Fifty-four forty or fight! War declared! That's the principle, all right—it's automatically news if it's in the newspaper. And thus was a routine waterfront brawl converted into the historical "Boston Massacre," and a negligible adolescent prank into the momentous "Boston Tea Party."

And thus, also, was an engaging and useful presidential aspirant made into a national hero—by having him lead his horseless "Rough Riders" into a colorful but utterly contrived "war" that existed only in the newspapers and the mind of The People—"Remember the Maine"; a war that the good Lincoln Steffens, for wise reasons of his own, acknowledges only by omission. He talked with Teddy at the alleged battlefront but only of politics, and there is not the least mention of cannon fire, bloody battles, uphill charges or casualties of any sort—not a word!

T.R.'s well-publicized little "war" was a trumped-up lark, a game of footsie with famous war correspondents and of skylarking in the Caribbean sun with his old college chums—all of it paving the way to the governorship of New York and then later to the presidency. F.D.R., then Undersecretary of the Navy, sent our fleet against Manila without a by-your-leave from anyone (anyone known to us, that is) and it was taken without bloodshed. And Guam fell to a single shot from one of our naval vessels, fired across the bow of a Spanish warship—whose commander thought it was a friendly salutation because no one had told him his country was at war and he was not even armed to fire back! Some fantastic war, Adam thought wryly— the seas were really churning red—ha!

Truly, an event is as little or as big as the media makes it. A little tremor along the San Andreas fault breaks a few windows, starts a couple of small local fires and topples a few old privvies. Properly covered in the tabloids it becomes the great San Francisco earthquake. Same for Mrs. O'Leary's fabled cow and the equally fabled Chicago fire. The Johnstown Flood. All those terrible wars. Hiroshima and Nagasaki. It all kind of makes a fellow wonder about those other biggies, too: Charles Manson (Oh, Son of Man!). The Kennedy assassinations. Watergate (a dumb scenario in my humble opinion, he thought impatiently). Patricia Hearst and the rest of them. And now religious brainwashing and deprogramming. International Terrorism. The revolution that wasn't? Think back, Adam.

The January 7, 1976 special bicentennial television program on the American Revolution celebrated the historic heroism of our ancestors beautifully, with a few admirable distractions thrown in. The on-location announcer in Boston did his dramatic speech amid present-day Bostonians, bustling, prosperous and happy. He also dramatically described the first encounter between the Minutemen and the Redcoats as the camera panned along the footpaths they marched. A few shots were fired, a few brave men fell, and the battle was over. As battles go—in movies like "D-Day" and "Bataan"—it didn't sound like much of a battle, despite all the publicity it's received in the past. So, now T.H.E.Y.'re letting it be known: it was all a great big beautiful phony charade?

And our great Civil War—same thing. The story on that is clear enough from any of those movies about it—where the big wars really happen—like *Gone With the Wind* and *Roots*. A formula scene: Someone announces that the big fiasco has begun and all the young firebrands go romantically ape-shit—up the wall with excitement and bloodlust. "We'll whup them Yanks!" "Gonna go down there and shoot me some Rebs!" And a few of them were undoubtedly killed—the ones who insisted on it—like Scarlett O'Hara's heroic young husband. A bunch of brave Yankee yahoos and courageous Confederate rednecks doing their instinctual number on each other.

"Thou shalt not kill!" Interesting book, the *Holy Bible*. It presents both sides of every moral dilemma, leaving us perfectly free to pick and choose—to take from it whatever we might need. At times it seems to get a little silly, like "He who lives by the sword shall die by the sword." That isn't a threat—it's a statement of the obvious. A sensible promise. If you like to fight you can always find someone else who also likes to fight—like those snarling dogs out on the sidewalk or the battling gamecocks in *Roots*. Like the Civil War.

But the bulk of it was pure pageantry, with the Illuminati directing the generals to lead their armies in opposite directions and ten miles apart from each other, while giving banner headlines to every little pasture brawl that the troops themselves insisted on having. A bunch of pitiful countryside ruckeses—the real war took place in the newspapers, history books, novels and movies!

Yes, he sighed, fighting dogs must fight. In his comical and *most* revealing social experiment with radical Reds and cops in New York, Steffens demonstrated how gladiators find their way into the arena, how masochists connect with sadists, and how the rapist and his victim tacitly conspire to fulfill their shared destiny—as in a precision waltz! He simply instructed the police not to attack the insulting soap-box orators, and as the peaceful day ended the wild-eyed Reds cursed him furiously for sparing them from the violence and spoiling their fun.[1]

Jesus! he thought, we really are surrounded by spectaculars. It's a continuous 183-ring circus, provided by malefactors or benefactors unknown. We never have learned who supplied the pure heroin that killed Janis Joplin and Jimi Hendrix, and yet the death of these two great artists lent a certain credibility to the administration's claim that drug abuse was its number one problem. Paranoid? Possibly, but it is strange that any retailer in today's highly competitive underground drug market would peddle the pure stuff, unadvertised as such, at the regular street price. The moral of the story: if you are famous and loved by many, know your supplier very, very well. Or, are Jimi and Janis—having done their job to a "T"—now living and well in Argentina? Or elsewhere in the galaxy?

As his private and rather hellish little mental marathon lurched spastically onward, his left cerebrum grappled relentlessly with the Great Puzzle at hand while his right one, simultaneously, passionately and devoutly bitched and berated the Gods for their sadistically inhumane treatment of his suffering clay. There must be an easier way to write, he groaned silently.

Why not? I suppose a lot of our music and novels and such are composed by the computer. To that Big Electronic Wizard in the Sky, all music and language would be dispassionately regarded and systematically dealt with like any other pattern of chorded cliches and coherent numerical sequences. A story plot is a formula, and "formula" is a mathematical notation. It really wouldn't be that hard to do. But I do know that this expose book on the Illuminati isn't being written by a computer, though I'm sure it could be. So why don't they just print it out and save me all this sweating? I know, I know—we have to learn it ourselves—thank you, Mr. Buddha, and thank you, Roc Gonman.

Drawing another momentary blank, he parted the drapes a few inches and looked down the darkened street. A theater marquee winked out but the image remained in his mind. Dustin Hoffman in "All the President's Men." The Watergate fiasco—and we're supposed to believe that the president of the United States—anyone for that matter—would really be dumb enough to record his crimes on tape and then forget to erase them before . . . what crap! Street theater, pure and simple.

Dustin? Not only a household word but a unique one. Probably the only Dustin in the whole world, except for the myriad boy children who've been named after him since he became a star. Why Dustin? Could be an anagram. In-stud. Studin. Indust. Damn!—*nudist!* In German, Hoffman would mean a man in his own courtyard—a nudist in his own territory. So, with thousands of little namesakes running around we'll have the name uttered millions of times a day to a large population, feeding a string of symbols into the unconscious mind of the masses where it is automatically unscrambled and recombined in every possible way. A new generation—household nudists all!

He sat down abruptly, took pencil and pad in hand and began to play with words and letters. We live in a sea of symbols—mostly visual and auditory—and most of them impinging on our senses through the media. Millions of bits of information a day from the newspaper, the tube, magazines, movies, street signs—all artifically generated. A program of some kind—could be.

Heston. There's only one Heston I've ever heard of—another household word. Teshon. Onhest. *Honest!* An honest charlatan! Very appropriate—playing all those Biblical roles he does so well.

Next he jotted down S-i-g-m-u-n-d F-r-e-u-d and immediately spotted the "guru." Staring at the combination intently he found himself forming it into syllables. Sig-mund-freud. Jesus! Literal translation: *sig*-victory, *mund*-mouth, *freud*-joy or pleasure. "Victory for Mouth Pleasure!" Perfect, for the one man who did the most to soften the Western mind toward the oral "perversions" and make them respectable again. Adam scratched his head. Damn. The problem is, how did his mother know what to name him? Figure that one out, my friend (And he would, a few days later.)

Big, oft-advertised and unique names. Movie stars and political heroes and villains. Try our friendly visitor from a small planet, Gore Vidal. Literal translation is *vital blood*, with a pure unmixed anagram to *ergo valid*. Not bad for an engaging chap who publicly admits that he might become something of a messiah. Now try some historically significant ones. Spiro Agnew *gains power*. Roosevelt is a *sole voter*, reconfirming that great man's observation that there are no accidents in politics and the whole thing is a fixed fight—not much doubt about that. Edward R. Murrow is *rumor rewarded*. De Gaulle—there's a giant among giants. Gaullede. Lagulede. *"La Deluge?"* Louis Catorce: "Apres moi l'deluge." La Deluge—absolutely perfect except for a negligible gender problem that wouldn't exist at all if he turned out to be Joan of Arc in drag. Hey, friend! cut the playing around—get back to work!

America as a real estate development. Past history and current events as staged drama—street theater. The European *Theater* of Operations. The Pacific *Theater*—Jesus! The brazen bastards were even advertising their chicanery. And what about those ICBM *silos* in the northwestern states? If they're not to be used for real warfare, then what is their purpose—food storage to support extraterrestrial colonizaton?

1. Steffens, p. 631.

23

It Makes the World Go 'Round

Come, come, Adam—back to earth—and is there anything earthier than money—those good old American dollars? Hamilton either had—or had access to—an almost bottomless supply of it. He arranged the loan from the Bank of New York to pay the initial salaries of our first president and first Congress,[1] and that selfsame bank—with branches all over the world—still boasts of the fact from the pages of *New Yorker* magazine. He was instrumental, too, in centralizing the national debt, which has gone on swelling voluminously ever since. And to whom is it owed? The American people? Some of it, to be sure, but no one quite seems to know just how much of it, or to whom the rest is owed. To banks and bankers, of course—the great and invisible international money managers.

Hamilton also had a strong hand in the setting up of state boundaries, economic laws, governmental land tracts and highways—the kind that made it possible for shrewd dollar manipulators like J.P. Morgan and Jay Gould and James B. Dill (whom Steffens called "just about the rightest man I ever met") to execute quasi-"fraudulent" rip-offs in the millions and millions. He also set the stage for the establishment of the Federal Reserve Board, (a *private*, not Federal

237

bank,) with its crucial role in regulating currency values—and later to be handily invaded and heavily influenced by the Warburg branch of the European Rothschild banking interests.[2]

A uniquely advantageous position, he reflected. Think what you could do with *that* set-up. Hell, a father can create an economic "depression" for his six-year-old son by limiting the number of pennies he doles out to the little boy, and if he's also the proprietor at the local candy store he can create "inflation" for the boy by jacking up the price of gum balls from one to three cents. The same thing can be done on a larger scale by those who control the flow of dollars and the price of goods. How marvelous, he congratulated himself wryly, that I who have never had a single course in economics and can barely balance my monthly household accounts—that I of all people should become almost overnight the world's foremost economic theorist. Money as a positive reinforcing CS in the training of an entire species! An astonishing thesis, and itself recently reinforced by a bottom-of-the-page squib of that grand old Illuminati publication, the *Reader's Digest*: in Japan the people commonly greet each other with a cordial, "Are you making any money?"

Yes, he concluded drily, quietly clucking his tongue, there are indeed some very persuasive indications that Mr. Hamilton came into this country with a full set of instructions on just how to proceed, and with plenty of ready cash to promote this very private looking program. A little checking into his background, his family history, his foreign business connections, could be very illuminating (you should pardon the expression) and Adam could not help but wonder if it might not, eventually, extend backward on through history to the Krupps and the Hapsburgs, the Genovese Bankers, to the popes of yore, to the publicity-shy Essenes of the Christian era (who, though devout and ascetic, were also said to have held control over great private wealth— the bankroll, perhaps, from which the modern banking industry was begun?) and on to Alexander, Solomon—and whatever "pre-historical" Cro-Magnon money barons may have preceded them; brilliant, powerful and ingenious mystery tycoons of the purportedly ancient past, shrewdly phasing themselves out of history, withdrawing into the wings, now the anonymous Silent Angels (of Darkness or of Light?) behind the Greatest Show on Earth—for that matter the only show on earth.

Trouble is, he had already tried the question of Hamilton's genealogy, personal and business, on the research department of the

Encyclopaedia Britannica, only to learn that their third-of-a-million references on almost every subject under the sun had nothing—*nothing*—on the financial backing of one of America's most illustrious founders! And as far as Adam was concerned that could only mean that all sources of information to the public, to all of us in the common herd—professors of history included—was under some kind of very careful and purposeful regulation.

Scanty clues. Bits and pieces. As well as Adam could tell, Lincoln Steffens and Professor Quigley were the only living people who had ever come within shouting distance of the outer perimeter of the Inner Circle. And, wonder of wonders, Quigley did not speak ill at all of these infamous "international bankers." Cosmopolitan one-worlders, they were not flag-waving, nationalistic superpatriots. They were "a constant, if weakening, influence for peace. . . . " (But did they not, Adam brooded, later throw their money behind Adolf Hitler's horrendous war machine?) According to Quigley they were conspicuously unwarlike; "civilized," cultivated and "cultured," generous patrons of art, science and education, who "set a pattern of endowed foundations which still surround us today."[3]

He even came right out and named some of these notable banking families, right there in black and white: Baring. Lazard. Erlanger. Warburg (especially noteworthy is their relationship, Adam underscored in his mind, to the American Federal Reserve Board). Schroder. Seligman. Speyers. Mirabaud. Mallet. Fould. And most prominent and best known of them all, of course, were the Morgan and Rothschild houses, both of whom linked later—by marriage and presumably by shared business interests—to the House of Rockefeller. (But they were all visible, and thus not of the *real* Inner Circle!)

These were not the same as ordinary bankers, perhaps chiefly because of their outspoken internationalism. And, sure enough, Adam recalled, that $8,000,000 tract of land for the United Nations site had been donated by the Rockefellers—true! Not at all surprisingly, he noted, was their intimate closeness to governments and to national debts—even (or *specially*) in underdeveloped, "poor risk" countries of the world. In money matters they were, or still *are*—he emended—the sharpest of the sharp, handling it by methods and standards that are simply incomprehensible to the unschooled (like me! he declared almost proudly). Finally, and again no great surprise, was their dedication to secrecy, especially in the exercise of money influence on the political affairs of the world's nations. And they scrupulously retained ownership of their businesses, as devoutly as they strove, and for the most part still strive to preserve their own anonymity. And they cling to gold!

The tie between big money and the operation of nations recurred time and again with interwoven expressions like the "money pyramid" (that grand old symbol of the Illuminatus, as routinely advertised on the back of your one-dollar bills, with the all-seeing eye peering out omnisciently from its apex), the "banking solar system," and "money power."

Ah, yes, he sighed, gradually becoming a little more philosophical about it all, money and government—and history. How many of us realize that such great American names as Edward Grenfell, Elihu Root and John Foster Dulles arose from the swirl of financial influence centering around the office at 23 Wall Street, New York City, home of the J.P. Morgan Company? And locally, here in the U.S. of A., the people of turn-of-the-century America were mildly scandalized to be told that Washington, D.C., was in simple fact, the "kept-mistress" of Wall Street, until the nation's capital was finally made an "honest woman" when President Herbert Hoover joined the two cities in Holy matrimony in the White House. And right in the public eye, with the nation's best-heeled tycoons on hand for the rites!

That T.H.E.Y. own national governments outright is neither a fanciful nor paranoid speculation, it's an unconcealed fact—a matter of public record. In the popular mind the American national debt is owed to the American people ("Buy Bonds!") but this accounts for only about one-fifth of the total debt. The remainder is owed to Federal Reserve, commercial and mutual savings banks, insurance companies, corporations and other large money combines. Once again Adam reminded himself of the difference between ownership and control; even if the Insiders had their paws on as little as ten percent of all that money they could still tune governmental mechanisms at will, by apathetic default of the securities-holder majority. But apparently T.H.E.Y. were not taking any chances—a little probing into the administrative structure of the Federal Reserve Board and the rest of the banking system would undoubtedly reveal that they literally *own* as well as control.

Flagrant corruption? Not according to Steffens—not at all. Adam read the passage again in the autobiography. This formal union between big money and government was, according to him (that liberal, Red-loving, Jeffersonian—Democrat-of-the-heart) just as it should be—even though the reasons for this were not known either to the president or the magnates, "as it was not in their habit of thought(!)." Adam scowled, backed up and read it again. *Not in their habit of thought?* American presidents and tycoons—not even they are let in on it! Then he relaxed; that is exactly what he himself had said to Bairny when discussing his overpass principle with her at morning rounds. Whatever was going on, it was happening *above* the highest heads known to us—in both government and finance. Sure. They had some inkling of it, as betrayed in FDR's remark about there being no accidents in politics, and in Churchill's odd little observation that national leaders exist only to fill available slots. It also helped explain Winnie's courtly declaration of war against the Japanese Empire during WW II, which he closed with a cordial "Your Most Obedient Servant." It was a ritual, not a declaration of war—not *real* war. Theater it was, and more theater.

But if the marriage of American money and government was not in the "habit of thought" of presidents and tycoons, what was it doing in the thought of Lincoln Steffens? Had he, by the time he got around to writing the story of his life, somehow fallen privy to an understanding of The System, of the Insiders themselves, that was *not* known to the wealthiest and most powerful creatures the world had ever hosted? The captains and the kings—and the billionaires? Possibly, possibly. Steffens was enormously trustworthy—protective of his news sources. It could well be that he, like the honorable and scholarly Professor Quigley, had for reasons unspecified been taken into the confidences of the Inner Circle. But therein lies a *most* distressing contradiction, Adam groaned, silently beseeching his aloof blank wall for succor and solution.

Steffens: A lifetime devoted to a penetrating analysis of the world scene, usually from The Inside, brought him to some very, very odd and interesting conclusions. The fathers of our nation, the designers of our Constitution, had no intention of establishing a democratic government.[4] That world history, from beginning to end, is "crying out to be rewritten."[5] Majoring in *Ethics* in Berlin, he was seeking for a science of behavior, not realizing *at that time* that there *is* such a science, and that *we are* and have *long been* on the receiving end of it. Those big bad tycoons, pawns of the Illuminati, he depicted as ". . . rogues outside, but inside, honest men."[6] And one of them, James B. Dill (anagrams to *J.A.M.S. billed*) speaking of the inexorable force of trusts and money power, favored "clearing the way for them," or, if they be deemed anti-social, for going to their origins and closing up their source[7]— which will happen when hell freezes over Adam reflected drily.

It was also Dill who taught Steffens that behind the public Wall Street there was another one that he, Steffens, a former Wall Street reporter, had never even glimpsed, one ". . . which the Wall Street men themselves did not really picture as it was."[8] Then, later, Steffens speaks again of dummy directors and dummy mayors, all run by the bankers—the "banker boss"[9] And he also refers openly to an invisible government behind "constitutional fronts."[10] His friend Jacob Riis, a noted reform journalist, explained the dynamics of the political jungle to him very simply: "God is running it."[11] But which God?

Steffens scorned New Jersey as a "back yard state" and a "Trust factory," and described in some detail Alexander Hamilton's judicious use of it.[12] The U.S. Senate he referred to as "the chamber of the bosses," with one senator representing his state's political machine and the other representing the big businessmen of the state—for whom the political boss invariably worked: "A chamber of traitors," he called them—or so he thought at the time.[13]

Then there was his commentary on "yellow journalist" Hearst as a wise man who". . . saw straight as far as he saw, and he saw pretty far, further than I did then. . . . "[14] *Further than I did then?* Then? What about later, L.S.—exactly what did you learn *later* that put you one-up on the rest of the world?

A lifetime of muckraking and that's what he'd concluded. Big business bosses politics, and for much of his life it was old J.P. Morgan who "sat on the American throne as the boss of bosses, as the ultimate American sovereign."[15] And toward the end Steffens had decided that all of these wicked arrangements were exactly as they should be. Business and politics should be one! Using whatever methods necessary, by bribery and corruption even, business should buy out government and *become* government.[16] On one occasion he even reassured a conscience-troubled Andrew Mellon, "You can't run a railroad without corrupting and running the government."[17]

The great journalist's notions on warfare, derived especially from one strenuous personal experience, were just as shocking. Did the people of the United States hate war? Not at all, he discovered, when he was sent out by President Wilson and Colonel House to soften them up for peace. The people were outraged—they did not want a reasonable peace—they wanted dead Germans! Their tears, their despair at hearing of the coming of an Armistice was so great that Steffens could no longer bring himself to inflict such cruelty on them— the cruelty of denying them their bloody revenge![18] But did they ever, really, get their revenge—or were they only led to believe that they had?

Wars. Wars. The Great Russian Revolution—the infamous Red Terror—had been brought off as smoothly as a chess game between masters. The railroad and telegraph systems simply routed the Czar's train to his fateful rendezvous with the "revolutionary" democrats, blocking the tracks behind him as the right switches were pulled in front of him. All rigged, and altogether a very quiet and peaceful sort of rebellion, the *War and Peace* and *Doctor Zhivago* versions notwithstanding.[19] So—what of all the other great wars?

Curious book he mused, dropping it to the floor and stretching, and with an even stranger conclusion. And there's that peculiar, rather crude little line drawing at the bottom of the last page of the autobiography. Not a sketch of a wizened, goateed little old man, but of a naked toddler, like Baby New Year, walking way from the reader and into the page—into the future? Add to that the closing lines from the new Kaplan biography of Steffens quoting the great and aging journalist as telling his young son: if a boy knows how to ride a horse and swim he can make good his getaway in the dark of night—or even in broad daylight? Getaway? From what and to where? Incognito—disguised—would make it possible to get away in broad daylight. Steffens really hit on something in his analysis of the system—something *big!*

But those good men, Steffens and Quigley, so blissful and accepting of the stranglehold that T.H.E.Y. hold on a helpless world populace. Just look! Quigley himself quotes the international financier, Walter Rathenau, as saying outright in 1909 that "Three hundred men, all of whom know one another, direct the economic destiny of Europe and choose their successors from among themselves." And more than a half-a-century before that the great Gladstone, Chancellor of the English Exchequer, candidly announcing aloud that the crux of the whole situation was very simple: government should know and keep to its own place, and "leave the Money Power supreme and unquestioned." Not to mention the report of Montagu Norman's modest claim, "I hold the hegemony of the world," at a time when he and J.P. Morgan dominated the financial world (roughly 1913-1930).[20]

Then there was Steffen's good friend and co-muckraker, Ida Tarbell, who devoted a good measure of her life to writing a monumental expose of the Standard Oil Company. And what came of it? Nothing. However sincere she may have been, the book itself had accomplished nothing. It was like Teddy Roosevelt's empty gesture at trust bustin'— all show and blow—a poppin' little ladyfinger of a firecracker amplified by the newspapers and elementary history texts to sound like a ten-inch cannon. No trust, no monopoly, no international cartel has ever been busted—not really. Big business has long since surpassed mere nations in wealth and in power, but they somehow manage to perpetuate the illusion that they are subordinate to government. How? Why, with their oft-publicized carpings and complaints about governmental controls, of course.

That was one way of concealing T.H.E.I.R. power. Another required a simple little sleight-of-hand flourish—now-you-see-it, now-you-don't. Hell, anyone who goes to the trouble of taking a good look at the trust bustin' scam can see it's a pretty transparent stunt. Every now and then T.H.E.Y. stage a lower level bust of some minor price-fixing conspiracy, say, like the big bakery scandal in Arizona. Then they create an illusion of massive trust busting by giving it banner headlines in the newspapers and playing it up big on the tube. "Ha!," we gloat, "some of those big bastard tycoons really got it in the neck that time! We got laws! That'll make good Christians of 'em, and serve as a powerful deterrent to all those other would-be grafters!" But the amount of money involved is peanuts, and the impact of this petite legal action on high-level conglomerates is quite, quite negligible. Clever of them, it is.

Adam smiled to himself, suddenly remembering his brief and friendly acquaintance of many years before with Larc Growlpiler, Chairman of the Board of Dow Chemical, and of his statement in Washington in 1972—about dreaming of the day when Dow headquarters might be relocated to an island with no national affiliations, there to do business freely with all the people of the world, "beholden" to no one, unfettered by the regulations of any government, there to buy and sell as a true citizen-of-the-world. Well, sir, Adam muttered sourly, Dow is free to do that now—as are all the other multinational (and supranational) corporations. It's the governments that aren't free—they're all toadying bootlickers to the big money boys.

So the Growlpiler dream—why announce it? Diversionary, of course. Declaring a hope like that simply helps conceal the fact that it's already been attained. But ... but ... but! He shook his head in another burst of bewilderment. What of Mr. Growpiler himself—a vicious, ruthless, heartless robber baron? Not at all! Gentle, considerate, courteous and law-abiding—there is no way he would countenance the peddling of Napalm to spray a-burning all over innocent women and children in Southeast Asia. Where do all those outlandish horror stories come from, anyway? The newspapers, of course, and television and radio—public gossip. But why, oh *why!?*

He tossed up his hands, exasperated. None of it made any sense at all. It just didn't add up. Unless, of course, one were willing to settle for the old profit-motive theory. Profit and power. Or the swollen ego thing—because what does a person or a company do with millions and billions of dollars of profit—except compete for more for the sheer fun and excitement of the game? Is that it?

Time and again he found himself running into this same stony blank wall: money. T.H.E.Y. had incomprehensibly large sums of it, were apparently contemptuous of it, so what in Heaven's name did they want with *more?* After all, it's been millennia since T.H.E.Y. perfected the alchemical transmutation of the lower metals to pure gold—so a bottomless supply is available to them. And, small wonder that the world economy still runs on the gold standard, and is faithfully maintained there even today by the international bankers and financiers, the eastern establishment—the Cliveden Set types. So, the question stands: if the money itself is intrinsically valueless, or has value only because we believe it has—and T.H.E.Y. know all that— then exactly what purpose is it serving? *CS?* Reinforcing or rewarding CS? Apparently so. There seems no other reasonable explanation. But to what end?

Banking, he mused, is a lot like religion and other bad habits—if you get hooked early enough it can stay with you for a lifetime. They started us in the first grade of public school, he recalled, with our own little savings account book, and every Tuesday morning we dutifully brought in a few pennies to deposit and record, and watched our holdings grow. Little capitalists, sucked into the system before we even knew what we were doing. Give us a child till he's six years old and he'll be a Catholic—or a Capitalist—for the rest of his life. Devilishly clever, those Insiders.

Devilish!

"How was your week at home?" Jasmyn asked brightly as Sandol entered the dome.

"Peaceful and serene as ever," he replied, trying vainly to keep the pain from his voice. "But I missed you. Did you visit him again?"

She turned to him and spoke out in a determined monotone. "Your acting on jealous impulse is a very serious and primitive violation of Law, Sandol. I have been too tolerant."

"I know," he nodded sadly. "It's taken control of my entire affectual system—it is no longer susceptible to rational regulation. So what do you plan for me—indefinite commitment to Earth?"

"That is by Law the designated disposition for chronic offenders, miscreants and the dysfunctionally retarded."

"Ah," he said, "but I think you like my jealousy."

Jasmyn was indignant. "That would be as primitive as the jealousy itself!"

"Even so . . . even so . . . "

She turned away from him slowly, thoughtfully, then reluctantly conceded. "Discretion would advise that we not inform on one another."

"Yes. We need more time—perhaps some professional help."

Jasmyn looked back at him once more. "If I read him correctly he has resigned from all couples counseling. We shall have to help ourselves."

Sandol nodded. "I have long suspected that was why we were assigned here. And so, I shall continue to work on wanting you without needing you. Agreed?"

1. On September 13, 1789, the "Temporary Loan of 1789" was made to the U.S. Government to pay the salaries of the president and of Congress. It was in the amount of $191,608.81, arranged by Hamilton from the Bank of New York and the Bank of North America, and at 6% interest. It was also an illegal transaction.

2. Allen, Gary, *None Dare Call It Conspiracy* (Seal Beach, California: Concord Press, 1971).

3. Quigley, pp. 51-52.

4. *The Autobiography of Lincoln Steffens*, p. 125.

5. *Ibid.*, p. 126.

6. *Ibid.*, p. 194.

7. *Ibid.*, p. 196.

8. *Ibid.*, p. 199.

9. *Ibid.*, pp. 233-4.

10. *Ibid.*, p. 235.

11. *Ibid.*, p. 257.

12. *Ibid.*, p. 495.

13. *Ibid.*, p. 504.

14. *Ibid.*, pp. 541-2.

15. *Ibid.*, p. 590.

16. *Ibid.*, p. 606.

17. *Ibid.*, p. 609.

18. *Ibid.*, pp. 774-5.

19. *Ibid.*, pp. 752-3.

20. Quigley, p. 62.

24

In Good Hands With Allstate?

It was dark again before he realized it, and once more he braced himself for the perpetuation of his mental marathon with another belt of barley. A most dangerous principle, he realized, this artificial stimulation of the mind with toxic excitants, but for him, at times, it did the job. Like the kids and their "mind expansion" with acid and peyote and hashish—most of them just got stoned blotto and that was it, but perhaps a few of them did succeed in making the Timothy Leary trip to some expanded consciousness. For now, he could feel himself accelerating, a second wind coming on strong.

He glanced at the monitor and saw that Goldy's working day was done. Now it was social hour, and she was getting it on heavily with a pretty young red-headed girl whom Adam didn't recognize. He thought momentarily about asking if he might join them but quickly checked the temptation and resolved not to lose his head of steam at frivolous romping. He was, after all, up against people who were themselves systematic, self-disciplined and dedicated, and for the time being—at least until he found the keystone to his puzzle—he could do no less. There would be plenty of time to play later.

The all-white, Anglo-Saxon American male—the most powerful

creature ever to walk the earth; mightier by far than Tyrannosaurus Rex, the mastodon or the sabre-toothed tiger. And the roots of his power must then lie in Western Europe—and most of all in Mother England. To be sure, nineteenth-century Britain had been effectively governed by a small, tightly-knit "society," a little clique comprised of no more than six families along with a few of their choice allies and an occasional recruit (Steffens' famous protege, Walter Lippman, was one of them) from Balliol, New College at Oxford or Trinity College at Cambridge. (Like that chilling television movie, *Brotherhood of the Bell*, that had caught his attention several years earlier—a clue, perhaps? Or a *reverse* clue?) They did reign supreme, this group, controlling both the Conservative and Liberal parties, between which there was little more than an outward appearance of competition.

They were united, and at one point closely banded around John Ruskin and Cecil Rhodes, the diamond czar, in a secret society known as the Circle of Initiates, who were intent upon extending upper-class English benevolence to the whole world—whether they wanted it or not! They did indeed link themselves clear around the world through such fraternal internationalist organizations as the Round Table Group, the Royal Institute of International Affairs, and, later, through our own Council on Foreign Relations, which so inspired the outraged indignation of the John Birchers. And closely allied with the Astor, Rhodes and Milner families was the elite "Cliveden Set" of transworld influence peddlers and political meddlers. (Stalling himself for time, bemused, Adam idly anagrammed "Cliveden Set" to *decent lives* and was mildly amused by it, though the real significance of it would not be understood by him until later.)

Yes, they controlled enormous wealth, and newspapers and universities, and were dominant in the Royal Institute of International Affairs. They sided with Neville Chamberlain and company in his appeasement policy toward Hitler, but were also evidently in some kind of private liaison with the German high command. The Round Table Group in London held hands across the sea with J.P. Morgan and Company in New York, which was instrumental in setting up the Institute for Advanced Study at Princeton (modelled after the English establishment's All Souls College—with the blessings and the backing of the Carnegie and Rockefeller fortunes).

This American arm of the British money-power nobs worked much of its influence through five powerful newspapers: the *New York Times* and *New York Herald Tribune*, the *Christian Science Monitor*, the *Washington*

Post (most recently of Watergate fame) and the now defunct *Boston Evening Transcript*—with all of them painting pictures on the American mind as they would.

Then, around 1925, with Lionel Curtis at the helm, a third international network was added to these other two, to extend the total organization's sphere of influence even farther. The transglobal interlock now included the Netherlands, China, France, Japan, Russia, Canada, Australia and New Zealand, and they operated with an abundance of financial backing from the ubiquitous if ultimately invisible "International Bankers"—the Inner Circle of the Illuminati. And all to what purpose? Ostensibly good ones, though Adam found himself battling, valiantly, this Quigley version of munificent manipulation in high places. According to him they did indeed favor peace, assistance for "underdeveloped countries," boosting neglected minorities —and generally upgrading the entire world by the good old Anglo-American standards of civility.

This complex and semisecret network's influence over the press, the universities and the foreign policies of many nations appears to have been even greater than was publicly acknowledged by them, but their benevolence was roundly doubted and soundly challenged by many: by the Senate's Reece Committee to investigate the interlocking network of the Ford, Rockefeller and other tax-exempt foundations; by the John Birch Society—who named and still names them as strictly a treasonous Communist-front organization (Nelson Rockefeller a Communist! Mind-boggling! Adam shook his head) and by one Senator Richard M. Nixon, who declared Truman's firing of Douglas MacArthur an act of appeasement toward world Communism.

At about that same time Senator William Jenner really laid it on the line, right up front, on the Senate floor: "This country today is in the hands of a secret inner coterie which is directed by agents of the Soviet Union. . . . Our only choice is to impeach President Truman and find out who is the secret invisible government which has so cleverly led our country down the road to destruction."[1]

My God, Adam moaned, they're giving it to us both ways—all is confusion! Good guys or bad guys, that is the question! Take it again, from scratch. The big money runs government—including the world's nations—and Lincoln Steffens knew both money and government as few mortals did. Get back to him. Yes, he does seem to have made it into the Inner Circle, while reading some curious conclusions about ethics on the way. *There are no ethics!* Don't try to be ethical—be intelligent.

Bribery and corruption are *the will of God* and do-good reformers are agents of the Devil." The guilty are in so many ways superior to the innocent, and . . . bribery is in a very pious sense an act of God."[2]

He plainly approved Herbert Hoover's marrying the Federal government to the Wall Street tycoons even though what came of that union was not enough to cure the big depression of the thirties. Damn! The Big Depression, " . . . which has causes beyond their ideas and habits of thought . . . "[3] Damn!!! An economic depression which *has causes beyond the ideas and the habitual thinking of presidents and billionaires?* What causes, then, and arranged by whom? Bankers, naturally—big bankers. Even Henry Ford had to hoard huge surpluses to protect his operation from the banks, " . . . which were after him as they are after all industry and business."[4]

Here, Adam suddenly recalled a recently televised Dick Cavett interview with the heads of four of the Country's biggest publishing houses. Their recurrent, collective and plaintive lament? "Someone is buying up our companies—and we don't even know who they are!"

All right then, big business owns the nations of the world—and the banks own big business. Some four hundred supra-national business corporations with resources greater than those of mere governments, and all of them controlled by banks. Query: who controls the banks? Not the stockholders, that's for damn sure. They hold paper, sit on their asses and clip coupons. "Owning" is one thing and controlling quite another. Those great, dramatic, grass-roots proxy battles only happen in movie and television plays. The transworld conglomerates are really, actually controlled by? There can only be one answer to that. Just one.

Any running inventory of megacorp mergers could go on forever, to a point at which any further accounting would soon become meaningless to us. Again, such a degree of complexity is deliberately created in order to exceed the reach of our finest minds. It is *beyond us*!

Here he found himself once again having to deal with the quite literally imponderable complexity of the international monetary system and, inevitably associated with it, the equally complex organization of the world's top business and financial combines. Most of us avoid the distress of confrontation through the familiar mental mechanism of *denial*, and thus we simply decline to deal with it. And in so doing, we are surely justified; it's enough to dazzle our finest minds, and to abrupt all further thinking about it.

Meanwhile, as we are busily occupied with neglecting the incomprehensible, great pains are taken to maintain the illusion of financial vulnerability, fragility, and the occasional impotence of the megacorporations, and to promote the associated illusion of governmental solvency and superiority. This double-duty illusion is laughable, as it presents us with the picture of munificently capitalized megacorps (e.g., Chrysler or General Motors) floundering helplessly until a thoroughly bankrupt national government finally takes mercy and comes to their aid.

Hence, the question: did Lee Iacocca really save Chrysler, or was Chrysler deliberately put in jeopardy, then "saved" by methodical design, with Mr. Iacocca serving only as a colorful front man who could then boast, "The Pride Is Back," once again reaffirming the ever-inspiring message of The Little Train That Could?

A "hero" for a piece like this is dramatically necessary. Any megacorporation that falters, struggles, and then survives does little to excite the interest of the masses. There must be a conspicuously visible protagonist to be identified as Hero or Villain in this kind of street theater, to carry authentic dramatic impact to the audience. This is a standard principle in all fiction writing. A nation or a company cannot be an effective dramatic figure. We can be annoyed with Russia but need a Kruschev to really hate. We may see Germany as a military threat but require an Adolf Hitler to properly serve our need to fear and villify. Hitler was, after all, a professional clown—one hired by the Invisible Big Money manipulators to function as a worthy target of our hatred, and as a transnational object lesson.

So, where do any of us fit in with the big corporations, huge, distant, and aloof as they are? I, for one, feel no intimacy with them. How do you love a Lipton's Tea Company? And how can it love you—except to use you as the city slicker uses a poor dumb country girl?

As David Hapgood says in his *Screwing of the Average Man* book, one way or another we're all working for the Hartford Insurance Company, or for A.T.T. or I.T.T. or Shell Oil or U.S. Steel. Another day older and deeper in debt, we owe our souls to the company sto-o-re! (The name Hapgood was familiar to him. It appeared several times in the Steffens autobiography, he recalled—a writer for the old *McClure's* magazine. Adam supposed that young David was probably a grandson or grandnephew of the older Hapgood, and probably a lower level agent of the Insiders who was handed a pile of facts and figures by T.H.E.M. and told to write a horror story on the multinational corporation conspiracy. But why?)

Well, the corporations and I may not be in love with each other but at least we have a correspondence club relationship. They send me computer cards filled with holes and covered with numbers, and every month I send them another bucket of my precious green pellets. And sometimes they behave like a bitchy, hysterical young girl who's about to be laid for the first time. Impulsive. Coy and teasing. Explosive— Seductive—Unfathomable—and damnably unpredictable. It's almost as if they're trying to elicit some sort of specific response from me—or trying to—to tell me something. He scratched his brow, troubled. So, the Universal Charge Card Company cancels my regular card for excessive use, then ten days later they issue me their platinum card with a $10,000 credit line. That's one.

Another: three months after applying for it, I get a credit card from the Avis Rent-A-Car Company, along with a routine questionnaire asking for my vital statistics and wanting me to fill in the "Name of Rental Company"—*like they don't even know their own name!* Trouble is, I'd applied three months earlier for a Hertz card—and I got an Avis. A pattern of some sort. Memory test? or it could mean that #2 just has to *appear* to be trying harder—that the two of them are actually one and the same company, just as those fifty big American oil companies are just one big conglomerate. Like love, and like God—there are a million corporations and yet there is but One!

But we very well know that they're neither hysterical nor capricious— far from it. Whoever they are and whatever they're up to, T.H.E.Y. sure are hell on organization and business methods. Scientific. Sound logicians—applying their rationalistic principles with fine discrimination to the design of weapons and war strategies, to economic analysis, market research surveys—even to "the games people play"—to the assessment (and to the conditioning? he wondered nervously) of human behavior in general. And computer technology, with its massive storage and lightning-like retrieval capacities, was the central nervous system of the entire operation. What incredible records T.H.E.Y. keep, and what a marvelously sophisticated personality profile the Master Computer could produce on any one of us, drawing as it does on the enormous amount of detailed, personal information served up by how we use our credit cards. This, combined with our other money-handling practices, our public and medical records, income tax returns, military service, job performance reports, school subjects and performance ratings. All of these added up and compared with similar data on huge populations, past and present, could easily serve up a solid basis for diagnosing our present status and predicting our futures (a la insurance actuarial predictions) far more accurately than we ourselves ever could. And that, he recalled, squares very nicely with the grand old Catholic concept of the omniscient God who sees all people of all time—past, present and future. Why hell, it's just market survey research! Like predictions of longevity and the frequency of heart attacks in the year 2001 from insurance company actuarial figures!

How many times, Adam now asked himself, had he scoffed at the computer as nothing more than an overgrown adding machine? That's what he wanted to believe, naturally enough, because who but the Starship *Enterprise's* Mr. Spock could equably tolerate the idea of being outsmarted by a machine?

Wishful thinking on my part, he finally admitted with a tremulous sigh. The mammalian neural impulse conduction rate is measured in seconds, or tenths and hundredths of seconds, whereas computer activities are reckoned in nanoseconds—billionths of a second! At that speed, and with enough hardware, it could easily "outthink" five billion people who hardly think at all—except about what they read in the newspaper or see on the tube. We think the same but not together— we're not hooked up in series.

Here he suddenly recalled Norbert Wiener's convoluted praise of the computer's vastly superior cognitive capabilities. It is programmed ahead of us, such that our criticism of it may be valid but, alas, too late to be relevant. It carries what is to us, plain and simply, an incomprehensible program. Amen.

Which says nothing about what that big undercover program is trying to accomplish. Yes, some kind of conditioning of the mass mind, with money as its principal reinforcing CS, and the media and the postal system as the main communication lines between the conditioners and the conditionees—the "subjects" of the great experiment.

The plot thickens. Human behavior, human subjective experience, is now being subjected to scientific regulation—adjusted and tuned like a piano. Is that how it's working? Jesus, he shuddered, 1984 moved in early—at least eight years (if not eight millennia) earlier than prophesied. But it never happened?

So you take a bunch of chimps and put them in a varied, open air environment and leave them alone. What happens? They play around, fight a little, groom each other, feed, empty body waste, copulate and spawn young. Eventually they multiply and overcrowd, whereupon they must start fighting and killing each other for food and *lebensraum.* Strong leadership, called despotism, becomes a necessity. Disease runs rampant. The strong prevail and the weak and the young die quickly. We, the experimenters, are saddened by this spectacle. We try to teach them agriculture, medicine, law, birth-control and other ecological principles—and morality. Some of them show flashes of intelligent interest and they learn a little bit. But most of them stubbornly resist giving up immediate pleasures for the kind of work that would offer them a longer, more varied and creative—more interesting life—and with this the time for even more pleasure of *all* different kinds.

We also note that they learn at different rates, and that they will not learn any faster than they want to. We could whip them and torture them and imprison them but that's been tried and we know it doesn't work—and we're not into that kind of cruelty anyway. No, the trick is to get them to *want* to learn and to let them believe they're doing it on their own. Hence, we fill their environment with interesting problems in the form of entertainment and drama, excite them with challenging games, give them clues to guide them through the pleasure mazes we prepare for them, then reward them when they punch the right button and leave them alone when they miss. And we feed them, of course, and protect them from each other. Though not too much from themselves! That would be much too sore an invasion of their privacy—a stealing of their lives.

Now, then, he thought, we have only to change the names of the players for a slightly different angle. We are the chimps, and T.H.E.Y. are the—the what? COs we might call them, standing either for commanding officers—or compassionate observers. Which is it? Yet another imponderable! If it is some kind of Skinnerian conditioning program, he decided, then exactly what are the most effective reinforcing stimuli for the human animal? That shouldn't be too hard—it was right in his professional ball park. Picking up his notebook and a ball-point pen he began to jot them down: affiliation with fellow creatures . . . money . . . prestige and other ego nutrients . . . drama that stirs and vents emotions . . . sex and other physical pleasures . . . entertainment that elicits laughter . . . a chance to look, hear and gratify innate curiosity—voluntary learning. Not bad. That about does it.

Poking his head through the door he found Goldy languishing contentedly in front of the tube watching Donnie and Marie. Glancing at the screen he noted absently that the orchestra for the "Donnie and

Marie Show" had their leader's initials, "J.O.," painted all over their music stands, and decided then and there to classify it with the Tickle and Bic-flicking commercials under "CS Masturbation Sanctions."

Interrupting quietly, he said, "Listen to this a minute, Goldy, and tell me if these are the things that you and other people want, and are willing to work for . . . "

When he had finished reading off the list, slowly, she thought for a moment then answered simply: "Sure, Adam—all of them things. But the biggest one, I guess, is jus' bein' alive, y'know?"

Taken aback, he withdrew into his own room and added her suggestion to his list—at the top. And that, he was reminded, posed the question of our most influential aversive conditioning stimuli. Pain. Disease. Monotony and inactivity—senility and death. Death, the ultimate conditioning stimulus—oblivion and nonexistence. But maybe that wasn't too bad. After all, why remain alive if you're doing nothing with it but converting oxygen to carbon dioxide and protein to urea? Remember that dreadful story in *Life* magazine a few years back— about the super-elderly people in that Rural Russian community— some of them 150 years or older—morosely wandering about, bored, and complaining because they were tired of life but couldn't seem to die? Same theme in the movie "Zardoz," where an inverted Messiah finally appears, bringing with him the blessed gift of death. If life is meant for the living, then—for those who really want to use it—might it not also be true that we do not die until we really want to? It may be necessary for us to believe in deathly oblivion if we're to make the most of what little time we are said to have.

Yes, he reflected, perhaps we are being cultivated, and not *taught* or *trained*. We could be voluntarily teaching ourselves under the influence of a system that is standard operating procedure in any good animal behavior laboratory. There, the good primate subject, be he rhesus, chimpanzee or man, will eagerly perform onerous physical chores to earn the tokens that he can then use to purchase the privilege of solving higher level puzzles and problems. For us these reward pellets, or tokens, are called "money," and we dig ditches and wash dishes and wait on tables to earn enough of them to buy an electronic calculator, a microscope or a telescope—or to buy our way into medicine, law or engineering schools. And we must, indeed, be deemed a most promising species, considering the increasing rate at which new technology and fresh information is being let down to us—at a rate limited not in the least, perhaps, by T.H.E.I.R. selfish reluctance to disclose it, but only by our inability to make good use of it. Aye—there's the rub—the bottleneck: Us! Or, is it T.H.E.M.?

If there is in fact such a program, he sighed, does it aim for the enslavement or the improvement of the species? You've answered that once, Adam—in your big book. You voted for "improvement." Longer life. More education. A refinement of law. A reduction in punishment. A gradual coalescing of fragmental nations into larger and more peaceful ones. But hell!—That's written history! What have you seen with your own eyes, in your own lifetime?

There have been some big changes in the past three or four decades, he reminisced. Not only do people have more money, they also have larger vocabularies—more "smarts" all around. As a population our visual-motor reflexes and comprehension have increased. Popular literature has grown more voluminous, sophisticated and complex. Scenes in movie and television dramas are far shorter and faster than they once were—covert tachystoscopic training for the unsuspecting masses. And we're harder to fool that we used to be. During World "War" II we all bought that dumb newsreel of Adolf Hitler dancing his silly little looped cat food commercial dance, when he was informed of the "Fall" of Paris, but no one would believe it today.

Today's young people are also bigger, stronger, and healthier. No more of those scary red quarantine signs on people's front doors; scarlet fever is gone, along with smallpox, diphtheria, polio, lobar pneumonia. People are living a lot longer. Hell! funeral processions were almost a daily occurrence when I was a kid—and about every fifth woman was knocked up. Blacks are considerably freer and so are whites. Technology is booming, and business was never better. Yes, we are being brought along, it would appear. We're even beginning to spread out into the solar system, and from there—*quo vadis*? It occurred to him that he might even last long enough to provide a few shrinking services on some Fleet Starship touring the Milky Way.

Dream on, fool! he suddenly reproached himself. Picking up a B.F. Skinner book he hefted it without opening the pages. After all, he had lived most of his professional life in the company of Pavlov and Skinner, of operant conditioning and behavior-modification and brainwashing of all sorts—"A rose by any other name," he reflected grimly, "is still Big Brotherism—a filthy bit of business." Ring a bell as you show the puppy his Alpo and he begins to salivate, and before long you can have him salivating just by ringing the bell (thus saving greatly on your dog food bill). And we're exactly the same—just a little more verbal about it all. Instead of bells we get a newspaper headline here, a bar of music there, a presidential address now, a new sit-com on the tube tomorrow—all of it adding up to a program that has us salivating—and obediently lock-stepping—in time to the Master Program in the Sky.

Screw it all, he thought, with a sudden flooding sense of futility. How do you fight a system like that—beat a trail into the great wilderness of northern Idaho and live off the land, far beyond the reach of their infernal conditioning stimuli where you might at least, at last, think your own thoughts and behave your own behavior? The free man's last outpost, the wilderness—his last chance at Freedom and Dignity. Mind-control. Ruthless and rampant financial ripping off. The American insurance industry alone now sitting on a greater than billion dollar surplus, and all of it—and more, much more!—handily available to The System, to the care and feeding of the worldwide computer network, to the brain-painting brushes of the mass media, to the ghastly war machines of the militant nations of the earth.

Murder and folly and corruption most foul—a stinking miasmatic swamp of a world. And with it all his old idol, Lincoln Steffens, who was in the thick of its worst—a hobnobbing confidante to presidents and kings and international bankers—how could he, as his life was drawing to an end, conclude that the only thing wrong with the world, or that ever was wrong with it, is what we think? What we *think* is wrong with it! The great muckraker—did he finally succeed in tracking the corrupt alliance between dirty politics and the Big Business swindlers to their source—to the powers-behind-the-scenes? The Illuminati themselves? And, if so, why so sanguine about his discovery? A sell-out? All's well with the world, he says. The best of all possible worlds—a world in perfect harmony. Variations on the eternal theme—The Establishment theme song. Or is it only the best we can receive?

In a petite pique of despair he backhanded a stack of his books and sent them scattering across the floor, then sat staring at them. Piss on it. There is no missing key—no hidden answer—it's all what it appears to be.

Downing a searing draught of boubon he sat back against the wall and gazed morosely, unthinkingly, at the traitorous array of scholarly tomes that had led him down so many blind-alleys and into so many dead ends. An eternal maze for human rats to run in, a labyrinth of frustration with No Exit and No Answer. We are like mice in a maze—no!—a Skinner box. Every time we cash a check or make a deposit, use a credit card, buy a tank of gas, enter a sweepstakes, answer a questionnaire—virtually every move we make—is duly noted and tabulated by the Great Computer. Each response is numbered, significance assigned to it, and rewards granted or withheld accordingly. You don't believe it? Just check the next TV commercial for your friendly "Ugly Teller" bank. The conditions are identical to those in any good animal research lab. Step up to the machine, slip your card into the proper slot, push the correct button, and those crispy green pellets (that you worked to earn) are delivered right into your hot little hands.

Goldy and her red-haired lady friend were now sprawled out comfortably on the satin pillows watching the tube. He turned his ear indifferently to the audio coming faintly through his door. A Burger King commercial: "You'll have it *your* way, *your way*. . . . "

Certainly.

Of course.

All the big money grubbers are out to serve our every need—if the price is right. Speaking of recurrent theme songs, that swindling bit of swill is the biggest of them all these days. "At Continental Airlines— We Really Move Our Tails For You!"

And the Valley National Bank, "We-e-e-e go out of our way-a-ay for you!?"

We're in great hands with Allstate. They're *all* ready when we are.

And, at McDonald's—"We Do It All For Yo-o-ou!"

"You asked for it—you got it—Toyota." If we want it, we have only to ask for it, and—we get it. That's a lot of power, which means that we must be pretty important people—almost angels and a little lower than the gods. Can we doubt it, with all that tuneful ego-support they feed to us through the tube? "You—are—the—one. You—are—the—only One—at McDo-o-on-a-alds!" Ah, yes, they do it all for us.

He sighed absently, they're really inundating the common man with freedom and dignity. The "Mary Tyler Moore Show" theme song— she's gonna make it after all. "Laverne and Shirley," almost a straight steal from the Burger King commercial: "We'll do it *our* way—we'll do it *our* way. . . . " (What other?) And what a magnificent waste of time and energy! Million dollar commercials advertising armpit de-stinkums, shit paper, shaving cream, Kotex, Lysol and a thousand other brands of glop and goop. All?—all of it obviously unnecessary, and yet it's there, a part of The Program. Too bloody, bloody hell with it all!, he growled savagely. Might as well cash in my chips and commit myself to a home for the partially bald.

Well, maybe I'm wrong, but it sure looks like one big joke to me. Idly, he picked up a March 22, 1976 copy of *Time* and opened it. So, first we have a full page ad from Texaco pleading with the American public to not let the politicians dismember the fifty integrated oil companies who are supposedly out there madly competing for our business. Know what that's like? It's like when my kids were little tads. They'd rassle me to the floor and pummel my poor body with powder puff punches while I begged them, "Oh, please, please don't hurt me." That's the oil companies begging us to save them from Uncle Sam.

And on the next page, a smaller ad for a nice power mower, and another for polyurethane heel taps. Then we have Betty Ford rhapsodizing about the eight-generation American miracle as if it were all ancient history, when in fact my great-grandfather was around when our "founding Fathers" were still kicking. It *is* a cute trick. By repeatedly emphasizing those *two centuries*, T.H.E.Y. conceal the fact that the whole thing was pre-engineered by them while generating in us the comforting illusion that we did it all by ourselves, and virtually overnight.

And here's a nice, typical bit of their pixy hogwash—a story about Russian and American diplomats arguing about how much of those brain-frying microwaves the Reds will be allowed to direct toward the American embassy. And we believe it all, don't we? I wonder who writes their scenarios, anyway? Hollywood's best, I suppose.

Monkey see, monkey do. People see, people do. The meteoric rise and fall of comedian Joe Penner (Penner—one who writes) in the thirties—another early demiser. Every Sunday night his one big line— "Hyuck, hyuck, hyuck—ya wanna buy a duck?" Next day, back at school and at work, millions of Americans would greet each other with their own imitation of this immortal line: "hyuck, hyuck, hyuck—ya wanna buy a duck?" We're sitting ducks—patsies—for any message they choose to put on that silly tube. Jesus!—what a farce! A few spots on national television and you could get rich peddling caramel-covered camel droppings.

There is no hope, he quietly concluded. We are five billion retarded anthropoids with the dubious gift of gab and a sporadic sense of style. Hail Socrates, and to your hemlock highball.

Minutes drifted by as he sat staring at his wall-to-wall carpet of books, staring mindlessly, blankly. He was neither asleep nor sleepy, drunk nor sober—but in curiously comfortable repose, resigned. A brown study—but more like beige. An hour passed . . .

"Now is the time, Sandol. He is on the verge of giving it up—but he's so near! Time for the clue. He has fathomed the role of Money, the covert instructional function of the Media, even the mock Warfare. He's almost there—just the least nudge should do it for him."

Sandol struggled against panic. "And if he makes it, so much for the five billion. But what else will you win?"

Jasmyn turned to him with the faintest of smiles. "You mean, will I win him?"

He bit down manfully. "Yes, and if you want him then I want you to have him. I — will — take — pleasure — in — your — happiness."

"You would fit in well here, Sandol. I'm sure you would be regarded as one of their superior beings. At least you know what to strive for, as few of them do."

"Then you will choose him?"

Exasperated, she let it all out. "For a time, perhaps. Then you for a time—then another and another. Relationships never end—they merely change!"

Sandol remained thoughtfully silent as she brought Adam into sharp focus and transmitted at maximum amplitude: "Adam. You have it now! You have it!"

1. Quigley, pp. 977-8.
2. Steffens, p. 862.
3. *Ibid.*, p. 865.
4. *Ibid.*, p. 854.

25

The Big Brass Ring

Click.

Adam shifted his position slightly and dropped his head back against the wall.

Click. Click.

What the hell's going on? He squirmed restlessly and came alert.

Click. Click. Click, and with each click came a split-second visual image.

The jungle wedding of a Neanderthal princess and a missionary inseminator from the Ceti I solar system, or from the Pleiades. Click. Their offspring systematically bred with computer-selected inseminators from the third galaxy to the left. Click. A band of imported Cro-Magnons marching down to ancient Sumeria, there to be taught agriculture then left to fend for themselves.

Click. Gilgamesh, royal son of a neanderthal mother and a space god. Click.

Providers from outer space. Click. Like those lovely clue movies, "Network," the "Star Trek" episodes, "The Questor Tapes."

The Providers:

> They give you the day
>   And show you the way,
> Then leave you alone
>   To do it your way.

Click. We'll do it *our* way, *our* way. Click. "Mother! I'd rather do it myself!" Click. The *only* way!

Click. A gushing, plunging river of billions of American dollars a year flooding uphill to the coffers of the tycoons.

Click. Hong Kong merchants paying a million dollars a year for downtown frontage and happily making change in five languages.

Click. A massive electronic brain hovering in the clouds above Olympus's towering top, its sensory tentacles spanning the earth and absorbing, in-feeding information from its remotest nooks and crannies, integrating it, and feeding out a billion impulses a second through its motor network—out to the media.

Click. A lumbering mule-headed mule drawn forward by the succulent carrot on a string dangling in front of him.

Our galactic sires of yore who found the maids of Israel fair and bred them to produce us. Click. Genetic engineering.

Interplanetary outcasts, madmen, and felons, Lo these many millennia in galactic Coventry. Oh no, in vain we try to call them but they answer not—*they* will call us when we are ready to hear them.

Click Click. Money makes the world go 'round—a necessary evil!

Click. Mammals in a maze. Options and alternatives, or stay where you are!

Click. Click. Moses and the mass of mankind—Plato and the human herd.

Steffens on herding habits of thought.

Click. Organization.

Click. Dummy corporations and dummy directors.

Click. General Sarnoff, are you up there?

Click. Dummy nations and dummy princes.

Click. Click . . .

All the world's a stage and we're all actors . . . Click.

Don't believe the newspapers—Click!—Even though that's all you know.

Click. European *Theater* of Operations. The Show Must Go On!

Click. Dummy armies, the refuge of the poor and the biggest school in the world.

Click. Dummy generals and plaster admirals.

Click. Corporations and mergers and coalitions and aggregates to trust and combines and cartels by geometrical progression comprehensible only to the computer and its console masters. Economic Ceiling Zero—beyond our ken!

Click. Margaret Mead and "you've got to tell it to them both ways."

Click. Choice, and Freedom thereof.

Margaret Mead at the Club of Rome—250 Cities in Greece by the Periclean era.

Click. The Lumanians and the Cro-Magnons. Darwin transcended and human bioevolution by quantum leaps, courtesy of our starmen progenitors, the Prophets of The Old Testament—the local ETI's.

Click. Chariots of the Gods, and B.F. Skinner conditioning us all Beyond Freedom and Dignity by way of the master computer.

Click.

Public records, the census, bank accounts, credit cards, and purchase records—that Great MMPI in the Sky. Click. Man in a Skinner Box. Click. No! On a *Skinner Ball*. Click. *CS!* Push this button or that button. Click. It's your choice.

Click. Reward or punishment. Click.

So do it *your* way, *your* way!

Click. You're in good hands with Allstate.

Click! He's got the *whole* world in His hands, He's got the whole world in his hands . . . He's got you and me, brother . . .

Click. Aerial bombing of London, Berlin and Bremen. Click. Precisely controlled urban renewal on a grand scale.

Now Adam sat rigidly transfixed, staring into his own imagery, listening intently, raptly, as the slow clicking visions accelerated into a soft, steady and continuous purring. Fluttering computer cards, millions of them. Click. A print-out . . . A kaleidoscopic print-out!

Oh Jesus!

He fell back and let it happen, reading it as it came, every shred and particle of energy in him surging to his head, there burgeoning, blooming, bursting at last into an orgastic storm of vibrant, explosive excitement.

Oh, Jesus.

Slowly, he slid up the wall to a standing position, bracing his back against the wall, staring blindly, slack-jawed and stunned motionless. Motionless except for the fine tremor dancing through him.

J-e-e-sus . . . H. . . . Particular!

Another hour passed as he stood there staring, as if impaled, his eyes and ears tuned inward, seeing and listening, outwardly catatonic as he first generated and then reabsorbed the biggest jackpot of them all.

Oh! My . . . GOD!!!!!

A sound of thunder rumbled in his mind, an instant of darkness, then a blinding flash of light—but he did not fall unconscious.

He opened his eyes to find Goldy, her face wreathed with concern, staring at him fearfully.

"Adam? Are you okay, hon? Whassa matter?"

Cupping her face in his hands, his eyes bursting with the shock of realization, he whispered hoarsely: "Goldy. When I was young I went to war."

"I know, Adam. You told me. You was a Marine!"

He seemed not to hear her, merely repeating, " . . . I went to a war and . . . and . . . "

"What, Adam? What? You're lookin' kind of crazy—are you okay?"

Astonishment spread slowly across his face, then he finally got it out: " . . . and . . . *nobody gave one!*"

"Huh?" she asked blankly.

He threw back his head and deep chords of rising triumphant laughter rolled from him. Picking her up bodily from the floor he swung her around the room in a frenzied dance of sheer joy.

"Thank you, Goldy—thank you! I could never have found it without you!"

Puzzled, but infected by his hither and yon explosion, she broke from his grip and began jumping excitedly up and down, her great pillowy breasts bounding in their own self-chosen ways. "Whaddya find, Adam? Huh? Watcha got?"

"Can't tell you about it now, Goldy, but it's beautiful!"

Hastily pulling on his clothing he kissed her once more quickly and headed for the door, calling back over his shoulder: "Tell you all about it later. You're a sweetheart and I love you. Gotta walk now—I'm still printing out! Keep an eye on the van for me, okay? Later!"

Jasmyn was ecstatic, laughing, clapping her hands and dancing around the room. "He made it! He made it! I knew he could—I just knew it!"

Sandol smiled spontaneously for the first time in days, genuinely pleased by her unbridled joy. "I am frankly astonished. It seems quite impossible."

"Oh, my!" she exclaimed excitedly, "We shall have to report it at once. Our security is no longer perfect!"

"Perhaps not perfect, but still more than sufficient to the need," he grinned at her. "You now have only 4,999,999,999 more earthlings to go."

"Ah!" she laughed, "that will never happen. But we can no longer boast that the system is unblemished."

"And your favorite blemisher—what of him now?"

Still jubilant, Jasmyn turned to him and smiled warmly. "Sandol, I can see it in your eyes. You are no longer jealous of him. You like him!"

"Unbounded admiration is close akin to liking, Jasmyn. Right, I am no longer jealous of him. But what will he do next?"

"Surprise us, I should hope! Come, let's watch him now!"

26

PLANETARY PROGRAMMED SELF-INSTRUCTION

Long-striding, buoyant with the enormous energy of his discovery, he walked several blocks east then north, clear through the city and into the moon-drenched desert.

With surprising speed he cycled through several distinct layers of acute paranoia.

Now that he had discovered T.H.E.I.R. secret he could blackmail them for enormous sums of money. *No! No! My God, they're too powerful for that—they'll do me in! Must keep my mouth shut just to stay alive.*

Oh, my god, he panicked next. *They've got us all in a box, running a maze and pushing levers—we're just five billion inconsequential little nobodies, like rats in a maze—a Skinner Box! They know my every thought and move!*

By the time he reached the desert the last wave of paranoia had ebbed away and he found himself filled with a novel, and for him quite unprecedented sense of peace and serenity. *So that's it,* he thought—*that's all there is to it. No more worry about war—it's all taken care of.* The same for over-population, birth control, pollution, oil and coffee and all the other "shortages," corrupt government and crime in the street, the energy crisis and travel to outer space—rigged histrionics. It's all known, *planned* and *certain.* Same for the weather, assassinations and other atrocities and scandals. Profumo, Wilbur Mills, Pattie Hearst, The Teapot Dome—all of them!

But what of me, he wondered with untroubled curiosity? Or does that really matter? Now I can die happy, understanding at last that it's not a vicious and futile jungle but a plan of marvelous beauty, and where I fit into it really matters hardly at all. And yet, when I begin writing about this it's going to shake things up—like a magnificent multi-megaton bomb. But damn!—I don't want to be a prophet or messiah—let Gore Vidal do that number! And as I don't really want that role, I'll probably have to be "assassinated" like the others, or get involved in some colorful Watergate- or Wilbur Mills- or Jack Profumo- or Chappaquiddick-type scandal—to help amuse and educate the masses—to help create clues for them.

That way I'd be going to Heaven, I guess, which would only require a little surgical face changing, a new hairdo, some elixir of youth, some fresh I.D. papers—then just lie low for awhile (I could use a *little* vacation). Then I'd slip stealthily back into the scene and join my fellow angels in helping other people find what I've had such a blast discovering—and in their own ways! Like James Bond without danger. An actor at last!

But could it be possible that he—in this very writing—was betraying their monumental secret? Ratting on them? That would surely present no problem at all for them. If the writing were premature, or should miss the mark altogether, it would fall into absolute obscurity, perhaps to be "discovered" at some later date when the time was right—or perhaps not at all.

If now is the time, however, arrangements would be made for a few lively and warmly contended interviews on national television: The *Today Show, Good Morning America,* or even Johnny Carson's *Tonight Show.* In any case, the contention would be certain. His revelation would be ridiculed, applauded, scorned and theified and, above all, roundly discredited. Both sides would be presented, as is always the case in any well designed course in programmed self-instruction; and, as always, it would be for Everyman to reach his own conclusions. Hoax and humbug, or astonishing truth? Flim flam or *filet?* Will ye, or nil ye?

He wondered how his book would be received, then. A ludicrous romantic fantasy and an intellectual outrage, or a switch that would light up the world and awaken a drowsing species? Is it a negligible bit of literary pother, or the most momentous work in all of human history? The answer would clearly be the readers' choice—it could not be otherwise.

Although close to mania with his discovery, Adam was realistic enough to know that his broadstroke appraisal of this admittedly mind-dazzling subject was only a crude "first"—a pioneering yet fumbling breakthrough. It will surely be reinforced by a welcome flood of followup books and articles by experts in their own fields, specialists in economics, government, archaeology and business, who could contribute invaluably to our ever-widening grasp of this remarkable phenomenon that involves us all.

Yes, he printed on, They Have Everything In Reach—T.H.E.I.R. But who are T.H.E.Y.? And Where?—and *what*? Humanoids? Cyborgs? Have I ever unknowingly met and talked with any of them? You're moving in on the *how* and the *why* of it, my friend, but those other adverbial questions are still great big blanks. But they are devilishly tricky—perpetuating that convincing appearance of ferocious competition between the big oil companies and the MNC's. And they have some ingenious ways of making themselves look disorganized and out of touch, like those contrived errors in mailing duplicates to the same addresses, with an apology "if you have already received this."

The big city blackouts and brownouts, and New York City's big financial crisis—all in the script. Then there are those deviously calculated screw-ups on the tube—but there are no accidents on national television; no, not even the little "We have lost a portion of our audio—please stand by." Nothing goes on or off that tube without approval, so that *everything* there means something—like that sci-fi movie about the earthlings who gradually came to realize that they were living in a Skinner Box. It's neither an accident nor a fiction, he now realized. It's true. And then there was *Fortune* magazine's highly personalized sales letter: "Dear Dr. Solon . . . have we finally found you? Where have you been? You got away from us." Fat chance! There is no way out, but only an appearance of it.

Ah, yes. The system even provides for that—a spate of ways for letting us believe that we are "working outside of the system," but these are all illusory. There is no "outside" to this *Sapiens System*. We are all known, identified and registered. We are also observed, and, yes, incredible though it may seem, cherished and nurtured. And protected. We are not being culled but, somehow, cultivated. We are being brought along at our own rate, surely not as rapidly as we are able to move—not by any means—but only as fast as we ourselves truly want to move. It is purely and mercifully voluntary. There are many tempting blandishments to encourage our forward movement to be sure, but no punishments for our refusal to do so. None but those we visit upon ourselves by electing passive vegetation over vital and adventuresome living. But if we should choose to go native we are free to do that, too, and with impunity—a sort of guardless and wardenless captivity that allows us *all the freedom we can handle!*

But in all of this, our emotionally wanting species is hopelessly fettered by countless regional chauvinisms. The special rapture of patriotism is an expected extension of the herding instinct. Our very personal sense of worth begins with our attachment to—and identification with—our family, then good old P.S. 23, then secondary school, our *alma mater*, hometown, region and nation. Even today, our personal identification with One World has not yet been attained.

Although we are not ready for it emotionally, our imminent awareness of galactic neighbors may catalyze this movement and unify the planet, if only for the misguided purpose of self-defense. The very notion of our involvement in anything resembling a "star wars" encounter is sheerest nonsense. It must be said again: if they wanted to harm us, they could have done so millennia (eons) ago. Our own technology is pathetically primitive compared to theirs. After-the-holocaust movies remind us of what could happen were we left to our own devices. Happily, that is not the case. The good news is that there will be no nuclear war, no holocaust, no Armageddon. We truly are in good hands with Allstate and friends.

No, there is no "outside of the system." Ten-to-one, he reflected, smiling, that the John Birch Society is a loyal and strictly mock-front for the very Insiders they so viciously and regularly attack. Their grass-roots members may be true believers, but somewhere up the line they must be getting under-the-table funding from the Ford or Rockefeller Foundation—who likely put the organization together in the first place.

My God, he thought—the system itself must be all but perfect! They give us great heroes and religious leaders to cling to and emulate, and a thousand villains to spend our fury on—with Adolf Hitler perhaps the greatest of the lot. Soon after the wicked Kaiser Bill and his hated Huns became old hat to the easily-bored masses, history's most perfect villain—better even that Nero!—was swept in from the wings to indulge our need to practice the self-righteous vilification of evil personified. The half-mad leader of a band of adolescent ruffians, after years of unproductive beer hall bullying and soap-box oratory, suddenly—almost overnight—rises to great wealth and power. And where did the Little Corporal's money come from, and what invisible strings were attached to it?

Six million Jews gassed to death and burned in the ghastly crematoria of Dachau and Buchenwald? Explain that one, oh sage. Can't do it, Adam, though you have yet to meet one person who can give you a believable first-hand account of what *really happened* in those places. But you did see with your own eyes that *belief* in the stories all but cured the vicious anti-Semitism that prevailed in the good old U.S.A. before then, such that anti-Semitism and anti—Gentilism are now about equally balanced here. T.H.E.Y. have given us each other to satisfy our hate needs—and our fear needs. We have the Communists. The Jews. Jehovah's Witnesses. Blacks. Limeys. The Pope. The Catholics. The Protestants. Indeed, we are well provided for—how luxuriously we can revel in our hatred and contempt for them all—a balming bromide for the masses. This just could be, as Pangloss said, the best of all possible worlds—or the best we can receive!

As for your chronic guilt about making more money than the poor people—bag it! We're not competing with each other for a finite amount of money. It's like a game of twenty-one in Las Vegas. Each of us is playing against the house independently of the others—and in the earthly system "the house" belongs to The Insiders and their monetary resources are inexhaustible. So the person who manages to rake in a few million dollars for himself is not depriving one single starving soul of one single crumb of moldy bread.

Yes, these Old Ones—these Others—have been through it all. T.H.E.Y. know every dirty business trick that ever was. Every ersatz religion, every con in the book. The horrors of tyranny and the abysmal chaos of true democracy are well in their ken, and the system T.H.E.Y. have devised to resolve these evil extremes is a master work of psychosocial engineering. It is custom-made for every living person, hand-tailored to his uniquely individual needs and interests and capabilities. It empowers him to *choose*, freely and constantly, to go as far as he wishes and in whatever direction, without coercion. To get there it is required only that we really want to do it, and that this wish be demonstrated not merely in wordy declarations (for these are empty things) but as demonstrated in the maze of life. Awesome obstacles are placed in his way but, once faced, they prove to be only phantoms. There are no real ogres to be conquered but only things to be done—with passion and vigor and for the sheer joy of doing them. And this is, indeed, what we all do, and which inevitably brings us all to where we *really* want to be.

It's true—*true!* Morality can not be taught—only learned. The *Insiders* discovered this empirically, but how many millennia ago? How many "crops" ago? When did they finally realize that imprisonment, floggings, decapitations, propaganda, promises of assorted posthumous heavens and hells—that none of these could overcome the marvelous obstinacy of the human animal and lead him to truth. Oh, yes, a few conditioning stimuli could point the way a little, like formal teaching and that flood of subliminals on the tube, but in the end, one golden and irrefutable principle emerges: each of us learns only what he is able to and wants to, and he does it in his own way and at his own rate. And the system they've so ingeniously devised provides for just that. Choice and opportunities, tailored precisely to the capabilities and limitations of individuals and of entire populations.

And graduation day is almost here—pack another crop of happy workers off to new and grander tasks among the stars. Then tip the earth on its axis, create a Velikovskian wipeout of the archaeological record, plant a new crop, and start the whole program all over again. Some garden!

But we also have the right to bitch our hearts out about it all, to weep and wail and gnash our teeth, as these things, too, are a part of our instinctual legacy. We are fantastically talented complainers and self-pitiers. The most wretched subclinical mental symptom afflicting our species now or ever is boredom, an emotional state inevitably consequent to doing less than one is capable of doing. And delusions of victimhood and helplessness are the almost universal human neuroses. Ah, woe is me!

His mind raced on as he strode along the rocky desert trail in the gleaming moonlight. And even though I really know very little about them I'm now in a position to fairly surmise a *few* things even at this early juncture. T.H.E.Y. are far above national affiliations and they transcend ethnicity and formal religions. The major planks in their platform are peace, internationalism (if not interstellarism), active and energetic creativity—and growth. They learned long ago that work is the only effective antidote to the chronic siesta syndrome, and I suspect that their surest principle is that the best worker is a happy worker, and a good worker makes more money for himself and for the system. They're running it all, but they permit the fiction of nations to stand because of our fatuous emotional attachment to this archaic allegiance.

T.H.E.I.R. basic method is voluntary operant conditioning, or programmed self-instruction, conducted chiefly through the mass media, with periodic quizzes being tacitly administered through the postal systems of the world. They are benevolent and infinitely patient—cherishing, protecting, and cultivating their mortal charges with a perfect blend of affection, seduction, direction and firmness.

T.H.E.Y. are at least humanoid, perhaps grading to the Cyborgian. They are superscientists, geneticists, businessmen, legalists, ethicians, and linguists—everything—and they mightily favor reason over passion. Adam Weishapt—*man with a wise head!*

T.H.E.Y. are incognito but not invisible, appearing among us from time to time to help move their program forward in any possible way, and also for the sheer fun of it. They are especially active at indirect teaching and clue-giving. The most familiar common model to which the M.O. might compare are those of the Greek gods seated in the balcony of the World Theater and beneficially influencing—though not coercively regulating—the hectic affairs of its mortal minions. Another parallel concept is the popular Christian idea of angels, or messengers of the highest authority, known almost universally as "God."

Not unlike ourselves they are subject to the gray, near-death of boredom, which goes far toward explaining their intense voyeurism. They watch our comical caperings and calamities much as we watch bullfights and live sex shows. By their standards we experience but a few very primitive emotions, whereas they have a multitude—all positive?

T.H.E.Y. are extremely few in number, highly organized and specialized, and among them rational disputation is permitted—even encouraged—but arbitrary disobedience is not. No law nor courts are necessary among them because they all know the law and obey it devoutly, and they are giving us mere mortals every possible chance to do the same through the incessant street-theater they first produce and then report and dramatize in their media. They are law-and-order creatures, in other words, but they are not punishers—having arranged that we shall provide this for ourselves in our own self-chosen ways.

T.H.E.I.R. business is serious but not somber. On the contrary, they have a bright and eager sense of humor, and they can even afford to spoof disease, death and human tragedy because they understand something about these things that we mere mortals do not. Their J.O.K.E.R.S. Division (Justified Order of Kings, Emperors and Regents Surpassed) is especially active in creating educational, eye-opening mischief and they love their work as few of us do. (Robert Benchley, George Plimpton, Bill Cosby, George Burns, Dinah Shore and Carol Burnett are just a few of their lower level agents.)

Sex is treated by T.H.E.M. as trifling pleasure—and one of the lesser art forms. They practice every "perversion" known to mankind and quite a few that aren't, but all in casual good humor. It is all entirely divorced from our notion of "love," and among them there is no marriage, envy or jealousy. Nor is there complaining or self-pity, remorse or guilt—or any other sapping or painful emotion. Each is responsible for himself and, of course, to the system. They appreciate and vicariously enjoy each others' lives just as they do ours.

Child-bearing is eugenically planned and optional—and child-rearing is strictly by the law.

Even though T.H.E.Y. control the wealth of the world, they themselves are nonmaterialistic, most moderate in pleasurable self-indulgence because problem-solving is their greatest pleasure. "Ascetic" might be too strong a word. They don't deliberately mortify the flesh—they just don't swill and screw and gluttonize it to death. Eschewing drugs almost entirely, they might occasionally savor a small warmer of fine brandy or a glass of the very best wine.

Their chiefest pleasures, though, are of the mind. They are puzzle-breakers and chess masters. They are also outrageously voyeuristic and exhibitionistic. Of course, it is for the best of reasons that they watch us like hawks but they do enjoy the watching. And they get a real kick out of writing, producing, and staging their endless theatrical spectaculars. And, he concluded lamely, I suppose that one way or another—they are immortal.

He was suddenly beset by an unearthly feeling, unexplainable and inarticulate though it was, that somehow our very lives—like the great wars and epidemics and catastrophes, and assassinations—are also staged theater; assigned roles, parts in a play. And that, of course, makes sense only if one chooses to wax mystical and metaphysical, which is no place for a good working shrink to be frittering away his time. But if we're all in assigned roles, the assignment, he supposed, would have to have been made preincarnationally, followed by a memory erase, that the mortal experience be felt as *real*, and not simply abstract and rote memorized. Seth explained that well enough. A rich man can't really know what it's like to be poor by simply donning old clothes, putting himself on a tight allowance, and moving into a squalid ghetto hovel for a few days. He would still know how much money he had in the bank, and that he could move back to that big mansion in the suburbs any time he wanted to. Only if knowledge of these things could be erased from his mind, would the poverty experience be genuine, and his ineffable spirit—his consciousness?—thus somehow altered—perhaps even improved?

After all, he reflected, the now familiar helical DNA substructure of the mammalian chromosome is simply the physical template of the individual's *essential self* (spirit, soul, self—as you will). Those of us formally trained in the biological sciences, especially including medicine, have been so indoctrinated with the principle "function follows form" that we seldom, if ever, consider the alternative: That consciousness creates substance; that the *self* creates the body, and does so for a very good purpose.

Beyond that, we have apparently chosen to place ourselves in a community of beings very like ourselves, with enough similarities among us to remind us of the worst of which we are capable, along with the best. Declarations of good moral intentions amount to nothing. The considerable wear-and-tear of earthly life forces us face-to-face with ourselves—where we are succeeding and where we are still wanting. Adam found he could think of no crime of which he was incapable, and it is their actual commission by others that most deterred him from doing the same.

Well, he decided, I guess that's one outfit I'd like to be a part of. No, I'm already a part of it—there's no way for any of us *not* to be a part of it. Should I say I want to be promoted? Or does the system require that you promote yourself? Do I apply somehow, or do I wait until T.H.E.Y. call me? (Many are called but few are chosen, or, "We're Ready When You Are.")

Could be neither of the above. Their security is obviously super-tight, and I can be damned sure they don't hang it on solemn oaths sworn-in-blood or demoniacal initiation rites or any crap like that. You just don't move ahead until you've made the grade—pay as you go—in their running, open-air IQ-Vocational Aptitude-Awareness—and-Comprehension Test. I'd better keep a sharper eye on those funny little questionnaires from magazines like *Time, Newsweek,* and *Skeptic* and the rest of them. Also, the ones from Common Cause, all those big national scientific organizations I belong to—everything!

He surveyed the silent silvery desert as he walked. The noble diamondbacks were all laid back in their cozy granite crevasses, and even the coyotes had stilled their raucous yelping. Only the stately giant Saguaros, their arms upraised in perpetual reverence, seemed awake to the tranquil magic of the desert at night.

His thoughts quickly returned to The System, where he found himself wondering if T.H.E.Y. had any personnel spies in the field doing on-the-spot evaluations of promising candidates. Such agents, he quickly reasoned, could easily get close to him in almost any guise, as patients or staff or both. And I'm a real pushover for women—a round-heeled mattress-back. Gilth Ypres? He had known and trusted old Gilth for almost twenty years. And he'd known Kate Nay and Deb Suners and Geneva Spear for close to ten. Roc was obviously in T.H.E.I.R. picture one way or another, but what about Bairny? He had a gut-feeling that she was straight—just what she appeared to be. The Sapinet twins were young but, well, they *had* come on pretty strong, and they asked just a few too many innocent little questions.

He trusted his own people, like Kono, Dan and the rest, but certain of his "patients" would have to be held suspect. Especially that homicidal bitch, Theda Camian, who anagrams to *death maniac*. And Doby Clandas, that charming gay troublemaker who had once vainly tried to seduce him—*body scandal*. Anagrams, the art of linking letters, to which our chiefest clue is Mr. Art Linkletter himself. Hell, maybe our entire language is programmed. It's easy enough to adjust. You have only to get a Janis Joplin or a Bob Dylan—even a John Denver—to say "cool" or "far out!" "right on!" on the tube a few times and within a week or two every kid in the country is imitating them. When Alcibiades plays the flute, everyone plays the flute. And twenty-five years ago every fifth mother was naming her baby boy Dennis, after the then new comic character, *Dennis the Menace*—and Dennis anagrams to *sinned*. Ah, good for you, Adam, my friend—your paranoia swelleth by leaping bounds!

That, after all, is no longer necessary. As Bairny said, T.H.E.Y. know everything anyway so why try to hide anything? Just relax and enjoy it. You've already been called—now it remains only to see if you'll be chosen. Good luck, and remember: you can't take the Kingdom of Heaven by storm.

Then again, he ruminated, I suppose there may never be any *direct* contact between T.H.E.M. and me. I can expect to receive assignments though, or perhaps that's also automatic. It's quite conceivable that writing this book could be the fulfillment of such a task without my even realizing it. A noisome question, that: Do those really big actors in the show—like Nelson Rockefeller and Dick Van Dyke and Richard

Nixon and Patricia Hearst—do they *know* what roles they're playing, and why? Or are they really unconscious of all that. Don't even try to conjecture on that one, Adam—too little data. It does not compute.

As he resumed walking it seemed to him that the big game of life was over, in a way—that now he had only to settle back and watch the human comedy unfold before his eyes. But in this he was sorely mistaken. For now he wanted only to be home, see Candy and Brian, swim the dust and sweat from his body, dine—and then to sleep.

The light of the morning sun was showing over the far eastern horizon as he walked around the house and onto the deck, where Candy and Brian were snuggled together in a single sleeping bag. Bone-weary and completely happy, he slumped down into a chair and looked out across the lake, now a shimmering platter of hammered gold in the morning's first rays.

Candy awoke first, then Brian, and they both lay quietly for a moment staring at him. He looked exhausted, but his eyes were afire and a calm smile brightened his face. It was at once obvious to them both that he had found what he was looking for. Brian raised himself on one elbow and asked, his voice tense and expectant, as was the expression on Candy's beautiful face: "What is it? Can you tell us?"

Adam nodded his head slowly. "Yes, I can and I will. But the question is—can you believe it when you hear it? Probably not."

Now Candy was sitting too, her face bright with wonderment: "Try us, Daddy. Just try us!"

Holding up his hands, he shook his head incredulously and his smile deepened: "It's so simple I don't know where to begin. It's . . . well . . . good news. I mean—*The good guys won!*"

For the next two hours he sat where he was, quietly running it out for them. *Homo sapiens*—the latest crop of our *literal* Fathers from outer space. The mock wars and other staged spectaculars. The media as CS, and America as a planned real estate development, human history as a scripted scenario, as they listened open-mouthed and flabbergasted.

"And that's about the size of it," he concluded. "T.H.E.Y., the Illuminati, the Old Ones—The Ones Who Came Before—they have us all in a very private school—we're being cultivated . . . "

"Programmed self-instruction?" Brian asked, amazement showing in his eyes.

Adam nodded. "But all entirely voluntary, and no punishments—only rewards."

Candy was aghast: "And we're *all* in it?"

"Every last one of us," he smiled wearily, "and there's no way out—but I can't imagine why anyone would want to be out of it—unless they're just not able to see it for what it is."

A moment of silence passed, then Brian said, "I'm not sure that we—I—can see it for what it is—yet. It's so much, all at once. Gargantuan. Like it's completely backward from what you've always—always . . ."

Adam nodded. "Yes, completely."

Candy was saucer-eyed. "And you say all those big wars were hoaxes? I mean—I just don't get it! Why?"

Once again he quickly ran over the affirmative functions of sham warfare, then extended his critique to the present.

"But there are other ways of reaching the same goals. For example, the big draft-dodge emigration during the Vietnam era also accomplished the mass interculturation of American youth with their opposite numbers in Canada, Mexico, South America and Europe. And it threw them on their own resources. So, by that point in history the willful *avoidance* of war brought them the same kind of stimulation, inspiration, excitation, interculturation and learning previously provided for by warfare.

"Wars! War games is what they were! Hell, I was right in the middle of it for almost four years and there *was no war!* What I really got out of it was relief from the boredom of higher education. Separation from the hearth and home of my childhood, which most of us badly need then. Discipline, and a chance to learn how to wipe my own ass. One damn training school after another, and all of them top-drawer. Hokey heroism and a chance to strut. Booze, women, and animal high spirits—'There is nothing like a d-a-a-ame!' Free travel. Free benefits. Phony mines in the Irish Channel. Night bombings in the distance over Merrie Old England—and how kind of them to suspend the Battle of Britain for me during my two-week stay in Bristol.

"Jesus! A great big musical comedy, so beautifully produced and on such a grand scale—all for us! And it worked! Why, T.H.E.Y. even began dropping clues to the big hoax almost as soon as it ended. 'Hogan's Heroes.' 'Mr. Roberts.' 'The Caine Mutiny.' Mobile Army Surgical Hospital: M*A*S*H = SHAM = 1976—hot ziggety damn!" he exulted.

"Good God," Candy whispered, "I've never, *ever* heard a theory like that in my whole life!"

"It's pretty incredible I know," he added quietly, now restraining his excitement, "but I can't find any way to pick a hole in it. I just can't. The 100-year war, the 30-year war, the Battle of Britain, the Battle of Berlin, the great march on Moscow, Napoleon—it's fantastic! All staged. All rigged. All made totally believable and for the best imaginable reasons. In the military or out, we're all of us attending the biggest open-air entirely tuition-free university ever known. It's called The World, and it works something like a Skinnerball. It is the *Sapiens System*! Now then, can you believe that?"

Thoughtfully rolling a thin wake-me-up joint, Brian smiled sardonically and challenged: "If T.H.E.Y. have everything arranged so perfectly—custom-made programmed self-instruction for five billion people and all that—then why is the noble weed illegal here in the land of liberty? It's harmless, even medicinal—I've heard you say it yourself a hundred times. Yet they're throwing kids in jail all over the country for having it and dealing it. And you! You were fired from the University Student Health Service for doing nothing more than citing the Nixon Commission's marijuana report on television!"

Adam smiled wearily. "Good case in point. I was just too dumb, too long, to see what's been going on. The deliberately preserved illegality of marijuana serves two distinct and major sociopsychological functions. One of them, Brian, you know about from personal experience. Morally and intellectually you're a devout pacifist, and yet you're tormented by a powerful inner drive to fight and rebel—it becomes your biological age and masculine gender. A rough conflict for young men like you to deal with, yet the system has provided for it. You need to adventure, take risks, do things on your own, fight the system—flirt with danger. In the past, real booze and illusory warfare have met that need for many. But now booze is legal and warfare just isn't selling as well as it used to. So along comes the harmless—and happily illegal—"peace drug" for the kids to use in joyful defiance, risk-taking and money-making. You're also inspired to travel, and to learn some pharmacology and a lot of law—especially the Bill-of-Rights—because of it. Admirable pedagogic technique."

"But," Brian protested, "they're really throwing those kids into jails and prisons—wretched places!"

"I know," Adam tisked. "And ain't it awful? I should have caught onto that one long ago—even said it myself in print over twenty years ago in my book on adolescents: kids need the chance to rebel, to contest the system, but it must be a *real* contest—no counterfeit jousting would deceive them and thus meet their need. So there must be real cops and real jails, you see?"

Candy piped into her brother's baffled silence: "Then what's the second purpose it serves?"

"Ah, that. Lovely! It creates a new and wide-open territory for aggressive young businessmen who would not otherwise have a chance against the big tobacco and pharmaceutical companies. The giant corporations can buy Congressmen and bribe the FDA but they can't get away with wholesaling, jobbing and retailing illegal drugs. So that rich market is handed on a silver platter to a whole new generation of quick-witted, eagerly enterprising, wholesomely aggressive wheeler-dealer tycoons of tomorrow. And you know what most of these young dope-dealers are like: bright and bad, well-educated, moralistic, sensitive, interesting—good people all considered—and the last thing they want is the legalization of those gorgeously illicit drugs. That wicked system of ours, you see, has ingeniously arranged that those uncommon virtues shall bloom and flourish, in the thriving marketplace of marijuana, cocaine and smack."

Brian looked at him steadily for a moment then dropped his eyes, almost sadly: "Okay. Everything you just said is—absolutely true. But for me it's really going to take the kick out of dealing."

Adam laughed and gripped his shoulder reassuringly: "I suppose so, but there are other markets—markets galore—out there. I mean, even the legit ones like law and medicine and engineering can be pretty exciting and lucrative, if approached in that spirit."

Candy was also troubled. "Does that mean that now you can make everything fit into your system—like justify all the ghastly things that are going on in the world?"

"No, not at all. It means that our First Amendment guarantees are alive and well in the world today. The System does not queer anyone's game—from felons to saints. We are all very much at liberty to bow, scrape, and roll before our favorite idols, to adore the symbols of our choice—stars, crosses, or swastikas—and to devoutly revere our very own One True God, and surely there is an abundance of Those to choose from. We are all perfectly free to ecstasize at the feet of our freely chosen idols, from Jethro to Jesus to Johnny Unitas."

He patted her placatingly and continued. "Well, first off we don't know very much about what *really* is going on in the world—just what we get from a very carefully programmed mass media, eh? But I think you're actually wondering if I can fit everything into my new delusional system, right?"

"I didn't exactly mean that, but, well—what about the way the Feds treat those poor Mexican wetbacks, for example?"

He nodded briefly. "T.H.E.Y. reward them for having the balls to move off the dime and take some risks to earn more of those reinforcing reward pellets we call money."

"Reward! Prison?"

"They call 'em prisons, just the way they call the Marine Corps the military, but they're not quite what they appear to be."

"How so?"

"In the first place, U.S. Federal slammers aren't too bad at all. Pretty cozy, easy way of life, and I suspect most of those good wetbacks never had it so good. It's also a chance for them to learn English, along with the rudiments of business and agriculture—then they're released to compete in the illicit American job farm market with a far better chance than they had before."

"No kidding?"

"No kidding. I've seen it happen many times. And our upwardly mobile Chicano middle-class workers are really peeved about the competition, even though they've been out of the fields and into blue-and-white-collar jobs for years."

He paused and thought for a moment and then went on: "It works like that up and down the line, no matter where you are in the system—rewards are given for effective effort. Around the turn of the century Charles Evans Hughes went after corruption in the big insurance companies—one of T.H.E.I.R. vital organs. He probed, fought and attacked them for months, fang and claw. Did T.H.E.Y. destroy him? Not at all—they made him Chief Justice of the U.S. Supreme Court—damn near made him president. Same thing happened to that plumber who came out here to repair our septic tank. Montgomery Ward kept overbilling him for some merchandise, threatening to take him to court and wreck his credit, y'know? So he got a lawyer and took *them* to court—and won. Ten days later they issued him one of their Extra-Special-Person cards with an extended line of credit. T.H.E.Y. pay you for trying, thinking and doing."

Brian returned from a stunned silence to rejoin the conversation:

"But what about this expose you're coming up with now—they're going to be pretty pissed, aren't they—when they realize you're on to their game?"

"That's a small bout of paranoia I worked through while walking out here last night. No, T.H.E.Y. want me to do my damndest to try to expose them—anything that will excite people, alert them, and give them more clues to work with. As for my doing them any harm, T.H.E.Y. have as much to fear from me as Michael Spinks has to fear from Don Knotts—vastly less, actually."

Brian was still fighting it. "Well, T.H.E.Y. sure play pretty rough, though—making us work our asses off . . . "

"But we don't really have to, you see. Have you ever seen anyone starve to death? You can stagnate on your lazy ass and still live well on unemployment compensation, veterans' benefits—a bottomless barrel of freebies for those who really want to go that route. But most of us find that when we do go to work and make it on our own, we're glad we did it. It's like giving a dog a bath; you have to fight him all over the house to get him into the tub, but when it's all over he struts around the house like the whole thing was his idea from the start."

"Jesus, that's an awful lot to digest in one sitting. But I guess you really are sitting on something pretty big. . . . "

"Merely monumental and earth-shaking," Adam answered modestly, "and so brilliantly deduced, too."

Brian was still confused but trying hard to understand. "Then you are saying T.H.E.Y. will actually approve of your uncovering them this way?"

"Yes, T.H.E.Y. will. T.H.E.I.R. security is flawless. As soon as one of their little programs is identified—as it was *meant* to be (like those subliminals on the tube)—it's simply replaced by another, always a step or two ahead of us."

"And you really think—it's that carefully planned?"

Adam wagged his head and grimaced incredulously, not quite believing his own words: "When I stand back and take a good hard look at it I see such precision and complexity to The Program that, well, I think the whole thing could have been set in motion eons ago and left to run itself out to some well-foreseen conclusion."

"That's crazy!"

He nodded agreeably. "Yes, I know."

"But . . . but . . . " Brian stammered, " . . . the people of G.R.I.P.E.— what are you going to tell them at the quarterly meeting on Alpha Orion?"

"I thought about that coming home, Brian, and there's only one thing I can tell them: the truth—the Honest to God Truth."

"They tried to kill you!" Brian exploded.

"Nope. As Bairny said, just some beer'd up cowboy. Those guys will shoot at anything that moves—or doesn't move."

"But what you've come up with—that means it's all over! No nuclear holocaust! No fear! An end to epidemic paranoia!"

"Right and not right. An end to fear and paranoia, yes, but the game's not over. Who are they exactly? An ancient priesthood derived from the Lumanians? Benevolent extraterrestrials who are too smart to come down here directly and get themselves mugged, raped, or murdered? Or is it the tycoons, fed up at last with their trillions of dollars, gorgeous women, fancy yachts and other toys—who decided to make their game the rearing of a species? And where are T.H.E.Y. located—are the Insiders *inside* our hollow earth? How do they live? What are their laws, manners, morals? I want to know what *they* know about medicine, science, and a thousand other things! Oh yes—we're going after them with everything we've got!!"

Candy whistled her astonishment: "Well, how d'you like them golden apples?"

"And that one, too," Adam added, pointing at the huge fiery sun hovering above the horizon behind the mountains: "Night has come into day."